# Consensual
# Qualitative
# Research

# CONSENSUAL QUALITATIVE RESEARCH

A Practical Resource
for Investigating
Social Science
Phenomena

EDITED BY
## CLARA E. HILL

American Psychological Association • Washington, DC

Published by
American Psychological Association
750 First Street, NE
Washington, DC 20002
www.apa.org

To order
APA Order Department
P.O. Box 92984
Washington, DC 20090-2984
Tel: (800) 374-2721; Direct: (202) 336-5510
Fax: (202) 336-5502; TDD/TTY: (202) 336-6123
Online: www.apa.org/pubs/books
E-mail: order@apa.org

In the U.K., Europe, Africa, and the Middle East, copies may be ordered from
American Psychological Association
3 Henrietta Street
Covent Garden, London
WC2E 8LU England

Typeset in Meridien by Circle Graphics, Inc., Columbia, MD

Printer: United Book Press, Baltimore, MD
Cover Designer: Naylor Design, Washington, DC

The opinions and statements published are the responsibility of the authors, and such opinions and statements do not necessarily represent the policies of the American Psychological Association.

**Library of Congress Cataloging-in-Publication Data**

Consensual qualitative research : a practical resource for investigating social science phenomena / edited by Clara E. Hill.
  p. cm.
Includes bibliographical references and index.
ISBN-13: 978-1-4338-1007-7
ISBN-10: 1-4338-1007-7
1. Qualitative research. 2. Social sciences—Research. 3. Social sciences—Methodology. I. Hill, Clara E., 1948-

H62.C58497 2011
001.4'2—dc22
                                    2010054365

**British Library Cataloguing-in-Publication Data**
A CIP record is available from the British Library.

*Printed in the United States of America*
*First Edition*

# Contents

# Contributors

**Alan W. Burkard, PhD,** Associate Professor/Department Chair, Marquette University, Milwaukee, WI

**Harold T. Chui, MS,** Doctoral Student, Counseling Psychology, Department of Psychology, University of Maryland, College Park

**Rachel E. Crook-Lyon, PhD,** Assistant Professor, Counseling Psychology and Special Education, Brigham Young University, Provo, UT

**J. Jane H. Dewey, MA,** Doctoral Student, Counseling Psychology, Seton Hall University, South Orange, NJ

**Melissa K. Goates-Jones, PhD,** Psychologist, Adjunct Clinical Faculty, Counseling and Career Center, Brigham Young University, Provo, UT

**Shirley A. Hess, PhD,** Associate Professor, Shippensburg University, Shippensburg, PA

**Clara E. Hill, PhD,** Professor, Department of Psychology, University of Maryland, College Park

**Erin E. Howard, PhD,** Licensed Psychologist, Fayetteville Veterans Affairs Medical Center, Fayetteville, NC

**Teresa C. Huang, BS,** Doctoral Student, University of Maryland, College Park

**Arpana G. Inman, PhD,** Associate Professor and Training Director, Counseling Psychology, Department of Education, Lehigh University, Bethlehem, PA

**John L. Jackson, MEd,** Doctoral Student, Counseling Psychology, University of Maryland, College Park

**Sarah Knox, PhD,** Associate Professor, Marquette University, Milwaukee, WI

**Nicholas Ladany, PhD,** Professor and Director, Counseling Program, Loyola Marymount University, Los Angeles, CA

**Jingqing Liu, MA,** Doctoral Student, Counseling Psychology, University of Maryland, College Park

**Lewis Z. Schlosser, PhD, ABPP,** Associate Professor, Seton Hall University, South Orange, NJ

**Wonjin Sim, PhD,** Assistant Professor, Chatham University, Pittsburgh PA

**Patricia T. Spangler, PhD,** Instructor, Department of Psychology, University of Maryland, College Park

**Jessica V. Stahl, PhD,** Core Faculty, Massachusetts School of Professional Psychology, Boston

**Nicole E. Taylor, PhD,** Psychologist, Colorado Blood Cancer Institute, Denver

**Barbara J. Thompson, PhD,** Adjunct Faculty, George Washington University, Washington, DC

**Barbara L. Vivino, PhD,** Psychologist, Private Practice, Berkeley, CA

**Elizabeth Nutt Williams, PhD,** Dean of the Core Curriculum, St. Mary's College of Maryland, St. Mary's City

# GENERAL OVERVIEW OF CONSENSUAL QUALITATIVE RESEARCH

*Clara E. Hill*

# Introduction to Consensual Qualitative Research 1

W hen I started doing research, I used quantitative methods because they were the only approaches that I knew at the time. For example, I developed a category system for coding therapist behaviors (Hill, 1978). Using this system, I trained judges to code each therapist sentence into one of several mutually exclusive categories of verbal response modes (e.g., reflection of feeling, interpretation). Once the therapist behavior was coded reliably, I could calculate how often each verbal response mode was used within and across sessions. The proportion of response modes could then be examined descriptively (e.g., differences between Rogers, Perls, and Ellis in their use of response modes; Hill, Thames, & Rardin, 1979) or correlated with other variables (e.g., immediate client response, session evaluation; Hill et al., 1988).

This method for training judges and attaining validity and reliability on category systems has been well developed and has been used frequently (see Hill & Lambert, 2004; Lambert & Hill, 1994), and it is particularly good for behaviors that are easily observable and require minimal interpretation (e.g., head nods). Unfortunately, many of the behaviors of most interest to researchers are not so transparent. As Holsti (1969) so aptly noted, "If you can't count it, it doesn't count . . . if you can count it, that ain't it" (p. 112).

For me, the culmination of this quantification-based, and somewhat sterile, paradigm came in a study examining the effects of therapist verbal response modes within 132 sessions of eight cases of brief psychotherapy, where each therapist and client statement was meticulously coded. In this study (Hill et al., 1988), we found that therapist verbal response modes accounted for only 1% of the variance of immediate client outcome (reactions, experiencing levels) and dropped to 0% when therapist intentions and previous client experiencing levels were added to the regression equations! How disheartening! After more than a decade of developing measures and then painstakingly collecting and coding data, we found that therapist verbal response modes did not seem to matter, a finding that fundamentally challenged my expectations and clinical experiences. Around this time, I went into an existential crisis (see Hill, 1984). I had been brought up in this particular research paradigm, I had played the game—and it did not work. Either my suppositions were wrong, or the method was wrong or just not appropriate for my topic.

Around this same time, several people were discussing problems with quantitative methods (see, e.g., Goldman, 1976, 1979). I remember participating in many such discussions at conferences (see Hill & Gronsky, 1984) where we lamented what we could learn from quantitative methods. Many colleagues suggested qualitative methods as an alternative paradigm. Although intrigued by these new methods, largely arising from anthropology, sociology, and education, I was very reluctant to embrace them because they seemed to lack rigor and specificity—it was hard to discern what the methods were and how to implement them on a practical level.

Nevertheless, I continued to think about ways that I could loosen my quantitative ties. In Hill, Charles, and Reed (1981), we interviewed doctoral students about their experiences of becoming therapists. We "qualitatively" analyzed the data and published it along with quantitative data, but we did not use any specific method. In our qualitative analyses, students reported that graduate school was stressful but also growth producing. They also indicated that most of their changes were in higher order counseling abilities (e.g., timing) rather than in basic helping skills. These qualitative results greatly enhanced our findings from quantitative analyses of judges' codings of verbal response modes in brief counseling sessions showing that trainees decreased their use of minimal encouragers and increased their use of questions across each of the three years of training.

I also experimented with what has been called *discovery-oriented* (Mahrer, 1988) or *exploratory* research (Hill, 1990). In this method, the researchers ask open-ended questions and then allow categories to emerge from the data for the individual study; they then train a new team of judges to code the data, and they assess the reliability of these codings (e.g., Hill, Rochlen, Zack, McCready, & Dematatis, 2003). In this way, the method is bottom up (i.e., inductive) in that categories emerge from the specific data set and so provide a faithful representation of the data (within the limits of researcher bias and the researcher's ability to see what is in the data), in contrast to using preimposed categories placed onto the data (considered a top-down or deductive approach). Unfortunately, this approach still requires a second team of judges to abandon their clinical intuition and code data into the categories provided. See Chapter 17 on consensual qualitative research modified (CQR-M) for how we have now evolved using this method for qualitatively analyzing relatively simple data.

My next step in this journey came when I was sitting at lunch with Renee Rhodes after a talk I gave at Columbia University. We decided that we wanted to learn how to do qualitative research because it seemed so promising, and so we asked Barbara Thompson to join us in this endeavor because she was also intrigued by qualitative methods. We invited Robert Elliott to coach us because he had been experimenting with qualitative methods. Thus began a great adventure. We studied misunderstandings in psychotherapy, asking clients about what preceded the misunderstanding, what the event entailed, and what the consequences were (Rhodes, Hill, Thompson, & Elliott, 1994). In this first study, we asked participants to write their responses to our open-ended questions because we thought that it might be easier for them to reveal distressing information if their responses were anonymous. We quickly learned, however, that data collected through written response tends to be "thin"; after this experience, we used interviews. This first experience also provided a nice opportunity for us to get together and hang out. (In my mind, a major advantage of qualitative research is that it fills a social function for researchers.) The Strauss and Corbin (1990) book on grounded theory (GT) was enormously influential in our initial work because it provided a structure and examples for how to do qualitative research. We read this book many times, but we were nevertheless somewhat frustrated because so many details of the method were unclear (e.g., what exactly is open coding?), and it was hard to determine exactly how to do several of the steps (e.g., how exactly do you develop a hierarchical structure or theory?). It helped very much to have Robert Elliott guide us through the process on the basis of his experiences of an awareness of *hermeneutics* (i.e., the interpretation of written and oral texts), modifying GT, and developing comprehensive process analysis (Elliott, 1989).

As we conducted a number of qualitative projects, we kept tinkering with the method. We tried to remain true to the qualitative philosophy, but we also did not want to abandon some of the good things we had learned about doing research using quantitative and exploratory methods. For instance, because different people can view the same stimulus in quite diverse ways, we felt it was important to have a way to address discrepancies in perspectives. Hence, we built in a consensus process, which involves having multiple judges talk through their reactions so that different ideas can be examined, and then having the team decide together about the interpretation of the data as well as having auditors evaluate all the judgments. Furthermore, as we tried to teach our students how to use this method, it quickly became apparent that we needed to codify what we were doing and present the steps in a clear manner so that other researchers could use it. The first description of what we came to call *consensual qualitative research* (CQR; Hill, Thompson, & Williams, 1997) was quite a challenge because it forced us to capture our ideas on paper. The incredibly helpful and detailed feedback from Puncky Heppner (then editor of *The Counseling Psychologist*) and five anonymous reviewers forced us to clarify our fuzzy thinking and reexamine and clarify many issues in the final published version of the method.

After the initial publication, we kept trying and modifying the method as new issues arose in subsequent studies (e.g., using interviews rather than written responses). With each study, new challenges occurred that forced us to rethink procedures (e.g., do we really need to hold two cases out to see if new things are added [or what has been called a *stability check*], and what criteria should be used to determine stability?). Then, when Beth Haverkamp, Sue Morrow, and Joe Ponterotto invited us to contribute to a special issue of the *Journal of Counseling Psychology* on qualitative methods, this provided an opportunity to think about these issues more formally. We examined the 27 studies that had used CQR to that point and noted how researchers had actually executed the proposed steps (Hill et al., 2005). By studying actual practices and thinking through the methodological issues more, we were able to modify the approach. For example, we no longer suggested that researchers withhold two cases from the cross-analysis to test for stability; we realized that this step was not followed and researchers never changed their findings on the basis of this check, primarily because adding new cases at this point could result in very different data than the set of interviews all collected at one time before data analyses.

Once we had a fairly clear idea about how to do CQR with interview data, we began to tinker even more with trying to apply the basic approach to noninterview data. More specifically, we modified the approach to fit examinations of data from cases of psychotherapy (see in particular Berman et al., in press; Hill et al., 2008; Kasper, Hill, & Kivlighan, 2008). Most recently, I was invited to submit a chapter on CQR (Hill, in press) for a book edited by Gelo, and in that text I included our expanded thinking about modifications to CQR.

Now that many studies have been conducted and published using CQR, the time seems ripe for a book in which we can again take the luxury of thinking through the major components and steps of the model. In a book format, we can provide more detail and more examples, which should make it easier for people to learn how to use the approach.

The authors of these chapters are all people who have worked closely with me or who have worked closely with people who have worked directly with me. I have benefited greatly over the years from collaborating with so many talented people who have helped me think through the issues involved in CQR and who have helped me continue to modify and improve CQR. Having so many inputs into this book has served as a consensus process in and of itself.

## What Is Qualitative Research?

I particularly like McLeod's (2011) description of qualitative research. In his excellent text on qualitative methods, he said that

> at its heart, qualitative research involves doing one's utmost to map and explore the meaning of an area of human experience. If carried out with integrity, this is a process that can result in unique learning both for the person who is the inquirer, and for those who are his or her audiences . . . good qualitative research requires an *immersion* in some aspect of social life, in an attempt to capture the wholeness of that experience, followed by an attempt to convey this understanding to others. (p. ix)

McLeod then went on to define qualitative methods as contributing a special way of knowing, which can be summarized in the following definition: *"The primary aim of qualitative research is to develop an understanding of how the social world is constructed"* (p. 3), with particular emphasis on the idea that this knowledge is constructed given that we live in a complex world and that knowledge can be viewed from many perspectives without one absolute truth.

## Key Components of CQR

The CQR approach is defined by several key components. See also Exhibit 1.1.

### INDUCTIVE APPROACH

The first and perhaps most important aspect of the model is that data analysis is *inductive* or *bottom up* (describing a phenomenon and drawing

---

**EXHIBIT 1.1**

**Key Components of Consensual Qualitative Research (CQR)**

1. CQR is inductive rather than deductive.
2. CQR uses open-ended questions that stimulate participants' thinking and elicit rich responses.
3. CQR uses words (narratives and stories) rather than numbers.
4. CQR uses the context of the entire case to understand each element.
5. CQR studies a small number of cases in depth.
6. CQR relies on multiple perspectives with at least three primary team members conducting the data analysis and one to two auditors checking the work of the primary team.
7. CQR relies on consensus among the team members.
8. CQR places a strong emphasis on ethics, trustworthiness, and the role of culture.
9. CQR requires that researchers continually return to raw data to verify their emerging conclusions.

---

conclusions based on the gathered data) rather than *top down* (imposing a particular theoretical lens on the data or setting out to confirm or disconfirm existing theory). In other words, researchers allow the results to emerge from the data without imposing theoretical constructs on the data, or imposing as little as possible. For example, rather than setting out to investigate whether therapist self-disclosure leads to client disclosure and insight, researchers might ask clients how they respond to therapist self-disclosure and then describe systematically what the clients have said about different consequences of disclosure. In this way, researchers remain open to learning new and unexpected things rather than just setting out to prove what they had anticipated and thus measured. Because of this openness to learning from the data, we typically use research questions rather than hypotheses.

## USE OF OPEN-ENDED QUESTIONS IN INTERVIEWS

Following from the inductive approach, a second important component of CQR is the use of open-ended questions for collecting data. Researchers give participants a framework within which to respond (i.e., they indicate the general topic) but then ask participants to say whatever comes to mind about the topic (e.g., "What was your experience of your supervisor at that moment?") without imposing predetermined ideas about what their experiences were. This qualitative approach starkly contrasts with the constraints placed on participants when they must indicate on a 5-point Likert scale how much they agree or disagree with a statement presented by the researchers. Thus, in CQR the researchers learn about the phenomenon from allowing the participants to talk openly rather than only asking to what extent participants agree with researchers' thinking as represented by questions on a measure.

## RELIANCE ON WORDS

A third and related component of CQR is its reliance on words, narratives, and stories rather than numbers. Thus, researchers allow participants to talk about what they are thinking in an open-ended manner, asking for a full description of experiences related to the topic rather than trying to capture their experiences merely through numbers. We recognize that words, like numbers, are symbols that can mean different things to different persons (e.g., when one person talks about apathy, she or he may mean something very different than another person means, just as a 3 on a 5-point scale does not mean the same thing to each person); therefore, we remain as open as possible to understanding what these words mean to the participant rather than imposing our meaning on the words.

## IMPORTANCE OF CONTEXT

Not only are the specific words important, but the context within which the words are spoken is also important. Thus, a fourth component of CQR is the importance of putting the words within a context. To understand an individual sentence that the participant has uttered, the researchers need to be immersed in everything the person has said (which they do through reading or listening to the whole case to get a sense of context before making judgments). This broader perspective of context provides clues for how the participant views the world. For example, knowing that the participant had been sexually abused may provide an important context for understanding this participant's reactions to marriage.

## USE OF SMALL SAMPLES

Given the intensity of trying to understand each participant's story, it quickly becomes apparent that only a small number of cases can be examined. Thus, the fifth component is that CQR studies rely on small samples of participants studied in great depth rather than superficially learning a few things about a large number of cases. Researchers thus attempt to recruit a group of people who have experienced the phenomenon in question and who can speak articulately about their experiences.

## MULTIPLE VIEWPOINTS

Because of the inherent biases in this process of making meaning out of people's stories (it is difficult for people to articulate their experiences, and judges inevitably impose their own experiences on their understanding of others' experiences), the sixth component of CQR involves using a team of judges to analyze the data. Bringing multiple perspectives to the data allows different viewpoints to emerge and helps the team think about the data in new ways. As mentioned earlier, I learned very early on when doing quantitative analyses of data with large teams of judges that people see the same stimulus in very different ways. For example, if 10 people listen to a psychotherapy session, there will often be 10 very different perspectives about the therapist's empathy, given that each person brings his or her own background and experiences to the judgment process. We do not want to force all the judges into one way of thinking just to achieve a decent and publishable reliability statistic; instead, we want to hear all of the different perspectives and have the team come to consensus in understanding the data.

Nevertheless, every team inevitably encounters group dynamics. Some people may try to dominate, some remain comparatively silent, some try to maintain harmony, and some have difficulty articulating their thinking. Furthermore, people are influenced by events outside of the research process (e.g., they may have had a bad day, are tired). Thus, although the team approach provides the advantage of having many perspectives on the data, it also presents challenges in terms of working with people (e.g., resolving interpersonal ruptures) and having people agree to preserve group harmony (i.e., groupthink). Because the data can be compromised by group dynamics (e.g., one team member gives in to appease another), it is important to build in mechanisms to check the work of the group. Therefore, we also use one or more auditors to examine the work of the team and provide feedback. In effect, the auditors provide a check and balance for the team and yet more perspectives on the data.

## CONSENSUS

As the name implies, consensus is an integral part of CQR. *Consensus* can be defined as "an unforced unanimous decision" (Schielke, Fishman, Osatuke, & Stiles, 2009). During the consensus process in CQR, judges examine the data independently and then come together to discuss their ideas until all members of the team agree on the best representation of the data (Hill et al., 1997). In other words, researchers seek a common understanding of the data, and individual team members' perspectives are respected and encouraged (Hill et al., 2005). The use of multiple perspectives enables the team to capture some of the complexity of the data because different members of the team inevitably perceive different nuances (although they certainly can never capture all the complexity of the data because of inherent biases and expectations). A variety of viewpoints thus emerge, helping to circumvent the biases of any one person.

Given the emphasis on both acknowledging multiple realities and reaching consensus, diverse viewpoints are valued and honored in CQR. In fact, team members need to have the interpersonal skills to state their own perspectives, discuss disagreements, and reach consensus (see also Chapter 4). Hill et al. (1997) stated that the consensus process "relies on mutual respect, equal involvement, and shared power" (p. 523), which is consistent with feminist and multicultural approaches to psychology because the process places a value on researchers working collaboratively (Hill et al., 1997, 2005).

The consensus process is also central to the trustworthiness, or credibility (i.e., the qualitative parallel of validity; Morrow, 2005), of a CQR study (see also Chapter 14). Consistent with CQR's ontology, the consensus process allows equally valid, multiple realities to be combined during data analysis to represent the data richly and thoroughly. In a sense, the consensus process serves as a means of triangulating researchers' understanding of the data, thus contributing to the credibility of the results. Thus, if multiple people who have examined the data independently subsequently agree on an interpretation, researchers may have more confidence that other similar individuals would also agree on that interpretation (Schielke et al., 2009) than they would with only one judge, especially when the judges articulate the rationales for their judgments (Morrow, 2005).

Some evidence suggests that groups making decisions by consensus perform either equal to or better than each group's highest performing individual (Schielke et al., 2009). Schielke et al. (2009) have suggested that "unforced consensus may result in interpretations that are deeper, richer, and more thorough, precise, and realistic than one generated by a single individual" (p. 559).

## ETHICS, TRUSTWORTHINESS, AND ATTENTION TO CULTURE

Following ethical guidelines, trying to conduct the analyses in a trustworthy manner, and attending to the cultural context are major features of CQR. Because CQR involves so much subjectivity, it is important for researchers to be as careful as possible in their procedures. The quality of the data relies on how the data are collected and analyzed. We present more details about these issues in Chapters 13 to 15, but I just want to highlight here how important they are.

## CONTINUALLY RETURNING TO THE DATA

The final component of this method is constantly returning to the raw data to check for the trustworthiness of the team's emerging understanding of the data. When team members disagree on how they view a piece of data, for example, they return to the participant's words to resolve the disagreement. Rereading the words, listening to a recording of the interview, and thinking about the context of the case helps team members distinguish whether their interpretation of the data arises from the data or from their own biases and expectations. Thus, CQR is characterized by judges going back to the data to resolve any confusion or lack of clarity at every step of the way.

## Overview of the Steps of CQR

Figure 1.1 provides a graphic illustration of the major steps of CQR. The first step involves getting started, which typically means choosing a topic, selecting a research team, formulating research questions (based on reading the literature, thinking about one's own experiences, and conducting pilot interviews or focus groups), and recruiting participants. Researchers then collect their data in an open-ended manner, such that the participant can tell his or her story about the topic in his or her own way. The data can be collected through an interview, a questionnaire, or over e-mail, but the fundamental method involves asking open-ended questions without forcing participants to think only in terms of predetermined responses (e.g., "Tell me about your experience . . . " rather than "Did you like working with her?"). Data collected through interviews are transcribed verbatim (except for minimal utterances such as "mm-hmm") for further analysis; transcripts are sent to participants so that they can make corrections and additions if desired.

Once transcripts are obtained, researchers begin the analyses of individual cases (called *within-case* analyses). They first sort the data into *domains* (content or topic areas). Thus, the researchers think about the different types of ideas that have emerged in the data, develop labels for these different types of ideas, and then place the raw data under these domains. For example, when asked about corrective experiences (CE) in psychotherapy, clients might talk about what happened in the experience itself, how therapists contributed to the experience, how they (as the client) contributed to the experience, and outcomes of the experience. Note that at this point, we are only organizing the data into these domains or topic areas; we are in no way interpreting the meaning of the data.

Once data are organized into domains, we summarize what the participant has said in each domain. We call these summaries *core ideas* because judges take what the participant has said in a domain and summarize what the participant said more concisely in clear and understand-

FIGURE 1.1

**GETTING STARTED**

1. Choose a topic and review the literature.

2. Select a research team.

3. Develop and pilot test an interview protocol.

4. Select the target population and develop criteria for selecting participants from the population.

5. Recruit participants.

6. Conduct and transcribe the interviews.

7. Send transcripts to participants for corrections and additions.

**WITHIN-CASE ANALYSIS**

1. Develop domains.

2. Construct core ideas for each case.

3. Auditors check domains and core ideas for each case.

4. Revise domains and core ideas based on audit.

**CROSS-ANALYSIS**

1. Develop categories within domains across all cases.

2. Auditors check cross-analysis.

3. Revise cross-analysis based on audit.

**WRITING THE MANUSCRIPT**

1. Write, rewrite, rewrite.

2. Get feedback and revise.

3. Keep rewriting until you convey a good, clear story that reflects the data.

Steps involved in consensual qualitative research.

able terms that take the context of the case into consideration. In other words, we abstract the essence of what the participant has said when we create core ideas. At this point, the auditor or auditors examine everything the primary research team has done and suggest changes.

Next, we explore whether there are any themes or patterns across participants in terms of their responses within each domain. To answer this question, we perform a cross-analysis in which we cluster the responses within each domain into different categories that characterize the data. For example, within the domain of client contributions to CE, we might have categories of "client remained open to process of therapy" and "client diagnosis interfered with CE." Client diagnosis might be further subcategorized into acting-out disorders versus depressive disorders. As is true of all stages of the data analysis process in CQR, the categories emerge from the data rather than being imposed by theory, and all decisions are made by consensus.

## Applicability of CQR

CQR is ideal for studying in depth the inner experiences, attitudes, and beliefs of individuals because it allows researchers to gain a rich, detailed understanding that is not usually possible with quantitative methods. CQR is also particularly useful for investigations of inner events (e.g., secrets) that cannot be captured by observers watching the process. In addition, CQR can be used to study perceptions of events that occur infrequently (e.g., weeping) or at variable time points (e.g., mood) because these are often hard for researchers to find when searching through psychotherapy sessions. And researchers can study not just events but also attitudes (e.g., attitudes about psychotherapy) and beliefs (e.g., beliefs about social justice). Perhaps most important, CQR is particularly useful for topics that have not been explored previously and thus for which there are no measures available and little to guide researchers about even what questions to ask. Finally, although most of the examples in this book are about psychotherapy research because that is my field, CQR is equally applicable to other topics in education and the behavioral and social sciences (e.g., social justice, urban leadership development, effects of teachers on students).

I would not argue that researchers should use only qualitative approaches but rather that researchers should choose the approach that best fits their research questions. For example, if investigating the effects of two different psychotherapeutic approaches, a quantitative clinical trials method involving standardized measures and sophisticated statistics is probably better suited than a qualitative approach. A qualitative approach, however, would be better suited to answering questions about how participants experienced the two different approaches.

## Comparison of CQR With Other Qualitative Methods

Qualitative researchers (e.g., Bogdan & Biklen, 1992; Henwood & Pidgeon, 1992; Stiles, 1993) have noted several key features of qualitative research:

- Words are used rather than numbers.
- Researchers use themselves as the instruments for analyzing and gaining insight into data (e.g., serve as the judges to interpret the data).
- Researchers seek to describe naturally occurring phenomena rather than explaining or manipulating such phenomena.
- Inductive rather than deductive strategies are used.
- Researchers seek to understand phenomena from the perspective of the participant.
- The importance of the context is emphasized in understanding behavior or events.
- The causes of experiences are assumed to be complex and non-linear.
- The scientific process is viewed as generating tentative ideas rather than facts.
- Researchers stress the emergence of theory from the data rather than forcing data into existing theories.

CQR fits well with all these features. See also Chapter 2 for a discussion of the philosophical foundation of CQR.

CQR is closer in theory and procedures to GT (Glaser & Strauss, 1967; Rennie, Phillips, & Quartaro, 1988; Strauss & Corbin, 1990) than to other qualitative methods. Similarities between CQR and GT include the following:

- interviewing participants,
- developing core ideas and domains, and
- continually returning to the data to ensure faithfulness to the data.

Differences between CQR and GT include the following:

- CQR researchers use a semistructured interview protocol, such that the same set of questions is used with all participants but the interviewer is also encouraged to probe for individual information.

In contrast, GT researchers use an unstructured interview protocol that evolves as additional participants are interviewed, and as such, the same questions might not be asked of all participants.

■ GT researchers alternate between data gathering and data analysis, collecting data until stability is attained (i.e., no new findings emerge). In contrast, CQR researchers use a predetermined number of participants.

■ GT researchers often use only one judge to analyze the data, whereas CQR uses multiple judges and auditors.

■ GT researchers construct core ideas first and then arrange these core ideas into domains, which are then arranged into a hierarchical structure under one core category. In contrast, CQR researchers code domains, then construct core ideas, and then develop a hierarchical structure of domains/categories and subcategories.

■ GT researchers describe each category in terms of its characteristics, whereas CQR researchers do not.

■ CQR researchers specify whether categories and subcategories are general (apply to all or all but one of the participants), typical (apply to at least half up to the cutoff for general), or variant (apply to at least two up to the cutoff for typical), whereas GT researchers do not specify how many participants fit into various categories.

■ CQR has a relatively fixed method of data analysis, whereas a key feature of GT is its flexibility, such that researchers vary a great deal in how they implement the method.

By no means do we claim that CQR is the best qualitative approach. We assert, instead, that CQR is a relatively accessible, rigorous, qualitative approach that researchers can easily learn and apply in a trustworthy manner.

## Overview of This Book

In the second chapter of Part I of this book, Stahl, Taylor, and I present a historical and philosophical treatise on CQR so that readers can be aware of underlying philosophy of science issues. Readers can make a more informed decision about whether to use this approach if they know whether it fits their philosophical leanings (e.g., do you think that there is truth that can be found or that there are multiple truths and perspectives depending on context?).

In Part II of the book, we delineate the steps of CQR in great detail so that researchers new to this method can understand each part of the process and consider the essential choices they must make along the way. Crook-Lyon, Goates-Jones, and I get us started in Chapter 3 by describing how researchers select a topic, how they decide whether to use qualitative methods, and how they approach the extant literature on the topic. In Chapter 4, Vivino, Thompson, and I describe issues related to the selection, care, and "feeding" of the research team, given that the composition and functioning of the team is crucial to the success of a CQR project. Biases and expectations are the topics for Sim, Huang, and me in Chapter 5. Given that researchers bring so much of themselves to this approach, this chapter will help the reader think carefully about how, on the one hand, to limit researchers' individual influences on the data and on the other hand, to encourage the creative and thoughtful input of each team member. In Chapter 6, Williams and I discuss the selection and recruitment of the sample, focusing on the influence of such choices on the results. Data collection methods are the focus for Burkard, Knox, and me in Chapter 7, with a discussion of how to conduct interviews. Thompson, Vivino, and I (Chapter 8) describe how to generate domains and construct core ideas. Ladany, Thompson, and I (Chapter 9) describe how to conduct cross-analyses. Auditing is the topic for Schlosser, Dewey, and me in Chapter 10, with a focus on how to select auditors and a description of the essential role and tasks of auditors. In Chapter 11, Knox, Schlosser, and I discuss steps involved in writing the manuscript so that researchers can best tell their stories and bring the data to life for readers. In the final chapter in this section (Chapter 12), Knox, Hess, and I present a new method called *qualitative meta-analysis,* which allows researchers to aggregate results across CQR studies.

In Part III, we attend to broader issues that influence CQR. First, Williams and I tackle the thorny issue of trustworthiness or determining the quality of a CQR study (Chapter 13). Rather than talking about the psychometric properties of measures (i.e., validity and reliability) as is done in quantitative research but that is not appropriate for qualitative research, we examine ways that researchers can show that their methods are trustworthy or credible. Inman, Howard, and I explore the topic of culture and its influence on CQR in Chapter 14. Burkard, Knox, and I discuss the myriad ethical issues that arise in conducting CQR in Chapter 15. In Chapter 16, Chui, Jackson, Liu, and I provide an annotated bibliography of published CQR studies, along with a summary of the key features of CQR studies (e.g., authors, publication outlets, samples); this summary should be useful to researchers trying to understand how CQR has been used.

Part IV addresses recent modifications and extensions of CQR. In Chapter 17, Spangler, Liu, and I describe the application of CQR to simpler data, often collected via short answers to open-ended questions in written questionnaires by large numbers of participants (CQR-M). In Chapter 18, Jackson, Chui, and I describe the application of CQR to psychotherapy case studies (CQR-C). In contrast to the original CQR, which involves data collection through semistructured interviews, CQR-C applies the method to naturalistically occurring data such as psychotherapy sessions or cases.

Finally, in an Appendix to the book, I present an overview of CQR by answering frequently asked questions about the method. I hope that this will serve as a review of the constructs used in CQR.

## Conclusions

It can be daunting to learn qualitative research, particularly for those steeped in quantitative traditions. Qualitative approaches offer a new way of thinking about research and knowledge, but they often require that researchers struggle with many new ideas. In addition, each new study requires researchers to think through many questions and develop unique solutions to problems in data collection and data analysis. We can only provide general guidelines here for what researchers might encounter in planning and conducting CQR studies.

I encourage researchers to follow the methods presented in this book as closely as possible if they wish to say that they are conducting CQR. After researchers have tried this method, I encourage them to empirically examine its various aspects in a constant effort to improve the approach and develop better ways of conducting this type of research.

## References

Berman, M., Hill, C. E., Liu, J., Jackson, J., Sim, W., & Spangler, P. (in press). Corrective relational events in the treatment of three cases of anorexia nervosa. In L. G. Castonguay & C. E. Hill (Eds.), *Transformation in psychotherapy: Corrective experiences across cognitive behavioral, humanistic, and psychodynamic approaches.* Washington, DC: American Psychological Association.

Bogdan, R. C., & Biklen, S. K. (1992). *Qualitative research for education: An introduction to theory and methods* (2nd ed.). Boston, MA: Allyn & Bacon.

Elliott, R. (1989). Comprehensive process analysis: Understanding the change process in significant therapy events. In M. J. Packer & R. B. Addison (Eds.), *Entering the circle: Hermeneutic investigation in psychology* (pp. 165–184). Albany: State University of New York Press.

Glaser, B., & Strauss, A. L. (1967). *The discovery of grounded theory: Strategies for qualitative research.* Hawthorne, NY: Aldine de Gruyter.

Goldman, L. (1976). A revolution in counseling research. *Journal of Counseling Psychology, 23,* 543–552. doi:10.1037/0022-0167.23.6.543.

Goldman, L. (1979). Research is more than technology. *The Counseling Psychologist, 8,* 41–44. doi:10.1177/001100007900800306

Henwood, K. L., & Pidgeon, N. F. (1992). Qualitative research and psychological theorizing. *The British Journal of Psychology, 83,* 97–111.

Hill, C. E. (1978). Development of a counselor verbal response category system. *Journal of Counseling Psychology, 25,* 461–468. doi:10.1037/0022-0167.25.5.461

Hill, C. E. (1984). A personal account of the process of becoming a counseling process researcher. *The Counseling Psychologist, 12,* 99–109. doi:10.1177/0011000084123010

Hill, C. E. (1990). A review of exploratory in-session process research. *Journal of Consulting and Clinical Psychology, 58,* 288–294. doi:10.1037/0022-006X.58.3.288

Hill, C. E. (in press). Consensual qualitative research (CQR) methods for conducting psychotherapy process research. In O. Gelo (Ed.), *Psychotherapy research: General issues, outcome and process.* Vienna, Austria: Springer.

Hill, C. E., Charles, D., & Reed, K. G. (1981). A longitudinal analysis of changes in counseling skills during doctoral training in counseling psychology. *Journal of Counseling Psychology, 28,* 428–436. doi:10.1037/0022-0167.28.5.428

Hill, C. E., & Gronsky, B. (1984). Research: Why and how? In J. M. Whiteley, N. Kagan, L. W. Harmon, B. R. Fretz, & F. Tanney (Eds.), *The coming decade in counseling psychology* (pp. 149–159). Schenectady, NY: Character Research Press.

Hill, C. E., Helms, J. E., Tichenor, V., Spiegel, S. B., O'Grady, K. E., & Perry, E. S. (1988). The effects of therapist response modes in brief psychotherapy. *Journal of Counseling Psychology, 35,* 222–233. doi:10.1037/0022-0167.35.3.222.

Hill, C. E., Knox, S., Thompson, B. J., Williams, E. N., Hess, S.A., & Ladany, N. (2005). Consensual qualitative research: An update. *Journal of Counseling Psychology, 52,* 196–205. doi:10.1037/0022-0167.52.2.196

Hill, C. E., & Lambert, M. J. (2004). Methodological issues in studying psychotherapy processes and outcomes. In M. J. Lambert (Ed.), *Handbook of psychotherapy and behavior change* (5th ed., pp. 84–136). New York, NY: Wiley.

Hill, C. E., Rochlen, A. B., Zack, J. S., McCready, T., & Dematatis, A. (2003). Working with dreams using the Hill cognitive–experiential model: A comparison of computer-assisted, therapist empathy, and therapist empathy + input conditions. *Journal of Counseling Psychology, 50,* 211–220. doi:10.1037/0022-0167.50.2.211

Hill, C. E., Sim, W., Spangler, P., Stahl, J., Sullivan, C., & Teyber, E. (2008). Therapist immediacy in brief psychotherapy: Case study II. *Psychotherapy: Theory, Research, Practice, Training, 45,* 298–315. doi:10.1037/a0013306

Hill, C. E., Thames, T. B., & Rardin, D. (1979). A comparison of Rogers, Perls, and Ellis on the Hill counselor verbal response category system. *Journal of Counseling Psychology, 26,* 198–203. doi:10.1037/0022-0167.26.3.198

Hill, C. E., Thompson, B. J., & Williams, E. N. (1997). A guide to conducting consensual qualitative research. *The Counseling Psychologist, 25,* 517–572. doi:10.1177/0011000097254001

Holsti, O. R. (1969). Introduction of Part II. In G. Gerbner, O. R. Holsti, K. Krippendorf, W. J. Paisley, & P. J. Stone (Eds.), *The analysis of communication content* (pp. 109–121). New York, NY: Wiley.

Kasper, L., Hill, C. E., & Kivlighan, D. (2008). Therapist immediacy in brief psychotherapy: Case Study I. *Psychotherapy: Theory, Research, Practice, Training, 45,* 281–297. doi:10.1037/a0013305

Lambert, M. J., & Hill, C. E. (1994). Assessing psychotherapy outcomes and processes. In A. E. Bergin & S. L. Garfield (Eds.), *Handbook of psychotherapy and behavior change* (4th ed., pp. 72–113). New York, NY: Wiley.

Mahrer, A. R. (1988). Discovery-oriented psychotherapy research. *American Psychologist, 43,* 694–702. doi:10.1037/0003-066X.43.9.694

McLeod, J. (2011). *Qualitative research in counselling and psychotherapy.* London, England: Sage.

Morrow, S. L. (2005). Quality and trustworthiness in qualitative research in counseling psychology. *Journal of Counseling Psychology, 52,* 250–260. doi:10.1037/0022-0167.52.2.250

Rennie, D. L., Phillips, J. R., & Quartaro, G. K. (1988). Grounded theory: A promising approach to conceptualization in psychology? *Canadian Psychology, 29,* 139–150. doi:10.1037/h0079765

Rhodes, R., Hill, C. E., Thompson, B. J., & Elliott, R. (1994). Client retrospective recall of resolved and unresolved misunderstanding events. *Journal of Counseling Psychology, 41,* 473–483. doi:10.1037/0022-0167.41.4.473

Schielke, H. J., Fishman, J. L., Osatuke, K., & Stiles, W. B. (2009). Creative consensus on interpretations of qualitative data: The Ward method. *Psychotherapy Research, 19,* 558–565. doi:10.1080/10503300802621180

Stiles, W. B. (1993). Quality control in qualitative research. *Clinical Psychology Review, 13,* 593–618. doi:10.1016/0272-7358(93)90048-Q

Strauss, A., & Corbin, J. (1990). *Basics of qualitative research: Grounded theory procedures and techniques.* Newbury Park, CA: Sage.

*Jessica V. Stahl, Nicole E. Taylor, and Clara E. Hill*

# Philosophical and Historical Background of Consensual Qualitative Research

# 2

R esearchers should understand the history and philosophy of any method they use to determine if it is an appropriate fit for their views and purposes (Creswell, 2007; Hoyt & Bhati, 2007). Such understanding allows researchers to have a deeper understanding of the research process, think critically about their own and others' qualitative work, and explain and defend the relevance of qualitative methods and findings (McLeod, 2011). This chapter provides a philosophical and historical context for the consensual qualitative research (CQR) method to assist researchers in determining whether it is appropriate for their circumstances.

In this chapter, we first define three major research paradigms relevant to the understanding of CQR and the assumptions embedded within each. Then, following the recommendations of Elliott, Fischer, and Rennie (1999), we place CQR within the context of the aforementioned research paradigms to locate its philosophical underpinnings. Next, we briefly describe the history of qualitative approaches and note the emergence of each of the research paradigms discussed in the first section; we also note how CQR fits into the history of qualitative approaches and discuss the rationale for qualitative, discovery-oriented approaches such as CQR. The aim in each of these discussions is to help CQR researchers fully understand the assumptions, philosophies, and historical context inherent in choosing this approach.

## Research Paradigms

A *paradigm* can be defined as "the entire constellation of beliefs, values, techniques and so on shared by the members of a given community" (Kuhn, 1970, p. 175). All research paradigms are guided by assumptions about the world and how it should be studied (i.e., philosophies of science; Denzin & Lincoln, 2005; Ponterotto, 2005). These assumptions address the nature of reality (*ontology*), the relationship between the researcher and research participant (*epistemology*), the role of researchers' values in the scientific process (*axiology*), the language used to present the research to an audience (*rhetorical structure*), and the process and procedures of the research (*methodology*) used.

In this section, we rely extensively on Ponterotto (2005) and delineate the ontology, epistemology, axiology, rhetorical structure, and methodology for each of three different research paradigms (positivism, postpositivism, and constructivism) relevant to understanding the philosophical underpinnings of CQR (for discussion of other research paradigms, see Creswell, 2007; Denzin & Lincoln, 2005; for discussion of the philosophical history and context of these paradigms as they relate to qualitative approaches, see McLeod, 2011). In addition, we provide an example to bring to life how one might study the effects of different types of psychotherapy from each approach.

### POSITIVISM

The first of these paradigms, positivism, is exemplified by quantitative approaches and the true scientific experiment. The focus is on using a priori hypotheses, controlled experimental methods, and inferential statistics to predict phenomena and interpret results in order to discover an objective truth. In terms of ontology, positivists believe that there is one true reality that can be apprehended, identified, and measured. In terms of epistemology, positivists assume that the researcher and research participants are independent and that the researcher can objectively (i.e., without bias) study the participants; positivists do not believe that participants and researchers influence one another. On the dimension of axiology, positivists believe that researchers' values have no place in the research process. Given the focus on objectivity and true experiments, positivists use a detached, neutral, scientific rhetorical structure and method in which variables are carefully controlled and manipulated through rigorous procedures (Ponterotto, 2005; Wampold, Heppner, & Kivlighan, 2008).

If one were to examine the effects of different types of psychotherapy from a positivistic approach, the goal would be to design a methodologically rigorous study with experimental controls such as random assignment to discover the truth about the psychotherapies (e.g., which one is more effective). Thus, the researcher would set some a priori hypotheses (e.g., Treatment A will be more effective than Treatment B in decreasing symptoms of anxiety). The researcher might then, using random sampling, find individuals who score highly on the variables of interest (in this case, individuals could score highly on a pretreatment anxiety inventory) and randomly assign identified individuals to treatment groups. One set of individuals would participate in Treatment A for a set length of time, and the other set of individuals would participate in Treatment B for that same set length of time. After treatment is completed, the researcher would then administer quantitative measures of anxiety to participants in both groups and would use statistical methods to objectively measure and identify which treatment was more effective in reducing anxiety. The relationship between the researcher and participants would ideally be nonexistent, with a double-blind method used so neither the researcher nor participants knew to which treatment class the participant was assigned. The researcher would assume throughout the process that his or her own beliefs about the effectiveness of Treatment A versus Treatment B had no impact on the results of the study; any research report of the study would present the results in a detached and neutral manner, thus conveying the objectivity assumed to exist throughout the study.

## POSTPOSITIVISM

Postpositivism shares many similarities with, yet is subtly different from, positivism. Methodologically, postpositivists, like positivists, use experimental methods in which variables are controlled or manipulated (Ponterotto, 2005; Wampold et al., 2008). Thus, postpositivists' hypotheses and research design for the study on the effects of Treatments A and B would look identical to the positivists' study.

However, postpositivists' ontological view differs from that of positivists in that they acknowledge that although an objective truth exists, only an approximate understanding of this truth can be attained. To continue the previous example from the hypothetical study on the effects of Treatments A and B on participants' anxiety, the postpositivist researcher acknowledges that we can never know the truth about which treatment is more effective. Rather, the postpositivist believes that we can approximate that "truth"[1] by using rigorous experimental methods in a number

---

[1] From this point forward, the word *truth* is placed in quotation marks ("truth") to reflect the postpositivist ontological view that one can never fully capture a true reality and the constructivist view that a single true reality does not exist but rather that there exist multiple, constructed realities (Ponterotto, 2005).

of different studies in the hopes that findings are corroborated and replicated across studies, allowing us to be more certain that we are understanding the "truth" (Wampold et al., 2008). So rather than drawing conclusions about the "truth" from a single study (as a positivist might), the postpositivist believes that conclusions about the "truth" are made as the convergence of findings across multiple studies increases.

The researchers in our Treatment A versus B study of anxiety might acknowledge (to themselves, or each other—but typically not in research reports; Wampold et al., 2008) any biases they might have that would affect the study. Regarding the relationship between researchers and participants, postpositivists take the epistemological stance that the researchers and participants should remain independent, although they inevitably influence one another within the research process. (Note that this is a subtle difference from the positivist view, which posits that rigorous, standard procedures allow the researcher to objectively study their participants without bias and without influencing them.) Thus, researchers might have the data collected by research assistants who are blind to the hypotheses of the study and to the condition to which participants have been assigned.

Postpositivists agree with positivists that researchers' values have no place in the research process, yet they simultaneously recognize human limitations for objectivity in the research endeavor. Postpositivists advocate that researchers' values be removed (or bracketed) from scientific research, and they try to control the influence of researchers' expectations (e.g., by keeping experimenters blind to the hypotheses of the experiment and/or to the condition to which participants have been assigned). Thus, postpositivist researchers recognize that biases exist, but they aim to contain their biases when studying a particular phenomenon. As with positivists, this approach is reflected in a neutral, detached, objective rhetorical structure for the presentation of research results (Ponterotto, 2005; Wampold et al., 2008).

## CONSTRUCTIVISM

A constructivist approach to research differs in many ways from both positivism and postpositivism. Ontologically, constructivists believe that a single true reality does not exist; rather, there exist multiple socially constructed realities. Regarding epistemology, they believe that a close, subjective interaction between the researcher and participant is central to accessing the participant's "lived experience." Because they are intended to access this lived experience, methods used by constructivists tend to be more naturalistic (i.e., using observations and/or interviews) and qualitative. In terms of axiology, constructivists acknowledge that the values of the researcher cannot be removed from the research process because the researcher's own lived experience inherently affects his or her interpretation of the participant's lived experience. Researchers who believe in constructivism thus "bracket" their values, biases, and expectations by explicitly acknowledging and describing them. However, they do not seek to get rid of or control for their biases and expectations (as postpositivists do) because they acknowledge that it is impossible to do so. Given the focus on the subjectivity of the researcher and the interactive nature of the relationship between researcher and participant, it is not surprising that such research reports are often written in the first person and detail the researcher's expectations, biases, values, and thought processes throughout the research process (Ponterotto, 2005; Wampold et al., 2008).

If constructivists were conducting the comparison of Treatments A and B for anxiety, they might interview individuals who had participated in each treatment to get a full picture of how participants experienced the treatments. The researcher might look for themes that capture the participants' shared experiences while simultaneously acknowledging that each participant's experience of the therapy is unique. The constructivist researcher in this study would likely have deep interactions with the participants and would acknowledge that his or her own biases are inherently embedded in the research process. Research reports from such a study would describe in detail the nature of the interaction between the researcher and the participants and would describe the common and unique lived experiences participants had while in the treatment. Furthermore, the researcher would report his or her biases (e.g., expectations about the ways in which the effects of the treatments differ) in any research reports so that readers could take those biases and expectations into account when interpreting the findings for themselves. Thus, in contrast to the positivist and postpositivist goal of determining which treatment was better, the utility of a constructivist study would lie in its ability to provide a vivid description of the participants' experiences of the treatments from the perspective of the authors.

## THE PHILOSOPHICAL UNDERPINNINGS OF CONSENSUAL QUALITATIVE RESEARCH

As outlined in Chapter 1, CQR has four major steps: (a) collecting data in an open-ended way; (b) sorting data into broad categories, called *domains;* (c) creating summaries, called *core ideas,* of what each participant has said in each domain; and (d) looking for themes or patterns across participants' responses within each domain, called *cross-analysis.* Thus, CQR is an inductive process that allows the results to emerge from the data and uses words and stories rather than numbers as the raw data. In addition, attention is paid to the context within which the words are spoken in assigning domains and creating core ideas, and the research team constantly returns to the raw data to check for the trustworthiness of the analysis. Furthermore, CQR relies extensively on the use of a team of judges who collaborate to consensually analyze the data, and auditors examine the work of the research team to provide feedback about each step of the data analysis. All of these components of CQR are important to keep in mind as we discuss the philosophical underpinnings of CQR.

Hill et al. (2005) described CQR as "predominantly constructivist, with some post-positivist elements" (p. 197). From a constructivist standpoint, CQR relies on naturalistic, interactive, qualitative methods. The meaning of the phenomenon being studied emerges from words and text, the context of participants' words is taken into account, and interviewers interact with participants through the use of probes and clarifications (Hill et al., 2005; Ponterotto, 2005).

In terms of ontology (i.e., view of the nature of reality), CQR researchers recognize that there are multiple, equally valid, socially constructed versions of the "truth" (a constructivist view). Thus, researchers accept the uniqueness of each participant's experience while looking for commonalities of experiences among participants. Ontologically, CQR also has a flavor of postpositivism because the emphasis on consensus among team members and auditors implies that team members are working to coconstruct a "truth" as they seek to represent the data as faithfully as possible through integrating multiple perspectives (Ponterotto, 2005). During the consensus process in CQR, judges examine the data independently and then come together to present and discuss their ideas until all members of the team agree on the best representation of the data (Hill, Thompson, & Williams, 1997). However, even within the consensus process, individual team members' perspectives are respected and encouraged (Hill et al., 2005). Use of multiple perspectives, combined with constantly returning to the raw data, helps capture the complexity of the data because different members of the team inevitably perceive different nuances. It also allows a variety of viewpoints to emerge, helping to circumvent the biases of any one person. Furthermore, including the auditors in the consensus process controls for groupthink and provides an additional perspective that helps the team come closer to the "truth" (Hill, in press; Hill et al., 1997). This emphasis on consensus is one of the features that differentiates CQR from more clearly constructivist approaches such as grounded theory (e.g., Ponterotto, 2005; Strauss & Corbin, 1990), which often rely on a single researcher's understanding of the data.

From an epistemological standpoint, CQR is primarily constructivist in its recognition of the mutual influence between researcher and participant. In CQR, the interviewer learns about the phenomenon in question from the participant but also helps the participant explore his or her experience in depth by using follow-up probes (see also Chapter 7 in this volume). The postpositivist component of the epistemology of CQR is evident in the use of a standard semistructured interview protocol with flexibility to query for further information where needed in order to obtain the same types of information from each participant. This procedure stands in contrast to a protocol subject to change, as one would find in more constructivist approaches.

Regarding the role of the researcher's values (axiology), CQR again resides between postpositivism and constructivism. In CQR, we acknowledge that researchers' biases are inevitable and should be discussed explicitly (a constructivist approach) but suggest that these biases can be bracketed such that the degree to which they influence the results is minimized. This bracketing of biases is consistent with both constructivist and postpositivist approaches. The goal of CQR is to present how participants (not the researchers) view the world, and the assumption is that as a result of bracketing, different teams would see the data in approximately the same way. Furthermore, in CQR, researchers all use the same interview protocol to minimize the impact of individual interviewers (a postpositivistic approach) but simultaneously acknowledge that the researchers' biases influence the way in which they conduct the interview (e.g., what follow-up probes they use, and when; see also Chapter 5 in this volume).

Finally, the rhetorical structure of CQR is primarily postpositivist because researchers present results as objectively as possible, avoid broad interpretations, and use the third person to report data. The goal is to summarize participants' words and find themes across participants with the hope of transferring results to a larger population if adequate sampling has taken place (Hill et al., 2005; Ponterotto, 2005). However, the use of participant excerpts that bring to life the "lived experience" of participants highlights the touch of constructivism present in the rhetorical structure of CQR (Ponterotto, 2005).

Finding the right balance of rigor and relevance has been an ongoing struggle for qualitative researchers. Qualitative research has been haunted by what Denzin and Lincoln (2005) called a "double-faced ghost," where one perspective emphasizes the assumption that qualitative researchers can report their observations of the world with some level of clarity, objectivity, and scientific merit (*rigor*) whereas the other perspective posits that the unique life stories of participants should be maintained with as much richness as possible (*relevance*). This double-faced ghost has led to a vacillation between experimental and postpositivist methods on one hand and more constructivist and narrative models like grounded theory on the other hand. The struggle between objectivity and richness has troubled qualitative researchers throughout history, but one of the greatest strengths of CQR is that it was designed with both rigor and relevance in mind, thus providing a resting place for the double-faced ghost.

## History of and Rationale for Qualitative Approaches

The research paradigms discussed in the previous section are embedded in the history of philosophy and the history of qualitative approaches; the history of qualitative approaches is briefly discussed next (a detailed account of the history of philosophy relevant to qualitative approaches is beyond the scope of current purposes; for more information, see McLeod, 2011). Prior to World War II, researchers using qualitative data (e.g., sociologists and ethnographers in their accounts of field experiences) did so from a positivist perspective: They sought to offer valid, reliable, and objective accounts and interpretations in their writings. In psychology, this approach to studying human phenomena was exemplified by behavioral traditions that were especially focused on quantifying human behaviors and implementing reinforcement strategies that would allow for consistent behavior change across many different groups (Denzin & Lincoln, 2005).

However, beginning in the middle of the 20th century, a paradigm shift from positivism to postpositivism occurred across social science disciplines. This shift occurred as social scientific researchers realized the importance of contextualizing data and describing phenomena in a rich way. In psychology, the groundwork for the emergence of qualitative methods was laid by dissatisfaction with behavioral approaches, which were seen as too simplistic in their attempts to generalize truths about human behavior. Postpositivism reigned as researchers sought to make qualitative research as rigorous as its qualitative counterpart, using probability and frequencies to support the likelihood that a conclusion applies to a specific situation (Denzin & Lincoln, 2005).

By the 1970s, constructivist approaches to qualitative data emerged as social scientists turned to the humanities for models, theories, and methods of analysis of qualitative data. Hermeneutics, structuralism, semiotics, phenomenology, cultural studies, and feminism enabled researchers to take a more critical, narrative, and interpretive look at human phenomena (Denzin & Lincoln, 2005). Across disciplines, scholars began to take a more complex view of human behavior and to evaluate cultural and social phenomena in new critical and contextualized ways. For example, sociologists and anthropologists began looking at social institutions and began to question the traditional assumptions and accepted truths about race and gender. This emphasis on understanding the social construction of variables like race and gender was a radical departure from previous paradigms (Denzin & Lincoln, 2005).

Qualitative research probably gained acceptance in fields like sociology and anthropology because the methods were complementary to the traditional practices within those fields, like studying social groups and engaging in fieldwork. In anthropology, in particular, the qualitative approach of ethnography became especially important as researchers traveled to foreign lands and sought ways to understand, document, and translate their experiences (Denzin & Lincoln, 2005).

Researchers in the social and behavioral sciences, on the other hand, were more reluctant to accept these new methods, and we would be remiss not to mention the history of resistance to qualitative work from our colleagues in the experimental sciences. Arguments against qualitative research tend to claim that it is not "real" science, is not objective, and is merely one researcher's version of the truth (Denzin & Lincoln, 2005). Psychology and other behavioral sciences are often considered natural sciences, and psychologists have historically attempted to distance themselves from the sciences that are too "soft." Unfortunately, this segregation between fields may have contributed to the slower acceptance of qualitative research within psychology. Many psychologists have attempted to adhere to positivist methodologies to keep up with their natural science colleagues, cleverly coined "physics envy" (Nichols, 1993).

The first movement in psychology and psychotherapy research toward more qualitative-like methods involved discovery-oriented approaches. Mahrer (1988) highlighted the limitations of hypothesis testing (i.e., quantitative approaches) for advancing knowledge about psychotherapy. He said that "hypothesis testing is essentially unable to fulfill its self-assigned mission of confirming or disconfirming psychotherapeutic propositions or theories" (p. 696). Rather, he suggested that

> researchers adopt the rationale, aims, and methods of discovery-oriented psychotherapy research . . . [because] the whole basis for designing discovery-oriented studies is the intention to learn more; to be surprised; to find out what one does not already expect, predict, or hypothesize; to answer a question whose answer provides something one wants to know but might not have expected, predicted, or hypothesized. (p. 697)

The limitations of hypothesis testing and quantitative research are significant, and researchers embarking on any new research project (not just those about psychotherapy) can benefit from taking a more discovery-oriented approach. Although Mahrer advocated more discovery-oriented approaches, he still retained many positivist elements in his approach (e.g., after deriving or discovering categories from the data, he advocated having a new team of judges trained to high reliability to code the data).

Qualitative approaches, which are of course discovery-oriented, emerged out of the discovery-oriented approaches and dropped many of the positivist elements. These discovery-oriented qualitative approaches are designed to understand (i.e., describe and interpret) the complexity of a phenomenon within its context. They focus on understanding a few individuals in great depth (an *idiographic* approach) rather than on general or universal patterns of behavior (a *nomothetic* approach; Ponterotto, 2005). Thus, the purpose of qualitative research is to "describe and clarify experience as it is lived and constituted in awareness" (Polkinghorne, 2005, p. 138). Fitting with Mahrer's ideas about discovery-oriented research, qualitative studies are usually driven by open-ended research questions rather than hypotheses because studies are often conducted in areas without much existing research and so hypotheses would be difficult to develop; in addition, studies are also conducted in areas where an idiographic approach is preferable to a nomothetic one (Wampold et al., 2008). Conclusions are made from the data by cycling between the inductive process of generating themes and categories from the data, and the deductive process of checking if those themes appear in new data (Morrow & Smith, 2000). This process keeps researchers grounded in the actual data—for example, the text of an interview—rather than focused on hypothesis testing.

The first three qualitative approaches that were developed and used within psychology and psychotherapy research were grounded theory (Strauss & Corbin, 1990), phenomenological approaches (Giorgi, 1985), and comprehensive process analysis (Elliott, 1989). These three qualitative methods have many beneficial uses within psychology, but Hill et al. (2005) expressed their frustration that the approaches seemed "vague, difficult to understand, and equally difficult to implement" (p.196). Given their desire to create an approach that could easily be taught and used, Hill and her colleagues developed a new approach to integrate the best features of the three existing approaches and thus created CQR (Hill et al., 1997). See Chapter 1 in this volume for more details about the history of the development of CQR.

In discussing the history and philosophical context of CQR, it bears noting that although the method was not developed specifically for psychotherapy research, the counseling psychologists who developed it had primary research interests in that field. Above and beyond the philosophical paradigms discussed earlier, the underlying biases and assumptions inherent in CQR are similar to those in counseling. Rennie (1994) described how qualitative researchers and counselors are both interested in the narratives of human experiences and the meaning individuals make out of them. Both counselors and qualitative researchers emphasize the empowerment of the individual research participant or client while still attempting to understand the person in the context of the whole (Rennie, 1994). Furthermore, the overlap between the skills and processes involved in qualitative research and counseling practice are extensive. Staying focused on the actual words that a participant uses in an interview is similar to using good listening and counseling skills in a therapy session; both require intense focus and empathy. Although this overlap makes CQR especially beneficial for counseling process and outcome research, CQR has increasingly been used with a variety of different topics, ranging from health psychology to sociology (see Chapter 18 in this volume). The possibilities for use in other disciplines are vast because CQR is easily adapted to any research project that involves interview data or textual analysis. Within psychotherapy research, CQR has continued to prove useful in understanding new aspects of psychotherapy and case analysis.

## Conclusions

We believe that CQR is an important research method that has built on the storied history of other qualitative methods and will continue to develop and change in the future. After reading this chapter, readers should have an understanding of where CQR fits within research paradigms and how it builds on the history of other qualitative methods. We encourage readers to keep in mind the historical context and philosophical assumptions of CQR discussed here as they learn more about the method in subsequent chapters.

## References

Creswell, J. W. (2007). *Qualitative inquiry and research design: Choosing among five approaches* (2nd ed.). Thousand Oaks, CA: Sage.

Denzin, N. K., & Lincoln, Y. S. (2005). *The SAGE handbook of qualitative research* (3rd ed.). Thousand Oaks, CA: Sage.

Elliott, R. (1989). Comprehensive process analysis: Understanding the change process in significant therapy events. In M. J. Packer & R. B. Addison (Eds.), *Entering the circle: Hermeneutic investigation in psychology* (pp. 165–184). Albany: State University of New York Press.

Elliott, R., Fischer, C. T., & Rennie, D. L. (1999). Evolving guidelines for publication of qualitative research studies in psychology and related fields. *The British Journal of Clinical Psychology, 38,* 215–229. doi:10.1348/014466599162782

Giorgi, A. (1985). Sketch of a psychological phenomenological method. In A. Giorgi (Ed.), *Phenomenology and psychological research* (pp. 8–22). Pittsburgh, PA: Duquesne University Press.

Hill, C. E. (in press). Consensual qualitative research (CQR) methods for conducting psychotherapy process research. In O. Gelo (Ed.), *Psychotherapy research: General issues, outcome and process.* Vienna, Austria: Springer.

Hill, C. E., Knox, S., Thompson, B. J., Williams, E. N., Hess, S.A., & Ladany, N. (2005). Consensual qualitative research: An update. *Journal of Counseling Psychology, 52,* 196–205. doi:10.1037/0022-0167.52.2.196

Hill, C. E., Thompson, B. J., & Williams, E. N. (1997). A guide to conducting consensual qualitative research. *The Counseling Psychologist, 25,* 517–572. doi:10.1177/0011000097254001

Hoyt, W. T., & Bhati, K. S. (2007). Principles and practices: An empirical examination of qualitative research in the Journal of Counseling Psychology. *Journal of Counseling Psychology, 54,* 201–210. doi:10.1037/0022-0167.54.2.201

Kuhn, T. S. (1970). *The structure of scientific revolutions.* Chicago, IL: University of Chicago Press.

Mahrer, A. R. (1988). Discovery-oriented psychotherapy research. *American Psychologist, 43,* 694–702. doi:10.1037/0003-066X.43.9.694

McLeod, J. (2011). *Qualitative research in counselling and psychotherapy.* London: Sage.

Morrow, S. L., & Smith, M. L. (2000). Qualitative research in counseling psychology. In S. D. Brown & R. W. Lent (Eds.), *Handbook of counseling psychology* (pp. 199–230). New York, NY: Wiley.

Nichols, D. P. (1993). Outgrowing physics envy: Reconceptualizing social research. *Contemporary Family Therapy, 15*(1), 51–72. doi:10.1007/BF00903487

Polkinghorne, D. E. (2005). Language and meaning: Data collection in qualitative research. *Journal of Counseling Psychology, 52,* 137–145. doi:10.1037/0022-0167.52.2.137

Ponterotto, J. G. (2005). Qualitative research in counseling psychology: A primer on research paradigms and philosophy of science. *Journal of Counseling Psychology, 52,* 126–136. doi:10.1037/0022-0167.52.2.126

Rennie, D. L. (1994). Human science and counseling psychology: Closing the gap between research and practice. *Counselling Psychology Quarterly, 7,* 235–250. doi:10.1080/09515079408254149

Strauss, A., & Corbin, J. (1990). *Basics of qualitative research: Grounded theory procedures and techniques.* Newbury Park, CA: Sage.

Wampold, B. E., Heppner, P. P., & Kivlighan, D. M. (2008). *Research design in counseling* (3rd ed.). New York, NY: Brooks/Cole.

# CONDUCTING CONSENSUAL QUALITATIVE RESEARCH

*Rachel E. Crook-Lyon, Melissa K. Goates-Jones, and Clara E. Hill*

# Getting Started | 3

W e offer some ideas in this chapter for researchers to consider when planning CQR studies. We discuss how researchers choose topics, decide on the appropriateness of the topic for qualitative analysis, state the purpose of the study, and develop research questions (see Table 3.1 for a summary). As a foundation, we encourage researchers using the consensual qualitative research (CQR) method to adopt a framework in planning that includes critical elements such as trustworthiness, ethical, and cultural considerations (see Chapters 13, 14, and 15, respectively, in this volume). At each step in the process, CQR researchers should think about establishing the trustworthiness of CQR data and maintaining high standards of ethical and cultural sensitivity.

Although we present a clear set of steps, we recognize that not all researchers will approach their projects in the order outlined below. Some researchers first become interested in a topic, then review the literature, then develop their research questions, and only then decide that qualitative methods are the most appropriate because of reasons listed in the previous section. Others may start out wanting to do qualitative research and search for an appropriate topic.

**TABLE 3.1**

**Summary of Recommendations for Getting Started on a Consensual Qualitative Research (CQR) Project**

| Step | Recommendations |
| --- | --- |
| Choosing a topic | Select a topic because of strong interest, based on personal experience, or when more research is needed in an area. |
| Generating research ideas | Brainstorm with colleagues and students, attend conferences, review scholarly journals, reflect or meditate. |
| Deciding on a qualitative approach | Choose CQR if you want to study processes with more depth, investigate infrequent events, describe complicated phenomena, explore new areas, or build theory. |
| Approaching the literature | Review literature related to the topic of interest prior to collecting data; bracket information during data analysis. |
| Stating the purpose | Identify that the purpose of the study is to describe, understand, develop or discover some phenomenon using a CQR methodology. |
| Stating research questions | Specifically state the research questions or objectives of the study. |

## Choosing a Topic

It is important to choose a topic in which you have a strong interest. Because research projects in general, and CQR projects in particular, often take months to years to complete, only a personally fascinating topic is likely to sustain motivation and momentum through the process. For example, Sarah Knox described how she came to choose the topic of clients' internal representations of their therapists (Knox, Goldberg, Woodhouse, & Hill, 1999):

> I had always been, and remain, fascinated by how clients carry around the presence of their therapist with them between sessions. Far more of clients' lives are lived outside of therapy, so how do clients continue the work, how to they invoke the (hopefully) healing presence of the therapist when not physically with him/her . . . I wanted to hear from clients themselves about this phenomenon, and was fascinated by what they shared. (S. Knox, personal communication, February 18, 2010)

It is easy to see that Sarah's passion for this topic was instrumental in the completion of this study.

In addition, researchers also often develop research ideas based on their own experiences with various phenomena. For example, Williams et al. (1998) published the article "Perceptions of Serendipity: Career Paths of Prominent Academic Women in Counseling Psychology." The idea for this study came from the principal investigator's own serendipitous events:

When I was an undergraduate student at Stanford University (and nearing graduation), I went to the Career Center, simply to have a counselor look over my resume as I was about to start job hunting. He looked over my experiences and interests and said, "You know, my wife works at a small test publishing company just down the road and I think you would really enjoy working there. You should check them out." I did, and they hired me as their "Test Expert" (which was fairly ironic at the time). The company was Consulting Psychologists Press, which publishes the Strong Interest Inventory, Myers-Briggs, and a number of other important assessment measures. I ended up serving as the minute-taker for the Strong Advisory Board meetings, and, as a result, got career counseling from Don Super, Lenore Harmon, and John Krumboltz. Not too shabby! Because of them (and through meeting many great counseling psychologists), I determined that I should apply to counseling psychology programs where there was also a good I/O [industrial/organizational psychology] program. (E. N. Williams, personal communication, March 22, 2010)

A caution should be noted, however, about using personal experience to choose a research topic. Because it is hard to be unbiased in the interviews and interpretation if you are extremely invested in obtaining a particular result, it is probably best not to choose topics that evoke intense emotions in you. For example, it may be difficult for a researcher to be unbiased in conducting interviews on childhood sexual trauma if experiences of such trauma have not yet been resolved.

Another way that researchers choose research topics is when they see a need for more information about this topic. For example, Knox, Dubois, Smith, Hess, and Hill (2009) published a study investigating clients' experiences giving gifts to therapists. They became interested in the topic after Sarah Knox did a literature review and found that

> this was an area that really hadn't been explored, and thus seemed ripe for further examination. Much of the literature was theoretical, with few investigations of the actual experiences of client gifts in therapy. Given the provocative nature of this interaction, we wanted to hear directly from clients themselves how they experienced the gift-giving process. (S. Knox, personal communication, February 18, 2010)

## *Generating Research Ideas*

Researchers have many unique methods of generating research ideas. For example, the third author of this chapter likes to go on walks with students and colleagues to brainstorm ideas. Other people get research ideas by listening to presentations at conventions and consulting with colleagues. For others, ideas come from reading scholarly journals. We especially encourage researchers to read CQR articles so that they get an idea about the kinds of topics and questions that are possible to examine. Other researchers may have ideas come to them in dreams, in the shower, or just by pondering. Researchers also may benefit from keeping an "idea journal" where they record their ideas for research projects.

Researchers should be careful to pick topics that on the one hand are important and big enough to study but on the other hand are relatively limited in scope so that they are not too overwhelming and vague. For example, the topic of clients' emotional experiences in therapy may be very interesting but it is very broad. Instead, it might be more manageable to narrow down the topic to, for example, client experiences of crying in therapy.

## Is a Qualitative Strategy the Best Approach for Studying the Topic?

Several topic areas are especially suitable for a qualitative approach such as CQR. For instance, qualitative approaches are especially suited for studying the process of psychotherapy to a depth that quantitative methods often fail to achieve. Hill, Nutt-Williams, Heaton, Thompson, and Rhodes, (1996), for example, were interested in studying therapeutic impasses in long-term therapy. Although a quantitative method may have elicited data about the frequency or content of therapeutic impasses, the researchers chose CQR because they wanted to obtain rich contextual data about the factors that led to therapeutic impasses from the therapists' perspective.

Another ideal application of qualitative methods is when one is interested in understanding events that happen infrequently, especially because it is difficult to find such events through typical approaches such as reviewing psychotherapy sessions. For example, gift-giving in therapy is a relatively uncommon event but one that is important to understand because it can be very meaningful to clients in a therapeutic setting. Because gift-giving in therapy is infrequent, it might be difficult to find a large enough sample to yield adequate results in a quantitative study. Instead, Knox, Hess, Williams, and Hill (2003) conducted a qualitative study wherein they interviewed 12 therapists about their experiences receiving tangible gifts from clients; they were able to ascertain specific differences between "problematic gifts" and "unproblematic gifts."

Relatedly, qualitative methods are helpful for understanding complicated phenomena such as internal events. For example, therapists' reactions to their sexual attraction toward clients is a topic that presents an opportunity to gather rich data. Using quantitative methods, researchers might examine the frequency of therapists' sexual attraction toward clients, or correlates of sexual attraction, but using qualitative methods can provide researchers with important information about the lived experience of the participants because data can be gathered in depth and within a context. Ladany et al. (1997) thus used CQR to determine that therapists believed they were overly invested and attentive to clients to whom they were sexually attracted and that sexual attraction created distance, distraction, and loss of objectivity. People often need time and an interested listener to be able to delve into their thoughts and feelings about such complex and emotionally charged topics.

Another instance in which qualitative methods are especially appropriate is when little is known about an area, making it difficult to know what questions to ask and what measures to use. For example, Santiago-Rivera, Altarriba, Poll, Gonzalez-Miller, and Cragun (2009) were interested in the incidence of therapist and client language switching between Spanish and English, but there was "little published research about the therapist's strategic use of bilingualism in therapy" (p. 437). Because it was a relatively new area of research, these researchers needed to do some groundwork to understand even what questions to ask. Hence, CQR was ideally suited for exploring this topic; researchers learned that therapists often used language switching and idiomatic expressions to establish trust, bond with clients, and promote disclosure.

Yet another reason for using CQR is because it is ideal for building theory. In contrast to the quantitative methods in which researchers develop a hypothesis and then test that hypothesis, CQR allows researchers to collect data that then forms the basis of a theory (thus CQR is inductive rather than deductive). In their study of relational influences in career development, Schultheiss, Palma, Predragovich, and Glasscock (2002) noted,

> Despite the complex nature of relationships, most of the research supporting the facilitative nature of close relationships on career progress has been conducted with large samples, employing quantitative statistical analyses based on responses from forced-choice, self-report instruments. . . . Although qualitative studies are not completely new to the attachment and career domain of inquiry, previous investigations have not fully captured the specific relational factors associated with developmental progress in career decision making. (p. 219)

Because there was an identified need to build a theory of relational influences on career development, Schultheiss et al. chose to conduct a qualitative study, which yielded valuable data about the relationship as a multidimensional source of support.

Qualitative methods are also uniquely suited to understanding the inner experiences of people because researchers can probe at a deep level. For example, Ladany, Constantine, Miller, Erickson, and Muse-Burke (2000) interviewed 11 psychotherapy supervisors about supervisory experiences with predoctoral interns; they were specifically interested in manifestations of countertransference in supervision. Because countertransference is an inner experience, interviewers were able to probe in depth and found that supervisor countertransference manifestations consisted of affective (e.g., emotional distress), cognitive (e.g., questioning one's own competence), and behavioral (e.g., disengagement) components.

Qualitative methods are also useful for describing rather than explaining phenomena. Schlosser, Knox, Moskovitz, and Hill (2003) were interested in *describing* the advisee's perspective of the graduate advising relationship rather than creating a model or *explaining* causal relationships between variables. Schlosser et al. interviewed 16 doctoral students about their relationships with their graduate advisors and discovered that satisfied and unsatisfied students differed on several aspects of the advising relationship, including the ability to choose their own advisors, the frequency of meeting with their advisors, the benefits and costs associated with the advising relationship, and how the conflict was dealt with over time.

Finally, although many of our previous examples were of studying specific experiences (e.g., gift-giving), CQR can also be used for studying attitudes or beliefs more broadly. For example, researchers could study attitudes toward racism or beliefs about God.

It is important to note that although CQR is ideal for studying a wide variety of phenomena, it is not as useful as quantitative methods when one wants to know something about the population, quantify an experience, or develop norms. However, for many of these areas, a quantitative study might be followed by a qualitative study to allow researchers to more richly examine the phenomena.

## *Approaching the Literature*

After the researcher has selected a topic and decided on CQR as a method it is time to review the literature. Some proponents of qualitative research (e.g., Glaser, 1978; Shank, 2002) have argued that qualitative researchers should be familiar enough with the literature to determine whether their proposed study has been conducted but should not review the literature completely until after the data have been collected. Their rationale for this is based on the idea that a qualitative researcher must put aside preconceived notions and use an exploratory approach to analyzing the data. At the completion of data collection, the researcher then integrates his or her findings within the larger body of literature.

Hill, Thompson, and Williams (1997) argued against this approach because knowledge of the literature can sometimes help researchers steer clear of mistakes made in prior studies and identify ways to meaningfully contribute to the literature (e.g., "next steps" within a particular line of research). Reviewing the literature before conducting the study allows the CQR researcher to become familiar with concepts and relationships that other researchers have identified in previous studies and thus consider the role that such concepts and relationships play in the situation being investigated. For instance, if a CQR researcher is interested in investigating the experiences of psychotherapy clients, the researcher would find in the literature that clients' perceptions of the working alliance in psychotherapy have been consistently related to clients' ratings of psychotherapy outcomes (Horvath, 2001). On the basis of this review of literature, the CQR researcher might decide to include questions about the relationship in the interview protocol.

To conduct a literature review, CQR researchers can search books, journal articles, and computer databases (e.g., ERIC, PsycINFO). Once relevant articles are found, researchers can search their reference lists to find other articles. For more specific steps and descriptions of research planning and conducting a literature review, we refer readers to various chapters and books written on this topic (e.g., Johnson & Christensen, 2008; Leong & Austin, 2006).

## Bracketing of Knowledge About Literature

Although it can be important to utilize the extant literature to inform the development of the research questions and interview protocol, CQR researchers should make a concerted effort to bracket or set aside such knowledge when interviewing participants and approaching the data in the data analysis phase so as to have a fresh or unbiased point of view. "Forgetting the literature" (Hill et al., 1997) is an important feature of qualitative research so that researchers can allow the participants and data to "speak" for themselves (Hill et al., 1997).

Using the hypothetical study of therapy outcome as an example, we might have been alerted from the literature review about the need to include questions about the therapeutic relationship in the interview protocol. During the interview and data analysis phase, however, the CQR researchers would make a concerted effort to put aside their knowledge of the empirical findings and instead focus on the experiences of the individual participants, who may or may not think that the therapeutic relationship is important. And indeed, the CQR researcher may also find that other issues (e.g., timing of the termination or financial concerns) than found in the literature are critical to the experiences of recently terminated clients. Similarly, during the data analysis phase, researchers look closely at the actual words the participants used rather than what they would like the participants to have said. If the CQR researcher does not bracket knowledge during interviewing and data analysis, essential information may thus be overlooked. Hence, CQR researchers need to consider the relevant literature when getting started with a study, bracket the literature when analyzing the data in order to allow unexpected information to emerge, and then reconsider the literature when trying to interpret the results.

## Stating the Purpose of a CQR Study

In CQR, the purpose of a study is typically to explore or understand a phenomenon experienced by certain individuals. In stating the purpose, researchers can include the following elements:

- Identify that the purpose of the study is to describe, understand, develop, or discover some phenomenon.
- Identify and justify the choice of CQR as the method by which the researcher plans to collect and analyze data.

In the following example of a statement of purpose, Juntunen et al. (2001) clearly identified that the purpose of the study was to explore the meaning adult American Indians make of career and related concepts using a CQR methodology:

> Darou's (1987) observation raised several questions about the relevance of career development theory and prompted initiation of this study. If career choice, as such, is not a relevant concept, what are some relevant issues that might contribute to the meaning of career or career development among American Indians? On the basis of the question raised by Darou (1987), our goal was to hear from American Indians themselves about the meaning of career and the ideas related to it. We also wanted to understand whether some of the issues raised in the multi-cultural literature, such as cultural identity, acculturation, and family and community relationships, may also apply specifically to the realm of career development. To that end, we conducted a qualitative investigation, relying on the strategies of consensual

qualitative research described by Hill, Thompson, and Williams (1997). The purposes of the study were to explore the definitions and meanings of career and career choices or career development among an American Indian sample and to identify related concepts generated by the participants. (p. 275)

## Stating Research Questions

CQR researchers then specifically state their research questions, or what they will be investigating. In a study of medical professionals' perceptions of ethical and professional challenges in working with patients with genetic concerns, for instance, Veach, Bartels, and LeRoy (2001, pp. 98–99) identified three objectives:

■ to begin to describe the scope of ethical and professional issues encountered by genetic counselors, physicians, and nurses in their practice;
■ to identify categories for classifying professional and ethical issues; and
■ to compare and contrast these issues across professional groups and across geographic regions in the United States.

The authors then posed three major research questions

■ What are the ethical and professional challenges encountered by genetic counselors, physicians, and nurses when their patients have genetic concerns?
■ Do the types of ethical and professional challenges vary by profession?
■ Do the types of ethical and professional challenges vary by geographic region?

## Conclusions

Although we have provided ideas about how to get started on a CQR study, we want to emphasize that developing ideas and formulating a research design is a creative process and that researchers will differ in how they get started. If researchers are having trouble getting started, we encourage them to read other references about research methods (e.g., Johnson & Christensen, 2008; Leong & Austin, 2006). Finally, it is important to note that other chapters in this book refer to additional aspects of getting started such as selecting and training the research team (Chapter 4), thinking about biases and expectations (Chapter 5), selecting a sample (Chapter 6), methods of data collection (Chapter 7), trustworthiness (Chapter 13), culture (Chapter 14), and ethics (Chapter 15). For an overview of what has been studied in the past, see the annotated bibliography in Chapter 16.

## *References*

Glaser, B. G. (1978). *Theoretical sensitivity.* Mill Valley, CA: Sociology Press.

Hill, C. E., Nutt-Williams, E., Heaton, K. J., Thompson, B. J., & Rhodes, R. H. (1996). Therapist retrospective recall of impasses in long-term psychotherapy: A qualitative analysis. *Journal of Counseling Psychology, 43,* 207–217. doi:10.1037/0022-0167.43.2.207

Hill, C. E., Thompson, B. J., & Williams, E. N. (1997). A guide to conducting consensual qualitative research. *The Counseling Psychologist, 25,* 517–572. doi:10.1177/0011000097254001

Horvath, A. O. (2001). The alliance. *Psychotherapy: Theory, Research, and Practice, 38,* 365–372. doi:10.1037/0033-3204.38.4.365

Johnson, B., & Christensen, L. (2008). *Education research: Quantitative, qualitative, and mixed approaches.* Thousand Oaks, CA: Sage.

Juntunen, C. L., Barraclough, D. J., Broneck, C. L., Seibel, G. A., Winrow, S. A., & Morin, P. M. (2001). American Indian perspectives on the career journey. *Journal of Counseling Psychology, 48,* 274–285. doi:10.1037/0022-0167.48.3.274

Knox, S., Dubois, R., Smith, J., Hess, S. A., & Hill, C. E. (2009). Clients' experiences giving gifts to therapists. *Psychotherapy: Theory, Research, and Practice, 46,* 350–361. doi:10.1037/a0017001

Knox, S., Goldberg, J. L., Woodhouse, S. S., & Hill, C. E. (1999). Clients' internal representations of their therapists. *Journal of Counseling Psychology, 46,* 244–256. doi:10.1037/0022-0167.46.2.244

Knox, S., Hess, S. A., Williams, E. N., & Hill, C. E. (2003). "Here's a little something for you": How therapists respond to client gifts. *Journal of Counseling Psychology, 50,* 199–210. doi:10.1037/0022-0167.50.2.199

Ladany, N., Constantine, M. G., Miller, K., Erickson, C., & Muse-Burke, J. (2000). Supervisor countertransference: A qualitative investigation into its identification and description. *Journal of Counseling Psychology, 47,* 102–115. doi:10.1037/0022-0167.47.1.102

Ladany, N., O'Brien, K. M., Hill, C. E., Melincoff, D. S., Knox, S., & Petersen, D. A. (1997). Sexual attraction toward clients, use of supervision, and prior training: A qualitative study of predoctoral psychology interns. *Journal of Counseling Psychology, 44,* 413–424. doi:10.1037/0022-0167.44.4.413

Leong, F. T. L., & Austin, J. T. (2006). *The psychology research handbook* (2nd ed.). Thousand Oaks, CA: Sage.

Santiago-Rivera, A. L., Altarriba, J., Poll, N., Gonzalez-Miller, N., & Cragun, C. (2009). Therapists' views on working with bilingual Spanish–English speaking clients: A qualitative investigation. *Professional Psychology: Research and Practice, 40,* 436–443. doi:10.1037/a0015933

Schlosser, L. Z., Knox, S., Moskovitz, A. R., & Hill, C. E. (2003). A qualitative examination of graduate advising relationships: The advisee perspective. *Journal of Counseling Psychology, 50,* 178–188. doi:10.1037/0022-0167.50.2.178

Schultheiss, D. E. P., Palma, T. V., Predragovich, K. S., & Glasscock, J. M. J. (2002). Relational influences on career paths: Siblings in context. *Journal of Counseling Psychology, 49,* 302–310. doi:10.1037/0022-0167.49.3.302

Shank, G. D. (2002). *Qualitative research.* Columbus, OH: Merrill, Prentice Hall

Veach, P. M., Bartels, D. M., & LeRoy, B. S. (2001). Ethical and professional challenges posed by patients with genetic concerns: A report of focus group discussions with genetic counselors, physicians, and nurses. *Journal of Genetic Counseling, 10,* 97–119. doi:10.1023/A:1009487513618

Williams, E. N., Soeprapto, E., Like, K., Touradji, P., Hess, S., & Hill, C. E. (1998). Perceptions of serendipity: Career paths of prominent academic women in counseling psychology. *Journal of Counseling Psychology, 45,* 379–389. doi:10.1037/0022-0167.45.4.379

*Barbara L. Vivino, Barbara J. Thompson, and Clara E. Hill*

# The Research Team | 4

The richness and validity of the data obtained from consensual qualitative research (CQR) is in large part dependent on the functioning of the team, given that the team works together to transform the data into concepts that can be compared across cases. The purpose of this chapter is to discuss issues pertinent to the formation and functioning of the research team.

## Composition of the Team

### SELECTION OF THE TEAM

In an unpublished survey we conducted in 2004 of people who had participated in CQR teams, we found that the people who most liked CQR indicated that they enjoyed identifying and communicating the core themes of others' thoughts and that they enjoyed working collaboratively with others on a research project, suggesting that these are important elements for people to think about during team selection.

Who makes up a team? Essentially the research team can be made up of anyone with a basic knowledge of the research subject, training in CQR, and a commitment to the research project. Research teams have typically involved some combination of graduate students, professors, and practicing therapists (Hill et al., 2005). Although there is no "best" choice in selecting a research team, there are some important factors to be considered.

The first criterion in selecting team members is initiative and motivation. CQR requires a major commitment of the members' time and resources, and team members must actively participate and be willing to have and voice their opinions. Because motivation and enjoyment of the process are essential to the research team experience, discussing these factors as well as suggesting ways to enhance them could be emphasized during the selection process. Understanding the benefit of working on a research team could positively influence the team members' motivation. Often it is gratifying for members to work in a team situation, especially because research traditionally can be an isolating experience. If team members enjoy collaborating with each other, they have an opportunity for learning from each other and enjoying each other's company!

Another criterion to consider when selecting team members is level of experience. Experience can include experience with the subject being studied, experience on a CQR team, or experience with research in general. Experienced or mature team members are typically considered to be more desirable for topics that require specific knowledge or training (e.g., countertransference; Hayes et al., 1998), whereas less experienced undergraduates are often quite able to participate as team members for research on broader topic areas (e.g., women's career development; Williams et al., 1998).

There are also personality and skill factors to consider in the selection of research team members. Hill, Thompson, and Williams (1997) suggested that therapists and therapists in training are good choices for research team members because of their good interpersonal skills, openness to feedback, and motivation to work on interpersonal relationships. Although personality variables have not been formally assessed in CQR research teams, researchers of team effectiveness have consistently found that emotional stability, extraversion, openness to new experience, agreeableness, conscientiousness, and lack of dominance are important attributes (Driskell, Goodwin, Salas, & O'Shea, 2006; Driskell & Salas, 1992).

Finally, in the majority of previous studies, the core team members knew one another or had some sort of prior affiliation (e.g., as students or colleagues) prior to being asked to be on a research team. Having already established relationships probably helps the primary team jell faster and work together because of mutual understandings and caring. Selecting team members who add diversity, however, can also be beneficial. For instance, including members of different genders and different educational and cultural backgrounds can add to the richness of the team discussion. Decisions about the diversity or homogeneity of the research team should be made, in part, on the basis of the research topic. For example, if researchers are studying heterosexual marital relationships, having both male and female team members might enable the team to better understand both gender perspectives. Similarly, the ages of the team members might be important if researchers are studying a topic such as older adult clients' perspectives on counseling. In addition, it might be preferable to have female interviewers interview women who have post-partum depression. Thus, we recommend that when gathering a team, the diversity of team members should be considered both in terms of the perspectives that one wants to be sure are covered and also in terms of the diversity or special concerns of the participants in relation to who conducts the interviews.

On the basis of our experience and the experience of many of our colleagues, then, it seems that several things are important in selecting team members. It helps if everyone is interested in the topic, in doing qualitative research, and in working together as a team.

## Forming the Team

Methods for recruiting team members have varied across studies. Typically, psychology doctoral students have been asked by other psychology doctoral students or by professors to participate as research team members.

Teams can be formed at various times during the research process. Sometimes teams have been formed at the inception of the research idea. The shared enthusiasm for an idea can be the impetus for researchers forming a research project and a team. Other research teams are initiated later in the research process. For instance, a researcher may have already developed the research idea and then later recruits team members to assist in the interview process and analysis of the interviews. Thus, the formation of the team is subject to the needs of the team members and of the project itself.

Occasionally, there has been a quid pro quo in the sense that one researcher looking for team members is willing to serve as a team member on another researcher's project if the latter will return the favor. For instance, when graduate students are working on several studies together, they can assist each other by working together to analyze each other's data, or an individual might agree to be an auditor for one study in return for one of the other team members agreeing to audit for that individual's project.

## Compensation for Participation on the Team

The typical forms of compensation have been authorship on the article to be published and/or reciprocal participation on another research team. Research team members have never, to our knowledge, earned financial compensation, although undergraduate students have often received course credit (e.g., Sim et al., 2010; Williams et al., 1998). In general, participants choose to participate in CQR teams because they enjoy collaborative investigative processes. In addition, professors participate and publish as part of their position in academia, although many, including the third author of this chapter, are interested in and enjoy the research and the collaboration as well. As clinicians, the two first authors of this chapter have participated in CQR studies because they were intrinsically interested in the topics, enjoyed doing qualitative research, enjoyed working on a team and being involved in the investigative aspects of studies, and have felt that the topics studied enriched and informed their practice (e.g., compassion in psychotherapy; Vivino, Thompson, Hill, & Ladany, 2009).

## TEAM STRUCTURE

How many people are on a team? Research teams have typically consisted of three people on the primary team and one or two auditors. A variation is larger teams where people serve as both primary team members and auditors in rotating teams (e.g., Ladany et al., 1997).

## POWER DIFFERENCES AND HIERARCHICAL CONSIDERATIONS

Differences in power among team members often influence the team process (see also Hill et al., 1997, 2005). For example, when teams are composed of faculty members (who have formal social power) and students (who have less social power), students often are reluctant, especially initially, to voice their opinions because of concerns about alienating their advisors or mentors or out of deference to authority. An additional power differential can occur when some members of the team have more experience than others in conducting CQR. Team members new to the process may defer to the more experienced members regarding both the process and content.

A related issue to be considered is the role of the principal investigator (PI) in a qualitative research team. In all of the teams we have been a part of, the PI has been a member of the research team. Power differences emerge naturally and need to be addressed when team members defer to the PI or when the PI expects team members to defer. The emphasis on training and discussion related to the consensual process helps to mitigate such expectations. So although the PI might have some additional organizational tasks (e.g., keeping track of progress on cases from interview through final audit status), the PI's role in the consensual team is the same as that of every other team member.

The majority of CQR research teams have consisted primarily of a combination of master's and PhD-level students (see Chapter 18 in this volume). This combination suggests that some of the research team members had some prior training or experience with research as well as being experienced in the field of psychology and were training the younger members. More experienced team members need to be cognizant of their referred power. Training and early discussions of the process can be used to highlight the importance of everyone "arguing" to consensus.

It is interesting to note that culture may play a role in this process, as discussions with colleagues in other countries suggest. In our experiences in the United States, it has not been a problem to include people at different power levels as long as the individuals with more designated power do not claim expert status and individuals with less designated power are able to express their opinions freely. However, in other countries with more rigid hierarchical power structures or in any setting that has a strong hierarchical culture, as might be found in certain institutions or across genders or roles, it can be difficult for students or people with less power to disagree with authority figures. Therefore, it is important to consider possible hierarchical limitations when selecting team members and to choose members at the same level of power if differences seem likely to be an obstacle to group functioning. If power struggles emerge in a group after it has already formed then this can be discussed openly. It is a good idea to schedule regular dialogue about group dynamics and emphasize the importance of each person's experience in the group. In addition, a system for anonymous input regarding the members' experience should be established (see also the section on team process later in this chapter).

## TYPES OF TEAMS

Research teams can take on several different configurations, including *set teams, rotating teams,* and *multiple dissertation teams.* The first configuration has been the typical one, although rotating and multiple dissertation teams are useful in particular circumstances.

### Set Teams

There are two different types of set teams. A group of researchers (usually three people) can work on the study from start to finish together. They share the construction of the interview protocol, conduct the interviews, and analyze all the data together. In addition to the primary team, one or two outside auditors are also used. Another type of set team is where one or two researchers conduct the interviews and then are joined by one or two other researchers in analyzing the data along with one or two auditors; this method is often used in a dissertation study in which the dissertator does all of the interviews. Set teams offer the advantage of allowing all of the primary team members to be immersed in analyzing all of the data (domains, core ideas, and cross-analysis) for all of the cases. The disadvantage is that some aspects of the data analysis process (e.g., developing domains and creating core ideas; see Chapter 8) can become repetitive after several cases and may not be the best use of everyone's time.

### Rotating Teams

Rotating teams usually consist of four to 12 team members who rotate doing all of the tasks, including auditing (e.g., Ladany et al., 1997). With rotating teams, the core team members serve as "internal" auditors, and the team meets as a group to reach consensus on the work that the team has done. The team works together initially to ensure consistency across teams and then breaks into smaller groups of three once everyone understands the process and shares a similar focus. (See Chapter 8 for more details on the data analysis.) An advantage to this strategy is that rotating teams can analyze larger data sets and that more viewpoints can be obtained. A disadvantage is that not all the team members are as familiar with all of the cases, and thus their contribution may be limited.

### Multiple Theses or Dissertations Teams

Another type of research team is one where several students working on theses or dissertations at the same time use one interview protocol that incorporates questions related to different areas of inquiry (distinct areas for each student). The students can then either analyze the interview together as a team and use the data specific to their dissertation, or the students could form separate teams to analyze only their portions of the interview data. Committee members for the dissertators could serve as auditors to monitor the process. This approach can be excellent because students learn from one another and have a built-in support group to compensate for the often lonely task of writing a dissertation. Of course, it can also be disastrous if some students do not complete their respective tasks. It is especially important for these types of teams that all members are fully aware of the time commitment involved in CQR research.

## Training

Training is strongly recommended for researchers new to CQR (Hill et al., 2005). The degree of formal training will depend on whether there are members of the team who have used the methodology before. When there are one or two "trainers" (i.e., experienced CQRers) embedded in the team, training can be more informal and consist of reading this book and reviewing exemplar studies (e.g., Hill, Rochlen, Zack, McCready, & Dematatis, 2003; Knox, Burkard, Johnson, Suzuki, & Ponterotto, 2003; Ladany et al., 1997; Vivino et al., 2009; Williams et al., 1998). Practicing together as a team on developing domains and core ideas from previous studies is also useful and recommended to build team rapport. If the majority of team members are new to CQR, training with an experienced CQR researcher is recommended. Here is a suggested outline for training:

- Each team member reads this book and several CQR articles.
- The process is described and discussed in detail, with examples from previous studies.
- Team members practice reaching consensual agreements as they work through the steps of the process (developing domains, constructing cores ideas, cross-analysis) using a small sample from a completed study.
- The experienced trainer makes him- or herself available for consultation during the actual data analysis process, ideally serving as an auditor to provide feedback along the way.

A final point is that the training procedures used should be clearly described in journal articles that are written about the project.

## The Team Process

Researchers often find that rich data can be obtained from CQR and also that participating on the team can be fun! However the success of the team is dependent on several factors. Organizational psychologists (West, 2004) suggest that three steps are important for the successful functioning of teams:

- a shared goal or vision,
- commitment to the team or project, and
- trust.

### SHARED GOAL OR VISION

The shared goal for CQR research teams is usually to obtain rich pertinent data that honors the varied experiences of the participants (interviewees) and that adds to the knowledge base in regard to the focus of the study. However, commitment and trust of team members may be influenced by other sometimes unspoken goals. Members may be interested in publishing an article, obtaining tenure, gathering members for their own research team, learning from or pleasing colleagues and professors, completing a master's thesis or doctoral dissertation, or helping a fellow student complete a master's thesis or doctoral dissertation. These different goals undoubtedly influence motivation and commitment, so it is important to understand why members are participating on a team and to recognize that differences may affect the team functioning. For instance, if one team member is anxious to complete his or her dissertation within a specific time frame, he or she might be reluctant to go back and reanalyze data even if other team members feel it is important.

## COMMITMENT TO THE TEAM

When a research team is formed, it is important that all members agree to the meeting time and the anticipated duration of the team. People unfamiliar with CQR may underestimate the amount of time involved in the process. Issues such as completing a dissertation in a timely manner may impose potentially interfering dynamics. Some research teams meet every week for up to 2 years, whereas others meet multiple times per week for a year. An understanding of the commitment and a willingness to stay with the process is essential. In addition to meeting times, team members need to acknowledge that they will be expected to work independently at times. An expectation of promptness and a commitment to excellence also needs to be clarified.

When the team gets started, it is also important to outline the structure of the group. Taking time to define roles, set ground rules, delineate the timing of sessions (i.e., how long, time of day) can prevent future difficulties. Expectations about who is going to be PI and how to share the multitude of administrative tasks all need to be discussed and agreed on. An explicit agreement to openly communicate opinions and dissensions is also important. Motivation can be maintained in the team by members giving each other positive feedback and by having clearly defined goals that are met so that a sense of progress is felt.

Team members also need to make a commitment about sharing the workload. Because CQR studies involve a lot of data management, team members typically (unless the study is for a thesis or dissertation) share the tasks of managing the data for a certain number of the cases. Clarifying which members will keep track of what data is part of the group process.

Many primary research teams work together in person to analyze the interviews. However, sometimes it has been impossible to be in the same place at the same time, so telephone discussions have been used instead. Telephone meetings have seemed to us to be effective as long as we started with close relationships, but it is also true that some of the nuances of communication (facial expressions, gestures, etc.) are lost.

The effect of this loss has seemed minimal, although it may have contributed to misunderstandings or to slowing down the process. The use of other technology (i.e., Skype, video conferencing) has recently been used in CQR research teams and has great potential, especially because researchers often live miles from each other or even in different countries. In addition, communication with auditors is frequently done via e-mail and telephone if needed to clarify comments or feedback.

## TRUST

### Establishing Trust

Establishing and maintaining trust in the research group is important so that members feel open to sharing their thoughts and opinions. This process begins with the formation of the research team. In addition to discussing the structure of the team, we have found it helpful to begin the first meeting of a team with a discussion of group dynamics and process. Expectations regarding the group process can be clarified in the following ways:

- All members are expected to contribute equally to all discussions.
- Team members are encouraged to be sensitive to nonverbal communication (e.g., be aware that silence may indicate disagreement, or recognize that physical signs of agitation may indicate that someone is uncomfortable with a decision).
- Team members are encouraged to comment and intervene to correct a group process problem (group process discussion is as important as content discussion!).
- Support and respect for each other is essential (the use of active listening skills can be beneficial).

Another important element for promoting trust is to establish roles early on and thus clarify who is going to do what tasks. As discussed earlier, the PI often takes on more of the tasks, such as spearheading the institutional review board approval process, organizing and keeping track of the status of each case, and writing up the first draft of the manuscript.

### Managing Conflict

Although conflict is often viewed negatively, it is important to realize that constructive conflict can increase a team's energy level and provide greater creativity through allowing myriad viewpoints. Conflict can add depth to discussions as members are challenged to elaborate on their ideas so that others better understand them. If everyone already had the same point of view, there would be no need to bring a team together to do the work!

In a CQR team, in fact, too much agreement is often problematic. If a team member wants to get along and avoid conflict there is a danger of *groupthink*, when everyone goes along with a proposal even when they secretly have reservations about it (Janis, 1972). Highly cohesive groups are much more likely to engage in groupthink because their cohesiveness often correlates with unspoken understandings and the ability to work together with minimal explanations. Surowiecki (2004) warned against the loss of "cognitive diversity" that comes if team members share similar educational and occupational backgrounds. The closer group members are in outlook, the less likely they are to raise questions that might break their cohesion. Social psychologist McCauley (1989) noted that groupthink occurs when there is directive leadership, homogeneity of members' social background and ideology, and isolation of the group from outside sources of information and analysis. Hence, CQR teams might benefit from initially selecting diversity in the team members and making sure that members feel comfortable speaking openly. In addition, CQR teams that have worked together on multiple projects may be a danger of too much cohesiveness. Adding new members or changing the makeup of the group for different projects, encouraging the expression of dissenting opinions within the group, establishing a regular discussion of the group process, and utilizing the objectivity of an outside monitor all may facilitate diversity of opinions and help to avoid groupthink.

Typically, CQR teams have been able to work out difficulties in group discussion. However, occasionally a team member may have problems (e.g., does not do the work, does not attend meetings, engages in hostile interactions). When concerns arise and multiple group discussions have been futile in an attempt to resolve the concerns, then the PI might have to gently inform the person that it is not working out and ask the person to drop out of the team.

## Example of a Working Team

In an example of a CQR team experience, the three authors of this chapter worked together on a research team (Vivino et al., 2009). We had known each other for years and had developed an idea for researching the concept of compassion in psychotherapy. The idea developed casually in discussions at conferences and grew over time. The team typically worked very well together, and we were all comfortable voicing dissenting opinions and arguing to consensus. Difficulties arose, however, when we were analyzing transcript material that had a spiritual nuance. Two of us with Buddhist/spiritual leanings perceived the meaning of the material very differently than did the third member, who seemed unaware of the subtleties that the others had observed. Given that much of what has been written about compassion comes from a Buddhist perspective and that many of the therapists we interviewed had a Buddhist perspective, this issue was salient. Because one person wanted to include material that seemed relevant from a Buddhist perspective whereas another person thought that such material was irrelevant, a conflict thus arose about how detailed the core ideas related to spirituality should be. The tension over the disagreement was uncomfortable, and it seemed like a stalemate. We reached a compromise eventually after much discussion, and then the auditor provided further feedback. The variety of perspectives helped us look carefully at the data, but perhaps more important, we had to respect that we disagreed about some issues but still liked each other.

## Conclusions

Although challenging interpersonal issues often arise in working through group dynamics, research teams are an essential part of the CQR process in terms of providing multiple perspectives on the data. We encourage researchers to think carefully about whom they select to work with on teams and then to thoughtfully and empathically talk about feelings and negotiate procedures as conflicts inevitably arise during the process.

## References

Driskell, J. E., Goodwin, G. F., Salas, E., & O'Shea, P. G. (2006). What makes a good team player? Personality and team effectiveness. *Group Dynamics, 10,* 249–271. doi:10.1037/1089-2699.10.4.249

Driskell, J. E., & Salas, E. (1992). Collective behavior and team performance. *Human Factors, 34,* 277–288.

Hayes, J. A., McCracken, J. E., McClanahan, M. K., Hill, C. E., Harp, J. S., & Carozzoni, P. (1998). Therapist perspectives on countertransference: Qualitative data in search of a theory. *Journal of Counseling Psychology, 45,* 468–482. doi:10.1037/0022-0167.45.4.468

Hill, C. E., Knox, S., Thompson, B. J., Williams, E. N., Hess, S.A., & Ladany, N. (2005). Consensual qualitative research: An update. *Journal of Counseling Psychology, 52,* 196–205. doi:10.1037/0022-0167.52.2.196

Hill, C. E., Rochlen, A. B., Zack, J. S., McCready, T., & Dematatis, A. (2003). Working with dreams using the Hill cognitive–experiential model: A comparison of computer-assisted, therapist empathy, and therapist empathy + input conditions. *Journal of Counseling Psychology, 50,* 211–220. doi:10.1037/0022-0167.50.2.211

Hill, C. E., Thompson, B. J., & Williams, E. N. (1997). A guide to conducting consensual qualitative research. *The Counseling Psychologist, 25,* 517–572. doi:10.1177/0011000097254001

Janis, I. L. (1972). *Victims of groupthink.* Boston, MA: Houghton Mifflin.

Knox, S., Burkard, A. W., Johnson, A. J., Suzuki, L. A., & Ponterotto, J. G. (2003). African American and European American therapists' experiences of addressing race in cross-racial psychotherapy dyads. *Journal of Counseling Psychology, 50,* 466–481. doi:10.1037/0022-0167.50.4.466

Ladany, N., O'Brien, K. M., Hill, C. E., Melincoff, D. S., Knox, S., & Petersen, D. A. (1997). Sexual attraction toward clients, use of supervision, and prior training: A qualitative study of predoctoral psychology interns. *Journal of Counseling Psychology, 44,* 413–424. doi:10.1037/0022-0167.44.4.413

McCauley, C. (1989). The nature of social influence in groupthink: Compliance and internalization. *Journal of Personality and Social Psychology, 57,* 250–260. doi:10.1037/0022-3514.57.2.250

Sim, W., Hill, C. E., Chowdhury, S., Huang, T. C., Zaman, N., & Talavera, P. (2010). Problems and action ideas discussed by first- and second-generation female East Asian students during dream sessions. *Dreaming, 20,* 42–59. doi:10.1037/a0018993

Surowiecki, J. (2004). *The wisdom of crowds.* New York, NY: Doubleday.

Vivino, B. L., Thompson, B., Hill, C. E., & Ladany, N. (2009). Compassion in psychotherapy: The perspective of psychotherapists nominated as compassionate. *Psychotherapy Research, 19,* 157–171. doi:10.1080/10503300802430681

West, M. A. (2004). *Effective teamwork: Practical lessons from organizational research* (2nd ed.). Oxford, England: Blackwell.

Williams, E. N., Soeprapto, E., Like, K., Touradji, P., Hess, S., & Hill, C. E. (1998). Perceptions of serendipity: Career paths of prominent academic women in counseling psychology. *Journal of Counseling Psychology, 45,* 379–389. doi:10.1037/0022-0167.45.4.379

*Wonjin Sim, Teresa C. Huang, and Clara E. Hill*

# Biases and Expectations 5

I n a study about the problems and action ideas of female college students expressed during dream sessions, a research team listened to a session in which a client discussed her parents' divorce. During the session, the client mentioned that her father was absent in her childhood because of her parents' divorce. One research team member argued that the client's parental divorce was a problem for the client. Another team member disclosed that her own parents' divorce was not problematic for her and contended that the client might have felt a sense of relief that the divorce reduced the marital conflict between the parents. Yet another judge expressed her angst about her parents' divorce, her father's absence, and having to travel back and forth between two houses. These three judges became emotionally involved and argued with each other about whether the divorce was a problem for this client. It became clear that their biases were interfering with their abilities to listen to the client. To clarify the matter, they discussed their biases and expectations, went back and listened carefully to the client's tone of voice and the words she used, and finally agreed that indeed the client did not seem distressed about either the divorce or her father's resulting absence after the divorce.

As illustrated in the above example, researchers' biases and expectations are inevitable parts of the data analysis process and undoubtedly affect the coding process and results. Addressing such ideas is especially important in qualitative research, where the research findings depend heavily on the researchers' interpretations of the data. In this chapter, we begin by providing a rationale for addressing biases and expectations in consensual qualitative research (CQR) along with definitions of terms. Next, we discuss some of the major challenges researchers face in addressing biases and expectations as well as provide recommendations for how to think about these ideas in each step of the research process. Last, we provide some concluding remarks about biases and expectations in CQR.

## Rationale for Addressing Biases and Expectations in CQR

Addressing biases and expectations in CQR can enhance the quality of research in important ways. First, qualitative research that includes examples of assumptions that have been identified and managed is regarded as more rigorous than research in which researchers do not examine their assumptions (Fischer, 2009). Addressing biases and expectations thus allows CQR researchers to "ensure that our understandings are not just our own and that if other researchers studied our data that they would come to similar understandings" (Fischer, 2009, p. 584). This methodological rigor can be achieved by having research team members try to set aside their biases and expectations when examining the data (i.e., bracketing their biases and expectations during data analysis). The methodological rigor can also occur by having team members record their biases and expectations prior to data analysis and then compare those with the results at the end of data analysis to see if the results were unduly influenced by the researchers' preexisting assumptions; if so, then researchers can take steps to remove or acknowledge their biases or expectations.

A second reason for addressing biases and expectations in CQR studies is that doing so can enrich the research process itself. For example, by recording expectations and biases prior to data analysis and discussing them throughout the data analysis process, the researchers may increase their self-awareness and self-knowledge. Research team members may also respectfully point out other team members' biases and expectations, thus contributing to greater awareness. Improved self-awareness and self-knowledge can assist researchers in looking at the data from diverse perspectives instead of seeing the data only from their own perspectives.

Another important reason to address biases and expectations in CQR is that including researchers' expectations and biases in the final write-up benefits the research audience. Reporting biases and expectations allows readers to understand the findings within the researcher's context (Hill, Thompson, & Williams, 1997) and take the researcher's perspective (Fischer, 2009). Alternatively, an awareness of the authors' biases and expectations allows readers to purposefully take a different perspective than that of the researchers if they wish to do so (Fischer, 2009).

## Definitions of Biases and Expectations

*Biases* in CQR can be defined as "personal issues that make it difficult for researchers to respond objectively to the data" (Hill et al., 1997, p. 539). We would add that because researchers cannot avoid having biases and thus cannot be completely objective, dealing with these biases is a matter of knowing how to acknowledge and address their effects. Researchers might have positive or negative reactions to the data on the basis of their cultural backgrounds, values, beliefs, and direct and indirect experiences regarding the topic, which hinders objective data analysis (Hill et al., 2005). For example, if a researcher has the strong feeling that abortion is immoral, he or she might have aversive reactions to a participant's statement about choosing to have an abortion, inadvertently make judgments about the participant's morality, and assume that a participant's abortion is a problem for the client, no matter how hard the researcher tries to be objective and attend to just the data.

In contrast, Hill et al. (1997) defined *expectations* as "beliefs that researchers have formed based on reading the literature and thinking about and developing the research questions" (p. 538). In other words, expectations refer to researchers' anticipations about participants' probable responses to interview questions or the probable results. For example, in a qualitative study on international students' challenges, researchers may anticipate, on the basis both of personal experiences and awareness of the literature, that most international students would experience language difficulties and loneliness. As a result, researchers may report language difficulties and loneliness for a participant even if he or she gave a brief indication that loneliness was no longer a difficulty.

Biases might be more difficult to report than expectations. The term *biases* has a negative connotation, which may discourage researchers from being honest, whereas the term *expectations* has a more neutral connotation. For example, when researchers are asked about their biases about Asian Americans' family relationships, they are likely to think about their negative stereotypes (e.g., too much parental control, lack of open communication), which are not easy to report. In contrast, expectations about Asian Americans' family relationships might be more neutral, and hence researchers might be more honest and less concerned about such reporting.

In their review of the corpus of published CQR studies, Hill et al. (2005) noted that there has been a great deal of confusion regarding the reporting of biases and expectations. Many researchers have used the terms interchangeably. Because of the lack of adherence to reporting both biases and expectations as recommended in Hill et al. (1997), Hill et al. (2005) recommended recording and reporting only biases; their rationale was that expectations are often implied in introduction sections.

We think, however, that there is a need to address expectations as well as biases. By addressing only biases, some influential expectations that are different from biases may not be discussed. For example, in a qualitative study about the effect of immediacy, researchers' expectations about potential effects might come not from personal issues but from training, and these expectations might influence the coding process (e.g., researchers' beliefs about whether they consider immediacy an important technique and their definition of immediacy). The results may thus reflect expectations without these being taken into account.

## Addressing Biases and Expectations

In this section, we discuss challenges in addressing biases and expectations and include recommendations for how to do so in each step of the research process. We provide a summary of our recommendations in Table 5.1.

### SELECTING RESEARCH TEAM MEMBERS

One difficulty that can arise in addressing biases and expectations pertains to the selection of team members. Although it may feel more comfortable to choose team members who have similar backgrounds as that of the primary investigator or investigators, making a conscious effort to choose team members who have a variety of biases and expectations (as well as theoretical orientations and cultural backgrounds; Hill et al., 1997) can be helpful as long as the team members can communicate well with each other. Diverse team members may be better able to detect other team members' biases than team members who have sim-

## TABLE 5.1

**Addressing Biases and Expectations in Each Step of Consensual Qualitative Research**

| Step | Recommendations |
|------|-----------------|
| Team selection | ▪ Select team members with a diversity of biases and expectations who would work well together. |
| Recording biases and expectations | ▪ Define biases and expectations.<br>▪ Explain rationale for addressing biases and expectations.<br>▪ Set ground rules for addressing biases and expectations.<br>▪ Have each team member think about and record their biases and expectations prior to any discussion by the team of biases or expectations.<br>▪ Encourage team members to learn about themselves throughout the research process and to openly discuss biases and expectations in order to increase self-knowledge. |
| Data collection | ▪ Ponder, record, and bracket interviewers' biases and expectations during the interview.<br>▪ Conduct practice interviews and receive feedback from team members, auditors, and/or others about as to whether interviews seem to be unduly influenced by researcher biases and expectations. |
| During analysis | ▪ Discuss biases and expectations when there is a lot of agreement.<br>▪ Take a break after a heated debate to help team members step back, process the group dynamics, and discuss ways for all members to feel heard and understood.<br>▪ Read or listen to the raw data again non-defensively and focus more on content and tone of voices of participants.<br>▪ Rotate which team member is designated as the first one to express an opinion.<br>▪ Invite team members to disagree and model openness to dissenting opinions. |
| Postanalysis and write-up | ▪ Present the common themes and differences in biases and expectations rather than presenting each individual person's ideas separately.<br>▪ In the limitations section, report the effects of the researchers' biases and expectations. |

ilar backgrounds and cultural influences. Although selecting diverse team members is usually optimal, it is also important for team members to work well together to facilitate openness and honesty during the research process (see also Chapter 14, this volume).

In some cases, when a less diverse team is preferred because of needed experience and expertise in the research area, having auditors with different backgrounds or perspectives can add a diverse perspective. For example, in Sim et al.'s (2010) study on Asian American students' problems and action ideas, all therapists and judges were Asian because of the importance for the study of their familiarity with Asian culture. In this case, an experienced Caucasian auditor was included on the research team to balance out the assumptions of the Asian research team. For more discussion about choosing research teams, see Chapter 4.

## RECORDING BIASES AND EXPECTATIONS PRIOR TO DATA COLLECTION

Team leaders may need to train team members with no CQR experience about biases and expectations by providing rationales, definitions, and examples to make sure that the team members truly understand the importance of such awareness and know how to do the task. It may also be helpful for team leaders to initiate discussion about setting ground rules for addressing biases and expectations.

During the research process, it may be difficult to remember what biases one had prior to data collection. Thus, it is important for each team member to record biases and expectations before engaging in the research. It is also important to note that the team should not begin collectively discussing biases and expectations until everyone has had a chance to independently ponder and record their biases. If team members think of more biases and expectations at any point later in the research process, they can add to their list. It may be helpful to distinguish and discuss biases and expectations that were noticed prior to data collection compared with those noticed as the data were being collected or analyzed.

A number of challenges can arise during the recording of biases and expectations. One challenge is limited self-awareness (Rennie, 1996), due perhaps to minimal exposure to other ways of thinking. In some cases, limited self-awareness is due to psychological defenses when admitting such biases or expectations goes against one's identity or ideal self. For example, one may not want to think of oneself as holding any racial biases, so it may be difficult to admit to any racial assumptions, which could result in one having a biased interpretation of racially related data without one's awareness. To address limited self-awareness, research team members could seek out psychotherapy, multicultural training, or other opportunities to examine their biases and stereotypes. Team leaders can also encourage team members to learn about themselves throughout the research process and to openly discuss biases and expectations in order to increase self-knowledge.

Additional challenges can arise from fear of potential professional and personal consequences of disclosing one's biases and expectations. Even if team members are aware of their biases, it can be challenging and embarrassing to report some controversial biases for fear of facing overt or covert criticism and judgment by other team members. For example, in a research team comprising faculty members and students, it may be difficult for student researchers to share controversial biases that go against perceived values and beliefs of authority figures given that faculty members might remember student researchers' biases during evaluations of their progress in training. For instance, a student's negative biases toward undocumented immigrants might be viewed as a lack of multicultural sensitivity by a professor with an opposite opinion. On the flip side, faculty members may be embarrassed to admit certain biases to their students because of a desire to project an expert persona or fear that admitting certain biases could negatively affect their professional or personal reputation. Although it may be challenging at times, we encourage CQR researchers to be as open as possible about their biases and expectations and nonjudgmental about other team members' beliefs for the purpose of ensuring greater research integrity. Selecting team members who trust each other and working to create a safe and nonjudgmental atmosphere in the research team (e.g., by modeling an openness to dissenting opinions) can help in facilitating open and honest reporting and discussion of biases and expectations.

## DATA COLLECTION

Interviewers' biases and expectations can affect how they conduct interviews because interviewers could subtly influence participants' responses. Interviewers might ask leading questions or unwittingly give participants hints as to what they want to hear (e.g., ask for gratuitous reassurance; Fischer, 2009). For example, researchers might expect that international students suffer from adjustment problems and thus might ask more questions about negative aspects of adjustment and fewer questions about positive experiences. To address this challenge, interviewers can try to ponder, record, and bracket (i.e., set aside) their biases and expectations during the interview. In addition, it can be useful to conduct practice interviews and receive feedback on whether interviews seem to be unduly influenced by researcher biases and expectations.

## DATA ANALYSIS

Recalling and revisiting biases and expectations during data analysis is particularly challenging because it is so easy to neglect them while focusing on analyzing data. Hence, it is important to take extra care in thinking about and discussing biases and expectations during this stage of the CQR process.

We recommend discussing biases and expectations when some team members always agree with certain other team members without counterargument, perhaps indicating power dynamics or groupthink within the research team. More dominant or talkative members might affect other members' opinions or make them feel uncomfortable about voicing differing opinions. Nondominant team members may feel pressure to follow the opinions of dominant team members, fear that their ideas might be devalued, and refrain from reporting different ideas, which can bias the results toward the dominant team members' opinions rather than staying close to what the data indicate. For example, when examining a case in which the therapist gives suggestions to a client, if most team members' believe that giving suggestions to a client is not effective and hinders client independence, it may be difficult for a researcher with a different idea (e.g., one who thinks that giving suggestions is helpful) to express his or her opinion, and so this person may defer to the majority opinion regarding giving suggestions.

In addition, when there is prolonged or significant disagreement among team members, when judges' ideas are polarized, when judges cannot reach consensus after long discussions, when one judge seems to "win" all the arguments, or when some judges do not offer opinions, researchers might suspect the existence of conflicting biases and expectations among the team members. When these cues are present, it would be advisable to discuss the possible influence of biases and expectations. For example, when a team listens to a session in which a client talks about a negative relationship with his or her mother, a judge who has a negative relationship with his or her own mother may express strong negative opinions about dependence on mothers and not want to give up this negative opinion. This person may need to be gently confronted by other team members.

Our recommendation about addressing biases and expectations during data analysis is that if any member of the research team suspects that biases and expectations may be influencing the data, that person should call attention to the concern. The team may need to step back, process the group dynamics, and discuss ways for all members to feel heard and understood. After the team members acknowledge the existence of biases and expectations through processing and discussion, researchers might want to read or listen to the raw data again nondefensively and focus more on content and tone of voice of participants than on what they want to hear from the data.

In addition, the principal investigator might emphasize early on the desire to foster a collaborative and collegial team environment in which all team members, not just the team leader, initiate discussion of biases and expectations. Rotating which team member is designated as the first one to express an opinion may allow all team members to share their opinions with less influence by other team members. The principal investigator may also invite team members to disagree and model an openness to dissenting opinions (i.e., when someone does disagree, considering discrepant opinions and talking about them while being mindful of avoiding the use of power to "win" the argument).

In addition, when a team finishes all of the analyses, researchers can hold a postmortem and talk about the influence of biases and expectations on the results. It is important that all research team members openly discuss the power dynamics in the group, how the team managed these dynamics, and how they could have managed them better. It is also useful to ask all judges whether they felt heard and validated, especially when the team involves people of different power levels.

## WRITING THE MANUSCRIPT

After discussing and processing biases and expectations in the research team, the final step is to include biases and expectations in the write-up of the study. It is important to include biases and expectations of the interviewers, primary team members, and auditors in the Method section's description of participants. The challenge in writing about biases and expectations is to summarize disparate and voluminous data across many people involved in the research process within given page limits. Because of space considerations, we recommend presenting the common themes and differences in biases and expectations rather than presenting each individual person's ideas separately.

An example of a report on biases and expectations can be found in a qualitative study on immediacy in brief psychotherapy by Hill et al. (2008):

> In terms of biases, all five researchers reported before the study that they liked immediacy and found it to be a powerful intervention in therapy, although they ranged in how comfortable they felt using it themselves as therapists. All had read Dr. W's book but had not met him personally before the study. (p. 300)

Another example can be found in Knox, Dubois, Smith, Hess, and Hill's (2009) study on clients giving gifts to therapists:

> We felt that the appropriateness of client gifts to therapists depended on a number of factors (e.g., the gift itself and its timing, the client's therapy concerns and therapy relationship, the perceived intentions behind and meaning of gift) and that small or inexpensive gifts given to show appreciation would usually be appropriate and should be discussed, even if only briefly. More troubling would be expensive or intimate gifts, gifts intended to manipulate the therapist in some way, or gifts from clients with tenuous boundaries; we also felt such gifts should be discussed. (p. 353)

In addition, it is helpful to report the effects of the researchers' biases and expectations on research findings in the limitations section of the paper because this helps readers understand the results within the context of the composition and functioning of the team. Authors not surprisingly feel vulnerable about presenting limitations for fear of reviewers dismissing their findings as biased, but it is important to be aware and to present the results openly and honestly.

## Conclusions

Biases and expectations are inevitable in the qualitative research process and undoubtedly affect how researchers understand and interpret research data. A parallel can be drawn to the effects of undetected and unmanaged countertransference on the therapy process: When a therapist recognizes his or her countertransference and uses it for a better understanding of the therapy process, countertransference can positively influence the psychotherapy process (Gelso & Hayes, 1998). Similarly, researchers can make a conscious effort to understand their biases and expectations, work to minimize these effects, and use their understanding of biases and expectations to enrich the research process. Therefore, we encourage CQR researchers to become aware of and address their biases and expectations and approach the data with open minds and curiosity.

## References

Fischer, C. T. (2009). Bracketing in qualitative research: Conceptual and practical matters. *Psychotherapy Research, 19,* 583–590. doi:10.1080/10503300902798375

Gelso, C. J., & Hayes, J. A. (1998). *The psychotherapy relationship: Theory, research, and practice.* New York, NY: Wiley.

Hill, C. E., Knox, S., Thompson, B. J., Williams, E. N., Hess, S.A., & Ladany, N. (2005). Consensual qualitative research: An update. *Journal of Counseling Psychology, 52,* 196–205. doi:10.1037/0022-0167.52.2.196

Hill, C. E., Sim, W., Spangler, P., Stahl, J., Sullivan, C., & Teyber, E. (2008). Therapist immediacy in brief psychotherapy: Case study II. *Psychotherapy: Theory, Research, Practice, Training, 45,* 298–315. doi:10.1037/a0013306

Hill, C. E., Thompson, B. J., & Williams, E. N. (1997). A guide to conducting consensual qualitative research. *The Counseling Psychologist, 25,* 517–572. doi:10.1177/0011000097254001

Knox, S., Dubois, R., Smith, J., Hess, S. A., & Hill, C. E. (2009). Clients' experiences giving gifts to therapists. *Psychotherapy: Theory, Research, Practice, Training, 46,* 350–361. doi:10.1037/a0017001

Rennie, D. L. (1996). Commentary on "Clients' Perceptions of Treatment for Depression: I and II." *Psychotherapy Research, 6,* 263–268. doi:10.1080/10503309612331331788

Sim, W., Hill, C. E., Chowdhury, S., Huang, T. C., Zaman, N., & Talavera, P. (2010). Problems and action ideas discussed by first- and second-generation female East Asian students during dream sessions. *Dreaming, 20,* 42–59. doi:10.1037/a0018993

*Clara E. Hill and Elizabeth Nutt Williams*

# The Sample 6

I n consensual qualitative research (CQR), we ask people to tell us their stories. To obtain these stories, we recruit participants who have had the type of experience that we are interested in and who can describe their reactions in great detail. Hence, choosing the sample is of utmost importance to obtaining good data. In this chapter, then, we focus on issues related to choosing and recruiting the best samples for CQR.

## *Choosing the Sample*

The main consideration in choosing a sample is to select one that fits the research questions, which, one would hope, are well-delineated and specific. Thus, researchers need to have clarity about the research questions before determining the composition of the sample (see Chapter 3). If the question is about transference, for example, we need to select partici- pants who are knowledgeable about transference and who are "experts" in being able to talk about the phenomenon, as did Gelso, Hill, Rochlen, Mohr, and Zack (1999). For the topic of transference, then, Gelso et al. chose a sample of psychoana- lytically oriented psychotherapists because they spoke a lan- guage that includes transference, were likely to have thought deeply about transference, and were likely to have experienced transference both as clients and as directed at them as therapists. If our interest is in learning more about impasses in psychotherapy, we need to select a sample of either clients or therapists who have experienced impasses, as did Hill, Nutt-Williams, Heaton, Thompson, and Rhodes (1996).

Once we have broadly defined the population, we need to identify specific criteria for selecting participants within this population. Our goal is to select a sample that is clearly defined because too much variability within the sample (or the lack of clearly defined research questions) often leads to a lack of consistency in the results.

Although there is some controversy about generalizability in qualitative research, we believe that consensual qualitative researchers do indeed want to apply their findings at least tentatively beyond their sample (what has been called *transferability*). Given that we want to transfer our findings, it is important to define the sample carefully so that we can clearly identify to whom the results might apply or to what theory the results might apply. In addition, if researchers define the sample carefully and clearly, future researchers might study the same population, thus enabling researchers to conduct qualitative meta-analyses to determine the trustworthiness and credibility of the data (see Chapter 12).

In defining the population, researchers should think about demographic variables that might be relevant to the research questions, such as gender, age, sexual orientation, socioeconomic status, racial–ethnic status, country of residence, religion, disability status, and educational level. Thus, in investigating relational events within therapy, we might want to specify that we will recruit experienced psychoanalytically oriented therapists, given that both experience level and orientation might influence the results, but we might try to recruit equal numbers of male and female therapists so that our results could apply to both sexes (especially if we have no reason to expect that male and female therapists would have different reactions). If we were studying the effects of psychotherapy with clients who have experienced trauma, however, we might be more concerned with gender, race or ethnicity, socioeconomic status, and type of trauma, given that traumas occur differentially across groups and influence groups in different ways. Thus, we might decide to select only upper class African American men who had been sexually abused so that we would know to what population we are referring.

Of particular relevance when thinking about criteria is the recency and salience of the experience. If a psychotherapy client is asked about a fleeting experience of feeling understood in a therapy session, it is probably best if the session was relatively recent so that the details of the experience are clear in the client's mind. Otherwise, the participant is likely to "fill in the blanks" and not remember the experience as accurately as she or he would have if interviewed soon after the event. For this research question, then, it might be best to talk with clients immediately after the therapy session. In contrast, other events are more salient and can be clearly remembered years later. The problem here is that feelings about the event may change over time. For example, if the research question involves a perspective on the grieving process after the death of a child, researchers might think carefully about how the grieving process would be immediately after the death, a year later, 2 to 5 years later, and 5 to 10 years later. Researchers in this study would need to think about what they are most interested in because they might get too broad a range of results if they do not narrow the time frame. Researchers of such a study might also want to contemplate other variables such as type of death, age of child, and religion of parents, all of which might influence the results.

In addition, as these above examples illustrate, salience of the event interacts with the recency of the event, given that very salient events are milestones in people's lives and are thus remembered longer and with more clarity than are events that are less salient or important to the individual. That said, qualitative researchers should always remember that retrospective recall is always limited, and thus what we are studying is the subjective (and undoubtedly distorted) recall of impressions and experiences rather the accurate and objective reporting of events (see also Chapter 2, this volume, about the philosophy of science underlying CQR). It is also important to remember, however, that all memories of events involve retrospection, which is open to distortion.

Ideally, when choosing the particular sample researchers would select from the population randomly so that they would be more likely to have a representative sample than one that is unique in a way that is not what is desired in the study. For example, if a researcher only selected friends as participants, there could be a skew if the researcher's friends were all introverted or aggressive but this skew was not known or acknowledged. In fact, however, it is often difficult, in quantitative studies as well as qualitative studies, to choose a completely random sample, and of course this inability places limits that must be acknowledged in the write-up (i.e., that a convenience sample was used and that a different sample might have produced different results). Once the population has been clearly defined, however, researchers should try as hard as possible to choose a sample randomly from the population by announcing the study as widely as possible to potential participants and choosing randomly from among the volunteers. In addition, because there are typically self-selection factors operating, researchers need to describe their sample as clearly as possible so that readers know who they were.

A final decision we discuss here is whether the research team should contribute data to the study. In the first study using CQR (Rhodes, Hill, Thompson, & Elliott, 1994), some of the authors did provide data for the study (although they did not serve on the team when their own data were being analyzed). In response to queries from reviewers, the authors justified this inclusion of data by explaining that having experienced misunderstandings in therapy themselves helped them understand the phenomenon more deeply. In thinking about this issue now, we would not recommend inclusion of researchers' own data; it simply makes it harder to be unbiased, and so much more information is available about the authors' experiences than about those of other participants because the authors might continue to embellish their experiences as they hear what others say.

## Size of the Sample

Our goal in determining the size of the sample is to try to think about how many participants are needed to obtain some consistency of results. Although the range of sample sizes has varied in the literature (see Chapter 18) from 3 to 97 ($M = 15.7$, $SD = 11.5$), we generally recommend using 12 to 15 participants. This number typically provides a large enough sample to begin to see some consistency in results across participants, especially if the sample is relatively homogeneous in terms of their experiences.

If researchers think that there is a good possibility that there may be subgroups within the sample, a larger sample of 15 to 19 is advisable. With larger samples, researchers can subdivide the sample using either predetermined criteria or criteria that emerge during the analyses. For example, Williams et al. (1998) divided their sample of female counseling psychologists who had experienced a serendipity experience in the career path into those who had experienced the event pre-PhD and those who had experienced the event post-PhD because it became apparent during the analysis that these two groups of participants had different experiences. In a study on hostile or unasserted client anger directed at therapists, Hill et al. (2003) divided their results into events that were resolved versus those that were unresolved on the basis of analyses that revealed that these were quite different experiences. Similarly, Hess et al. (2008) divided their sample of psychology doctoral student interns into those who were satisfied with their supervisor's self-disclosures versus those who were not satisfied because results differed between the two groups.

If one is using a very large sample (>20), different issues emerge. If in-depth information is sought from each participant, researchers may end up with so much information that they have a hard time finishing the project. Some researchers solve this problem by asking for less information from each participant. In this situation, we recommend a modification to CQR called consensual qualitative research modified (CQR-M; see Chapter 17).

## Recruiting the Sample

Recruiting for qualitative studies is difficult because we are asking potential participants for a lot of time, investment of energy, and disclosure of personal feelings. Thus, it is not surprising that many people are reluctant to participate in qualitative projects. A couple of research findings provide evidence about this issue. Bednar and Shapiro (1970) reported that fewer than 1% of 16,100 therapists agreed to participate in research that involved audiotaping a therapy session and then spending an additional 3 hours evaluating the session. Another example is when Vachon et al. (1995) asked 845 therapists to participate in a study that involved audiotaping one therapy session and then being interviewed about the case for 2 hours, only 2% agreed. The primary reasons given for not participating were insufficient time, unwillingness to audiotape clients, and not having clients who were considered appropriate for the research.

In research using CQR, the participation rate has varied wildly from about 4% in Hill et al. (1996) to 93% in Vivino, Thompson, Hill, and Ladany (2009). In Chapter 12, we report a qualitative meta-analysis of 10 studies that queried participants about why they chose to participate in CQR studies. The two most salient reasons were the wish to be helpful and thinking that the topic was interesting or important. Other reasons mentioned less frequently were having had related meaningful experiences, wanting to educate or contribute to knowledge, liking qualitative research, being invited by a colleague or advisor, facilitating the participant's own research, the topic not being invasive or exploitative, and wanting experience as an interviewee. It is interesting to note that it appeared graduate students had different reasons for participating than did postgraduate professionals (the two most common samples). Graduate students were more likely to participate when they felt that they had experienced the phenomenon and when they wanted to help, whereas professionals were more likely to participate when they were invited by a colleague and when they wanted to educate or contribute to knowledge. Taking the above research findings and our personal experiences into account, we next cover factors that may influence participation.

## VARIABLES INFLUENCING POTENTIAL PARTICIPANTS TO VOLUNTEER

First, there is the topic. In the Gelso et al. (1999) study, therapists seemed to be more willing to participate because they were psychoanalytic and were interested in thinking about transference (participation rate = 13%). This topic seemed to spark a chord in these therapists, and so they were willing to talk about it. In contrast, it was harder to recruit therapists for a study on impasses in therapy (4% agreed; Hill et al., 1996), perhaps because the topic was of less interest to therapists.

A related issue is how vulnerable the topic makes the potential participant feel. For example, in the Hill et al. (1996) that had only a 4% participation rate, therapists may have felt very vulnerable talking about clients who terminated from treatment because of impasses, perhaps because this topic made them question their competence. Similarly, in a study of gifts in therapy (Knox, Hess, Williams, & Hill, 2003), the low participation rate (6%) might have been due to therapists feeling vulnerable about talking about clients giving them gifts when there is such a taboo against accepting gifts in some theoretical orientations. People have told us that they were nervous about what might come out in interviews about sensitive topics.

Another related issue is how much the potential participants trust the researchers. Especially in qualitative research, where the participant is expected to disclose honestly about deep and often difficult experiences, the participants have to trust that the investigators are going to be honest, fair, compassionate, and nonjudgmental. If potential participants do not know the investigators, at least by reputation, they may be reluctant to commit to participating and revealing deeply about themselves, and thus novice researchers will have to work hard to be credible (see later section of chapter about suggested procedures for recruiting).

In addition, if participants are busy, they are probably not going to participate no matter how wonderful and important your study is because time is a concern for many people. Picking the right time to ask is crucial, although often impossible to determine. But time and busyness are strange things—sometimes we find time to do things that we consider to be very important—so it is vital to convince the potential participant of the value of your study.

Wanting to be helpful, particularly if a colleague or person in authority asks for help, is a very salient reason for participating, especially for people in helping professions. Graduate students often mention *research karma*, or the idea that if they participate in someone's research, then others will feel generous and be willing to participate in their research when the time comes. In addition, if a friend, colleague, mentor, or someone familiar asks, it is probably more likely that people will respond than if asked by a stranger.

Incentives might work for some potential participants. For example, undergraduate students may be more likely to participate if given course credit or money. For professionals, however, any incentives that we can offer usually cannot match what their time is worth (e.g., offering $10 for 2 hours of their time is hardly adequate compensation if they make $100 per hour). We would also caution against using excessive incentives because potential participants might feel coerced into participating.

A general principle to think about in terms of recruiting is to know your population and think carefully and creatively about what would motivate these particular people to participate. Different groups present different challenges in terms of recruitment. For example, recruiting therapists can be difficult because therapists are often very good at defining boundaries and saying no, their time is valuable, and they are reluctant to make themselves vulnerable if they do not trust the researchers. Clients, in contrast, are usually more amenable to participating in studies, but it is hard to find a way to contact them. (A caution or consideration in using clients may be that they are more vulnerable to exploitation and less able to give informed consent.) College students in introductory psychology classes are easy to recruit if they earn extra credit for participating, but the topic has to appeal to them because they often have choices about studies in which they can participate. Finally, graduate students in psychology are often relatively easy to recruit, especially if the researchers are other graduate students who appeal the potential participant's sense of karma (i.e., paying back others who have helped you in your research either previously or who might help you in the future; the idea is that if you help others, others will be more likely to help you). Given that graduate students need to conduct research, they are often sympathetic to others in the same position.

## SUGGESTED PROCEDURES FOR RECRUITING

The participation rate can also be influenced by recruitment methods. For example, for the study in Hill et al. (1996), we sent a letter of invitation to therapists and asked those who were interested to respond using a self-addressed stamped envelope, and only 4% followed through and agreed to participate. We probably demanded too much of these therapists, and they were not motivated to take the time and energy to respond. In contrast, Gelso et al. (1999) reported a 13% participation rate when a letter was followed up by a phone call. Vivino et al. (2009) obtained a 93% return rate when therapists who had been nominated by a large sample of people in a metropolitan area as compassionate were personally invited and told that they had been nominated as compassionate.

We suggest several ideas that researchers can consider when recruiting, remembering that the recruiting strategy will differ depending on the target sample:

- Send a personalized e-mail or letter (rather than a mass communication).
- Begin the invitation with a catchy first sentence. You need to grab the reader's attention right away (remember how easy it is to hit the "delete" button or throw something away). Compare "We would like to invite you to participate in a study on the experiences of clients giving gifts in therapy" with "Has a client given you a gift recently and set you to wondering about how you should respond?" Which sentence is most likely to grab your attention and make you want to read further rather than hitting the "delete" button or throwing the letter away?
- In the recruiting letter (or e-mail), provide all the relevant information about the time commitment, nature of the study, and procedures for ensuring confidentiality so that the potential participant can be fully informed and make a wise decision about whether she or he wants to participate.
- For studies requiring that participants think about the topic prior to the interview (e.g., a therapist may need to review case notes to refresh his or her memory before talking with an interviewer about an experience of dealing with a hostile or angry client), we recommend providing a copy of the interview protocol so that potential participants can prepare themselves for the interview. When participants might prepare too much and give only socially desirable responses (e.g., when we want to know their immediate reactions to feminism and do not want them to have a chance to formulate a politically correct response), we would not give the interview protocol ahead of time. However, we typically are less concerned about getting only socially desirable responses than we are about providing people with enough opportunity to think over the details of events and perhaps review case notes. Providing the interview protocol ahead of time also allows potential participants the opportunity to make a wise choice about whether they want to participate. We are usually asking people to disclose to us, and they need to know what they are getting into.

- Follow the initial invitation with one more personal e-mail or phone call to invite the person to participate.
- Make it as easy as possible for the person to let you know that they agree to participate. Don't expect that they will take a lot of initiative to respond.
- Do not harass potential participants. If people do not respond after two or three invitations, researchers can safely assume that the potential participants are not interested.

It is important to recognize that our responsibility to participants does not end with recruiting them. Indeed, we must treat participants with care, respect their autonomy and right to withdraw at any time, and recognize their likely caution about sharing deep things with people who are strangers. We also need to offer to provide participants with a transcript of the interview so they can correct mistakes or provide additional information, and we need to provide them with a copy of the final draft of the manuscript so that they can assure us that their identities have been concealed adequately.

There are a number of other relevant cultural and ethical issues involved in recruiting participants. Cultural concerns are treated in depth Chapter 14 and suggest that researchers think carefully about the background of the people they are selecting. Ethical concerns are treated in detail in Chapter 15, but to summarize the issues here: We should not unfairly burden people who are vulnerable (e.g., use prisoners as participants just because they are available, especially if the topic is not directly about their lives), should not unduly pressure people to participate, should provide adequate information so that people can choose whether they want to participate, and should recognize that participants have a right to withdraw at any time with no penalty. We assume that good research involves sensitivity to culture and good ethical practices, so we strongly advocate such practices in CQR.

## Conclusions

We hope we have convinced readers of the importance of thinking through issues related to choosing and recruiting the sample. Given that the quality of the data yielded by the study depends on the quality of the sample, researchers need to be attentive to such details. We cannot provide criteria here for all possible scenarios, but we hope that we have provided readers with things to think about when selecting and working with samples. A summary of the points in the chapter is presented in Table 6.1.

## TABLE 6.1

**Issues to Consider in Recruiting a Consensual Qualitative Research Sample**

| Concern | Recommendation |
| --- | --- |
| Choosing the sample | Have clear research questions. |
| | The sample should fit the research questions. |
| | Identify specific criteria for the sample. |
| | Try to obtain a representative sample. |
| | Do not include own data. |
| Recruiting the sample | Choose a relevant topic for the sample. |
| | Reduce vulnerability. |
| | Enhance trust. |
| | Be respectful of time commitment. |
| | Maximize desire to be helpful. |
| | Consider incentives. |
| | Know your particular population. |
| Recruiting procedures | Send a personalized e-mail or letter. |
| | Immediately grab the reader's attention. |
| | Provide all the relevant information. |
| | Consider providing a copy of the interview protocol. |
| | Follow up initial invitation with personal invitation. |
| | Make it easy for the person to participate. |
| | Do not harass potential participants. |

# *References*

Bednar, R. L., & Shapiro, J. G. (1970). Professional research commitment: A symptom of a syndrome. *Journal of Consulting and Clinical Psychology, 34*, 323–326. doi:10.1037/h0029339

Gelso, C. J., Hill, C. E., Rochlen, A., Mohr, J., & Zack, J. (1999). Describing the face of transference: Psychodynamic therapists' recollections of transference in successful long-term therapy. *Journal of Counseling Psychology, 46*, 257–267. doi:10.1037/0022-0167.46.2.257

Hess, S. A., Knox, S., Schultz, J. M., Hill, C. E., Sloan, L., Brandt, S., . . . Hoffman, M. A. (2008). Pre-doctoral interns' non-disclosure in supervision. *Psychotherapy Research, 18*, 400–411. doi:10.1080/10503300701697505

Hill, C. E., Kellems, I. S., Kolchakian, M. R., Wonnell, T. L., Davis, T. L., & Nakayama, E. Y. (2003). The therapist experience of being the target of hostile versus suspected-unasserted client anger: Factors associated with resolution. *Psychotherapy Research, 13*, 475–491. doi:10.1093/ptr/kpg040

Hill, C. E., Nutt-Williams, E., Heaton, K. J., Thompson, B. J., & Rhodes, R. H. (1996). Therapist retrospective recall of impasses in long-term psychotherapy: A qualitative analysis. *Journal of Counseling Psychology, 43*, 207–217. doi:10.1037/0022-0167.43.2.207

Knox, S., Hess, S. A., Williams, E. N., & Hill, C. E. (2003). "Here's a little something for you": How therapists respond to client gifts. *Journal of Counseling Psychology, 50*, 199–210. doi:10.1037/0022-0167.50.2.199

Rhodes, R., Hill, C. E., Thompson, B. J., & Elliott, R. (1994). Client retrospective recall of resolved and unresolved misunderstanding events. *Journal of Counseling Psychology, 41*, 473–483. doi:10.1037/0022-0167.41.4.473

Vachon, D. O., Sussman, M., Wynne, M. E., Birringer, J., Olshefsky, L., & Cox, K. (1995). Reasons therapists give for refusing to participate in psychotherapy process research. *Journal of Counseling Psychology, 42*, 380–382. doi:10.1037/0022-0167.42.3.380

Vivino, B. L., Thompson, B., Hill, C. E., & Ladany, N. (2009). Compassion in psychotherapy: The perspective of psychotherapists nominated as compassionate. *Psychotherapy Research, 19*, 157–171. doi:10.1080/10503300802430681

Williams, E. N., Soeprapto, E., Like, K., Touradji, P., Hess, S., & Hill, C. E. (1998). Perceptions of serendipity: Career paths of prominent academic women in counseling psychology. *Journal of Counseling Psychology, 45*, 379–389. doi:10.1037/0022-0167.45.4.379

*Alan W. Burkard, Sarah Knox, and Clara E. Hill*

# Data Collection | 7

C onsensual qualitative research (CQR) data are language based, can focus on events or nonevents (e.g., attitudes, beliefs), and can be collected in several different forms. Most researchers have used in-person or telephone interviews (66 out of 90 CQR studies; see Chapter 16), but others have used journaling (e.g., Hill, Sullivan, Knox, & Schlosser, 2007), written questionnaires (e.g., Rhodes, Hill, Thompson, & Elliott, 1994), e-mailed questionnaires and correspondence (e.g., Kim, Brenner, Liang, & Asay, 2003), and focus groups (e.g., Hendrickson, Veach, & LeRoy, 2002). Given this clear predominance, the current chapter will focus on data collection via interviews. We pay special attention to the development of the interview protocol, address preinterview considerations, and also discuss factors that affect the interview process itself. Finally, we address other considerations that are important to the collection and handling of interview data. Steps of the data collection process are summarized in Table 7.1.

## TABLE 7.1

**Data Collection Steps**

| Step | Recommendations |
|---|---|
| Protocol development | Make sure CQR is the best approach for research questions. |
| | Review the literature but be aware of assumptions in literature. |
| | Use personal experience to develop questions. |
| | Use eight to 10 open-ended scripted questions per hour. |
| | Start with rapport-building general questions. |
| | Locate evocative questions later in the protocol. |
| | Use unscripted probes to help participants elaborate on details (generate possible probes prior to conducting interviews). |
| | End the interview with closure-type questions. |
| | Consult with content experts to ensure coverage of relevant topics. |
| | Conduct at least two pilot interviews to assess the quality of the protocol. |
| Prepare for interviewing | Decide whether to use telephone or in-person interviews. |
| | Require interviewers who are empathic listeners and train them to ask open-ended questions. |
| | Train interviewers on interview protocol. |
| | Discuss and document biases and expectations about topic. |
| | Check recording equipment to ensure that it is working properly. |
| Interviewing | Typically complete at least two interviews with participants. |
| | Send protocol to interviewees ahead of time. |
| | If the study focuses on specific events, these events preferably should have occurred within the past 3 years. |
| | Develop an alliance with the interviewee. |
| | Maintain the focus of interviews on the participant. |
| | Take notes during and after the interview. |
| | Debrief the research team who are empathic listeners and train them to ask open-sided questions about difficult interviews. |

# *Development of the Interview Protocol*

## USE OF LITERATURE AND CLINICAL EXPERIENCE IN DEVELOPING THE INTERVIEW PROTOCOL

To reduce bias in the development of the interview protocol, some qualitative researchers believe it is important to avoid reviewing the literature prior to the development of any interview questions (e.g., Charmatz, 1995). Disagreeing with this perspective, Hill, Thompson, and Williams (1997) encouraged CQR researchers to review the extant literature to develop an understanding of the empirical findings on a given research topic, to ensure that the study builds on this prior research, and to avoid mistakes made by other researchers. We assert that a solid understanding of prior research provides researchers a foundation for developing a study that is connected to and advances prior research and that also avoids any shortcomings in prior research. Additionally, we also caution researchers to be aware of the assumptions they may have regarding a topic from exposure to the extant literature because these beliefs may unnecessarily restrict their ideas in the development of a research protocol. (See also Chapters 3 and 5 in this volume.)

Those engaged in CQR, however, need not be limited only to developing questions that emerge from the literature. Another important source of ideas is personal experiences. For example, given that many qualitative psychotherapy researchers are themselves clinicians, they may have insights about attitudes, beliefs, and psychotherapy practices related to the topic of investigation from their clinical work. As an illustration, clinical supervisors have often asserted that difficult events in supervision influence supervisees' work with clients, although this connection has been elusive to establish empirically (Bernard & Goodyear, 2009). Using this clinical awareness, researchers in two studies of difficult supervision events recently included questions that asked supervisees to describe any effects that supervision had had on their work with clients (Burkard et al., 2006; Burkard, Knox, Hess, & Schultz, 2009).

## THE INTERVIEW PROTOCOL

The scope of the protocol is dictated by two important and related goals: the need to develop rapport with participants and the need to gather consistent as well as idiosyncratic information from participants about the phenomenon of interest. Interview protocols, then, often comprise three sections designed to accomplish these goals. In the opening section, researchers build rapport with participants by inquiring about topics that may be less emotionally evocative yet are still related broadly to the study's focus and thus serve to get the participants talking and to establish rapport. For instance, in the studies of difficult supervision events mentioned previously, we queried participants first about their supervisors' supervision style before exploring more evocative topics of difficult supervision experiences.

The second section of the interview protocol focuses on the main topic of interest. Typically, scripted questions are used to explore areas germane to the topic and to ensure consistent information across participants and may include discussion of events as well as attitudes, beliefs, and feelings about such experiences. For example, when the research involves questions about specific events, we often explore antecedents to the event of interest, factors that affect the event, descriptions of the actual event, participant reactions, and consequences for the participants and their relationships. Additional unscripted probes are used to help participants explain their individual experiences more deeply and richly. For instance, after participants have shared an experience, we might probe for their attitudes or emotions related to the events, how they behaved in such situations, what they were thinking during the event, or what they noticed about others' reactions. Such elaboration helps participants more fully explain their experiences. Although some researchers script their probes, this additional structure to the interview can again lead to thin data as noted earlier, and it also reduces the spontaneity of the interview. We have found that unscripted probes best allow the interviewer to explore areas that are uniquely relevant to the participant and can lead to unexpected findings. We do recommend that research teams discuss possible probes prior to interviews and practice probing for further explanation during pilot interviews. In our experience, these training approaches have been adequate for preparing team members to use probes to help participants further elaborate on their experiences.

In the final section of the interview protocol, participants are asked to reflect on broader issues related to the topic (e.g., advice about the topic; suggestions to clients, therapists, or supervisors related to the topic). We also frequently ask participants about why they chose to participate and about the effects of the interview. After disclosing what may be emotional information in the second section of the interview, this final section helps participants decompress from any intense reaction and allows the researchers to discern how participants are feeling emotionally. In cases where the interview was particularly intense and participants remain upset, we offer referrals to further assist participants with any distress they may be experiencing.

An important consideration for the interview protocol is the number of scripted questions to be included. Hill et al. (2005) found that CQR researchers were using between three and 30 questions in an hour-long interview, with 12 the median number and 15 the modal number. Using a large number of questions can lead to thin data that resemble questionnaire information rather than an in-depth description of a participant's experience; too few questions can lead to topic areas that are not consistently explored across participants (e.g., because researchers have not consistently probed the same areas). In seeking to balance depth with consistency across participants, Hill et al. recommended that interviewers use eight to 10 scripted, open-ended questions per interview hour for a typical study. This number allows interviewers to fully probe important areas and still maintain the consistent collection of information across participants.

Finally, interview questions are most productive when phrased as open-ended probes. These questions are often used to facilitate clarification; explore attitudes, thoughts, or feelings about experiences; and encourage participant elaboration of events without fear of judgment. Open questions specifically facilitate participants' exploration of feelings, thoughts, and meaning of events without setting limits on the type of response. These queries may be offered as questions (e.g., "What was your supervision relationship like?") or directives (e.g., "Tell me about your supervision relationship"). To probe participants' responses more deeply, we encourage researchers to be keenly attuned not only to the content of what is said but also to the manner in which it is said, both of which may yield additional rich data. It is also important to avoid leading questions (e.g., "Wouldn't it be helpful to you if your therapist self-disclosed?"). Ideally, then, open questions offer the interviewer the best opportunity for facilitating participants' in-depth exploration and elaboration of their experiences. (For more information about how to construct good open-ended questions, see Hill, 2009, Chapters 6 and 7.)

## CONSULTATION WITH CONTENT EXPERTS ON THE PROTOCOL

After the initial protocol has been developed, we consult with researchers knowledgeable about the topic area to ensure that our interview is capturing the relevant data. We often ask such individuals to review our interview questions to determine whether we have addressed the important areas of inquiry. We may also seek feedback from individuals who have experienced the phenomenon of interest. Such persons have "lived the experience" and can offer feedback on the protocol that may not be readily apparent to the researchers.

## PILOTING AND REVISING PROTOCOL

As an additional means of assessing whether the interview questions actually elicit the sought data, we pilot the protocol with at least two people who fulfill the participation criteria but are not part of the final sample. These pilot interviews allow researchers to determine whether participants understand the questions, whether the questions yield data about the specific area of investigation, and whether the questions flow logically. During such pilot interviews, we actively solicit feedback from participants about any troublesome parts of the protocol (e.g., unclear wording, overlooked topic areas, abrupt flow) and then use this feedback and our own reactions to revise the protocol. When we have revised the interview protocol extensively on the basis of the feedback, we often conduct a second round of pilot interviews to ensure the viability of the questions and the flow of the interview. Such efforts have been invaluable in developing effective protocols. No matter how much experience we have had with CQR, we find that developing effective interview protocols requires intensive work.

## The Interview

### PHONE OR IN-PERSON INTERVIEW

As noted by Knox and Burkard (2009), researchers must first decide whether to interview participants by phone, by Skype, or in person (i.e., face to face). Phone and internet interviews free researchers from geographic limitations. Drawing a sample from a broader geographical location may also be attractive to researchers who desire a pragmatic way to obtain the perspectives of nonlocal participants. In addition, participants who are themselves professionals in the mental health field may value the more concrete boundaries inherent in a phone or internet interview (e.g., a distinct block of time that they can set aside). Furthermore, phone and audio-only Internet interviews may provide participants greater anonymity through the use of a pseudonym.

In-person (also called *face-to-face*) interviews, however, offer access to nonverbal data, such as facial expressions, gestures, and other paraverbal communications and enrich the meaning of spoken words (Carr & Worth, 2001). In this vein, some researchers assert that because both researcher and participant occupy the same physical space in an in-person, face-to-face interview and thus have access to more than verbal data, they are better able to build the rapport so essential for participants' disclosure of their experiences than would occur in a phone interview (Shuy, 2003).

Video-based Skype interviews may be an alternative approach to phone or in-person face-to-face interviews. Skype may combine the benefits of in-person interviews (e.g., access to nonverbal data) with the advantages of phone interviews (e.g., low cost, no travel, ability to reach participants where the Internet is accessible). If researchers elect to use Skype in an investigation, we encourage them to review the limits of the Skype privacy policies and include a statement regarding the limits of confidentiality in their informed consent for potential participants. Although there are no current published CQR studies that have used Skype for interviewing, the technology is an important innovation for combining traditional phone and in-person interviews.

Across hundreds of phone interviews, we have encountered few participants who were hesitant to share their experiences (after all, they volunteered knowing what was expected). Most, in fact, have appreciated the invitation to share their stories; freely offering their perspectives and noting that doing so was helpful in allowing them to speak about often powerful personal experiences (see also Hiller & DiLuzio, 2004). For the reticent few, we surmise that had we been face to face, they may have been even less comfortable; the phone at least provided them physical and psychological space from the interviewer (Sturges & Hanrahan, 2004). Furthermore, participants' access to nonverbal data may heighten the potential for response bias, for they may "read" interviewers' reactions to their disclosures and then alter what they share (Marcus & Crane, 1986; Musselwhite, Cuff, McGregor, & King, 2006). There is no empirical evidence about which approach is preferable (although this would be an excellent area for research), and so at this point the ideal approach may vary from study to study (Shuy, 2003).

## SELECTING INTERVIEWERS

It is essential to select interviewers who can conduct a good interview. They need to be empathic listeners who can gently and competently elicit information from participants. In our own research teams, we typically seek individuals who have at least had a class in basic counseling skills (e.g., use of restatements, open-ended questions, reflections of feeling). Such training helps interviewers understand the purpose of these skills, how these skills affect interviewees, and the type of information likely to be gathered by using these skills. In short, trained interviewers are able to be more intentional during the interview process, thus leading to more in-depth information emerging from the interviews. We have also found that it is best to select people who have not only had helping skills training but who have also had substantial clinical experience because they are more adept at conducting interviews.

## NUMBER OF INTERVIEWERS

A second decision CQR researchers must make involves how many interviewers to use. If one person conducts all interviews, the interviews across participants are more likely to be consistent and uniform but of course reflect only that one interviewer's biases. Alternatively, as long as multiple interviewers adhere to the prepared protocol, a team of interviewers usually reduces the opportunity for a single researcher's approach or biases to adversely affect data collection. We must acknowledge, however, that multiple interviewers may introduce a wider range of biases, thus making it more difficult to understand how interviews were influenced by biases. The effects of the biases may be reduced, however, because these biases are spread more thinly across interviews. The team approach also brings the benefit of more equitably dividing the labor: The demands of data collection are dispersed across several people rather than being the responsibility of one person, potentially making researchers' involvement in the project more attractive and also eliciting a stronger investment from all team members because each has direct contact with participants. In addition, if a researcher knows a participant, the interview can be conducted by a different member of the team (see Chapter 15, on ethics, in this volume).

## NUMBER OF INTERVIEWS PER PARTICIPANT

Although some qualitative researchers or methods have used just a single interview with each participant, most CQR studies have used multiple interview contacts. Our concern with the former is that it may fail to capture important information: One interaction with a participant with whom the researcher has never before spoken may not yield the contextual data that would more likely emerge via multiple interviews (Mishler, 1986) and without which the experiences discussed in an interview may lose some of their meaning (Patton, 1989). Multiple interviews, then, may forge a stronger relationship between researcher and participant, enabling the latter to feel greater comfort in describing emotionally evocative experiences because he or she has had prior contact with the researcher (i.e., the first interview) and has established at least a basic level of trust. Moreover, researchers and participants may have further feelings and thoughts about or responses to the first interview that can be explored in a second contact. Furthermore, if either party ended the first interview feeling concerned or confused about some of its content, a follow-up interview provides an opportunity for clarification.

We thus recommend that researchers use at least two interviews. Doing so increases the likelihood of capturing the context, and thereby the meaning, of participants' experiences; helps participants feel safe with the interviewer; permits exploration of additional content that may be stimulated by the first interview; and lets both parties clarify any confusing content from the first interview. In this vein, some CQR interviewers are finding that during the second interview, participants disclose important information that was not examined during the first interview. In addition, it may be important to distribute substantive questions across the two interviews so that the second interview does not become only a pro forma procedure consisting of a check-in with the participant.

## RETROSPECTIVE NATURE OF INTERVIEW

Some CQR studies focus on attitudes or beliefs, which illuminate participants' immediate reactions; others, however, examine events or specific experiences, thereby yielding retrospective data. The greatest consideration in the latter circumstance, then, centers on the length of time between the participants' experiences and the interviews. In other words, how retrospective can the data be? Interviews completed relatively soon after the actual experience certainly bring immediacy and recency to the data. And because human memory is imperfect (Schacter, 1999), participants may have better recall for events and may thus be able to offer more details than in an interview occurring after a long passage of time. As Polkinghorne (2005) asserted, however, the purpose of such interviews is often actually *not* to derive an inherently accurate recall but instead to engender participants' examination of the meaning and import of their experiences. In interviews that necessarily occur after time has passed, then, asking participants to discuss especially salient or potent events may reduce distortion or loss of detail because such powerful experiences are often well remembered. Such retrospective interviews also enable participants to describe any shift in their perspective on the events themselves because with the passage of time, new insights may develop.

In our research on specific experiences, participants have discussed events occurring as recently as a few weeks before and as distally as several years before. We have not found any meaningful differences in the richness or quality of these data, although it should be noted that researchers have not empirically examined data for these differences or to see how perspectives change over time. We have found that participants are able to describe their experiences—whether recent or remote—quite powerfully. Our recommendation, then, is that although it may be preferable to capture data as soon after the experience as possible, researchers need not abandon the pursuit of data about experiences that occurred some time before. As long as participants can recall and share rich data about their experience, the purposes of the interview may be fulfilled. We do recommend keeping the elapsed time between the experience and the interview somewhat consistent across cases.

## *Conducting the Interview*

After developing the protocol, the next step is to implement it. Here, we discuss considerations related to the actual execution of the protocol.

## TRAINING INTERVIEWERS

Even when good clinicians have been selected, training is crucial to ensure consistent quality in the interviews. For training researchers new to CQR, we often ask them first to transcribe interviews because this allows them to develop a sense of the interview process, the scope of interviews, and how interviewers probe for depth on a topic. Second, we conduct mock interviews during team meetings using the protocol. Usually, we have team members experienced in CQR model the process during an hour-long mock-interview. After this demonstration, the team discusses the interview process and addresses any questions that have arisen. Some CQR teams listen to National Public Radio interviewers for an additional modeling experience to learn how to manage researcher biases during the interview process. Next, we typically have novice researchers conduct mock interviews during team meetings. These role-plays afford them the opportunity to receive direct feedback on their interviewing skills from experienced interviewers and to become comfortable with the interview protocol. We also encourage these novice interviewers to practice interviewing outside of team meetings, ideally by telephone because our interviews are usually conducted by phone. Finally, we have novice interviewers conduct pilot interviews, which reinforces their prior learning and offers further experience with the protocol. After data collection begins, we have more experienced members of the research team conduct the first interviews of the study and have the novice interviewers listen to the recordings of these initial interviews, thereby allowing the novice an opportunity to hear the interview with a "live" participant. In addition, we debrief after every interview that a novice researcher conducts, further helping to identify strategies for problems or difficulties that may occur during the interview process.

## INTERVIEWER'S RELATIONSHIP WITH PARTICIPANT

Consider, for a moment, the interview for a qualitative study from the participant's perspective. As a participant, you have agreed to share information about your attitudes, beliefs, or important events in your life, and in many cases these beliefs or experiences may be some of the most difficult or challenging intrapersonal concerns or interpersonal events you have faced. Interviewers use *probes* (i.e., open-ended questions) to gather further details, often asking you about your emotions, perceptions, or experience with regard to these situations. In short, they ask you to be open about intimate details of your life, and often you know little if anything about the interviewer. During the interview, you may feel vulnerable; may fear sharing a painful event; or may be exploring an attitude, belief, or topic that causes you embarrassment (Adler & Adler, 2002). In addition, you may feel evaluated by the interviewer, as if the interviewer is judging your experience. Finally, you are also aware that eventually your experiences will be presented in published form, where others will read your comments, emotions, and thoughts about these intimate experiences (albeit anonymously). From this perspective, the interview can certainly be intimidating and may well elicit anxiety, vulnerability, and concern for privacy.

Given this context, the interviewer bears the responsibility for developing a research alliance with each participant and thus establishing rapport, trust, and a sense of safety. This relationship is essential because the interviewer–participant relationship often determines the richness of data collected for a qualitative research project (Knox & Burkard, 2009) and strengthens the validity of the data (Adler & Adler, 2002; Kvale, 1996). As such, the alliance helps participants be forthcoming with information about their experiences and can help protect the integrity of the information (Thomas & Pollio, 2002).

While establishing such a research alliance, interviewers must balance the provision of support with the need to acquire information. Attaining this balance is challenging because disclosure does not occur equally for interviewer and participant, and as such they do not have equal status in the interview relationship (Collins, Shattell, & Thomas, 2005). For instance, interviewers seldom disclose personal information but request that participants fully disclose. Encouraging participant disclosure requires interviewers to be empathic, which helps participants feel safe and develop enough trust with the interviewer to fully describe their experience. In these circumstances, interviewers often use the same skills during interviews that are used by therapists (see Hill, 2009). For example, restatements, reflections of feelings, and open-ended questions are vital for facilitating participant exploration, which often leads to further insight, which in turn promotes further disclosure of feelings and thoughts. It is important, however, that interviewers maintain a focus on the study at hand and remember that the purpose of the interview is to gather data rather than to create insight or therapeutic change.

Perhaps most important, we stress that interviewers maintain a sense of curiosity and not be judgmental because participants are likely to shut down if they feel that the interviewer is evaluating them. In addition, we suggest that interviewers offer minimal self-disclosure during the interview process because excessive interviewer self-disclosure may bias participant responses and divert the focus of the interview to the researcher rather than to the participant. We acknowledge, however, that it would be impossible (and probably undesirable) for interviewers to remain wholly neutral during the interview process because such neutrality could result in a sterile, uncompassionate tone to the interview. Participants' retelling of a powerful experience or a tightly held belief is likely to influence researchers' perceptions and interpretations of the events or attitudes and may then affect their interactions in the interview. We encourage researchers to examine and discuss their biases prior to each study, discuss their evolving perceptions of the phenomenon of interest with the team during the data collection process, and examine if and/or how their biases and perceptions may have influenced the data collection at the end of the interview process (see also Chapter 5 in this volume).

## RESPONDING TO DIFFICULTIES IN THE INTERVIEW PROCESS

Regardless of the quality of the interview relationship, researchers will inevitability face difficulties during the interview process. These difficulties often emerge from participant anxiety and vulnerability, which can be challenging for interviewers to manage (Adler & Adler, 2002). For example, participants may provide little information, offer vague or unclear responses, seek to take over and control the pacing of interview, or request self-disclosure from interviewers.

In responding to these difficult behaviors, interviewer compassion and patience are crucial as participants work through their thoughts and emotions about experiences that may have remained unexamined until the interview. Sending the protocol in advance helps interviewees be aware of the questions and also gives them the opportunity to reflect on their related attitudes, beliefs, and experiences prior to the interview, perhaps further reducing the potential for surprise when discussing some topics. In addition, we often come back to the questions that were not directly answered by participants and try to rephrase them in a way that participants can hear. For instance, we often query participants about their reactions to specific events. In cases where they do not respond, we rephrase questions by asking about feelings they experienced or thoughts that arose during the events. If the question remains unanswered, we note this and attempt to probe the area later in the first or the follow-up interview. On occasion, we also might gently interrupt participants if they are responding tangentially to topics and refocus them to get the desired information. In the following section, we address some additional specific concerns that have been identified during the interview process.

### Nonresponsiveness

In our experience, participants who interpersonally withdraw or shut down during interviews do so because they are experiencing intense emotions. Although these participants are usually able to continue with the interview if they are given support and reassurance, in a few cases participants have needed a short break to enable them to refocus in the interview. In addition, interviewers might also consider using the therapeutic skill of *immediacy* (i.e., talking in the here and now about the here and now relationship; Hill, 2009) to address participant affect. For example, interviewers could ask participants if there is something about the interview content or relationship that is contributing to their discomfort and then change their approach if necessary.

## Controlling the Interview

When participants attempt to take control of interviews by asking and then answering their own questions, the interviewer may need to gently interrupt the participant to ensure that the integrity of the study is maintained and that rich data are collected. It may also be important to talk with the participant about the best approach for the interview (e.g., remind the participant that the researcher should ask the questions and have room to pursue follow-up questions as well).

## Requests for Interviewer Self-Disclosure

For the reasons noted earlier, some participants ask questions of interviewers, which could lead to interviewer self-disclosure. In these circumstances, we have briefly self-disclosed a shared experience or belief but also asked if our feelings, beliefs, and observations were similar to those of the participant, thereby ensuring that the focus remains on the participant and her or his experience. Such interviewer self-disclosure is frequently used among feminist researchers who seek to lessen the hierarchical relationship between interviewer and participant (Edwards, 1993); we support this strategy as long as the researcher moves the focus of the interview back to the participant. Researchers are cautioned against extensive self-disclosure during the interview process, however, because it may indeed change the information that participants are willing to share or affect their perceptions of their experiences, thus altering the data collected.

## Misrepresentation

Some novice researchers have asked whether participants misrepresent or lie and how interviewers have handled these situations during the interview. In our experience of hundreds of interviews, we have never known of a participant to intentionally misrepresent or lie about her or his beliefs, feelings, or experiences. Although it is possible such misrepresentation could occur, we suspect that it happens infrequently. If, however, the research team suspects that a participant is not being truthful, we encourage them to discuss the case in detail. If the team concludes that the participant is intentionally misrepresenting her or his beliefs or experiences, we recommend that the case not be included in the analysis process with the deletion mentioned in the write-up.

## Other Considerations

We recognize that researchers using CQR face multiple decisions on other elements of the data collection process. In the following, we briefly address these topics and offer some suggestions.

### GIVING PARTICIPANTS THE INTERVIEW PROTOCOL IN ADVANCE

We wholeheartedly recommend that researchers send the protocol to participants prior to the interview itself. At a practical level, participants' review of the protocol helps ensure that they have indeed had the experience or attitudes on which the research depends. When reading in the protocol that the interview will examine clients' experiences of giving their therapist a gift, for instance, participants clearly see the intended focus of the interview and thus either confirm or disconfirm their appropriateness for taking part. Furthermore, seeing the protocol prior to the actual interview enables participants to give fully informed consent: They know the questions they will be asked, are aware of the nature of the interview, and thus can make an informed decision regarding their participation. In addition, having the protocol in advance allows participants to reflect on their experiences before the interview itself. Many CQR studies examine emotionally evocative phenomena, so participants may benefit from the opportunity to carefully examine their thoughts and feelings about the events under examination.

Some journal reviewers have been critical of the CQR practice of sending interview questions in advance because doing so allows participants to prepare for the interview and perhaps divulge only socially desirable responses. Although we acknowledge the possibility that seeing the protocol ahead of time facilitates socially desirable responses, we firmly believe that the ethical concerns of informed consent should prevail in these circumstances. Furthermore, we note that no empirical evidence exists at this time to suggest that sending the interview questions in advance affects the social desirability of participants' responses. Once again, however, the choice about whether to send the protocol ahead of time depends on whether the research question requires extensive self-reflection or checking of documents.

# RECORDING

Researchers need to make an audio recording of each interview because without it, accurate transcription (see the following section) is not possible. Researchers should test recording equipment before any interview process (we can attest to the disheartening effect of losing an interview because of faulty equipment). In addition, we recommend using equipment with the best audio quality, such as digital recorders. Our practice has been to record each interview; make a back-up copy of this original recording (we keep the original to ensure that we have a record of the interview); and then give the back-up copy to a transcriber, who completes the transcription. Once the transcript is finished, the transcriber returns the back-up recording to us, and we delete the recording as per our agreements on the informed consent.

# TRANSCRIBING

Transcribing is an absolutely crucial part of CQR because it is through this process that the interview data are made available for analysis. We may have had deep and rich interviews and memorable interactions with participants, but until we secure the transcripts we lack data in a usable form.

We provide our transcribers (often undergraduate or graduate students seeking research experience) with clear instructions about how to do the transcription. More specifically, we talk with transcribers about the importance of confidentiality in terms of not talking about the interview content and keeping the recordings of the interviews in a secure location. We also ask them to use initials rather than people's names and also not to use the names of cities, states, countries, businesses, or universities. The transcript format that we suggest (see the example in Exhibit 7.1) involves using *I* for interviewer and *P* for participant. We tell transcribers that they need to transcribe all utterances verbatim, although they should exclude stutters, minimal encouragers (i.e., "mm-hmm"), and verbal fillers such as "you know." Additionally, we request that transcribers acknowledge nonverbal data such as pauses, sighs, laughter, or crying in brackets. We also often ask them to complete the transcript within a defined period of time (e.g., 2 weeks). Once the transcript is returned to us, we review the document to ensure that all meaningful data have been included, usually by having a second person listen to the recording and review the transcription for accuracy. Assuming that the transcript is indeed complete, we ask the transcriber to delete the transcript from her or his computer.

In a few instances, we have discovered that we did not record the interview or that the recording was entirely inaudible. To protect against such circumstances, we take detailed notes of the interview and then

---

**EXHIBIT 7.1**

**Sample Transcription Format**

---

*I:* First question [name of participant] is, how if at all, have LGB [lesbian, gay, bisexual] issues been addressed in your graduate training?

*P:* Well they've been addressed very sparsely, and they've been addressed in the context of multiculturalism. I would have to say almost as an aside or an afterthought as it may be brought up specifically by members of my cohort. For example, [long pause] Classmate A said something the other day. There are a few of us who identify as LGB and we feel almost a certain level or responsibility to make sure that the issue is brought up because if we don't, sometimes it isn't.

*I:* Can you say more?

*P:* Sure, [sigh] there were a couple of specific times when it was, one was in the context of a class on relationship counseling. And two individuals, one was bisexual and one was gay were invited into the class. They were both therapists and were invited to share perspectives on counseling lesbian and gay individuals and their relationships.

---

*Note.* I = researcher/interviewer; P = participant/interviewee.

---

create the transcript from these notes. We also inform the participants of the error and ask that she or he carefully review the transcript for accuracy and completeness. On a rare occasion, we have also reinterviewed participants. These occurrences have been rare, but they emphasize the importance of checking recording equipment to ensure that it is working properly prior to the interview process.

## TAKING NOTES DURING AND AFTER INTERVIEWS

Our final recommendation is that researchers take notes both during and after the interview. Thorough interview notes help the interviewer stay actively involved in the interview process and may prove vital in reviewing transcriptions for accuracy or filling in omitted words or phrases that were unclear in the recording. In a few instances when parts of an interview have been inaudible, our copious notes were helpful in filling in these gaps in the data. In addition, we suggest that researchers briefly note their experience of the interview at its conclusion (e.g., sense of rapport with the participant, richness of the participant's responses, reactions evoked in the researcher by the participant or his or her responses). Such a record sometimes proves useful later in the data analysis process, providing context for puzzling interview content or information that seems unclear. For example, during a study of clients' experiences of giving gifts to their therapist (Knox, Hess, Williams, & Hill, 2003), one participant's responses were consistently brief and nonelaborated. In addition, the researcher sensed some reticence, perhaps even some fragility, in the participant, which she noted in the postinterview notes. When later analyzing this participant's data, such information helped the research team better understand the data. Similarly, if a participant is struggling with bipolar disorder and presents as depressed in one interview and manic in another interview, we would encourage researchers to document these differences.

## Concluding Thoughts

In this chapter, we have offered an overview of the interview process commonly used in CQR. These procedures have been developed, refined, and implemented in dozens of research studies and reflect the strategies in use by many experienced investigators in CQR. These guidelines should provide information important to planning a CQR study and the opportunity for the researcher to develop or refine her or his interview skills to ensure the collection of rich, high-quality interview data.

In closing, we also hope to encourage researchers to examine several methodological features of the CQR interview and data collection process. First, the influence of specific interviewers needs to be investigated. From the psychotherapy literature, it appears that therapist characteristics have a major influence on psychotherapy outcome (Wampold & Bolt, 2007). Likewise, different interviewers may obtain different amounts and quality of data from participants. Further research would also be useful on the relationships between the richness of data obtained and how recently the interview occurred after the experiences being described as well as the method used for the interview (e.g., telephone, Skype, face to face). Finally, the viability of alternative data collection methods such as e-mail questionnaires (e.g., Kim et al., 2003), journaling (e.g., Hill et al., 2007), written questionnaires (e.g., Rhodes et al., 1994), and focus groups (e.g., Hendrickson et al., 2002) could be explored to determine whether there are differences in terms of richness and depth of description of participant experiences.

## References

Adler, P. A., & Adler, P. (2002). The reluctant respondent. In J. F. Gubrium & J. A. Holstein (Eds.), *Handbook of interview research: Context and method* (pp. 515–536). Thousand Oaks, CA: Sage.

Bernard, J. M., & Goodyear, R. K. (2009). *Fundamentals of clinical supervision* (4th ed.). Boston, MA: Allyn & Bacon.

Burkard, A. W., Johnson, A. J., Madson, M. B., Pruitt, N. T., Contreras-Tadych, D. A., Kozlowski, J. M., . . . Knox, S. (2006). Supervisor cultural responsiveness and unresponsiveness in cross-cultural supervision. *Journal of Counseling Psychology, 53,* 288–301. doi:10.1037/0022-0167. 53.3.288

Burkard, A. W., Knox, S., Hess, S., & Schultz, J. (2009). Lesbian, gay, and bisexual affirmative and non-affirmative supervision. *Journal of Counseling Psychology, 56,* 176–188. doi:10.1037/0022-0167.56.1.176

Carr, E. C. J., & Worth, A. (2001). The use of the telephone interview for research. *Nursing Times Research, 6,* 511–524. doi:10.1177/136140960100600107

Charmatz, K. (1995). Grounded theory. In J. A. Smith, R. Harre, & L. Van Langenhone (Eds.), *Rethinking methods in psychology* (pp. 27–49). London, England: Sage.

Collins, M., Shattell, M., & Thomas, S. P. (2005). Problematic participant behaviors in qualitative research. *Western Journal of Nursing Research, 27,* 188–199. doi:10.1177/0193945904268068

Edwards, R. (1993). An education in interviewing: Placing the researcher in the research. In C. M. Renzetti & R. M. Lee (Eds.), *Researching sensitive topics* (pp. 107–122). Newbury Park, CA: Sage.

Hendrickson, S. M., Veach, P. M., & LeRoy, B. S. (2002). A qualitative investigation of student and supervisor perceptions of live supervision in genetic counseling. *Journal of Genetic Counseling, 11,* 25–49. doi:10.1023/A:1013868431533

Hill, C. E. (2009). *Helping skills: Facilitating exploration, insight, and action* (3rd ed.). Washington, DC: American Psychological Association.

Hill, C. E., Knox, S., Thompson, B. J., Williams, E. N., Hess, S.A., & Ladany, N. (2005). Consensual qualitative research: An update. *Journal of Counseling Psychology, 52,* 196–205. doi:10.1037/0022-0167.52.2.196

Hill, C. E., Sullivan, C., Knox, S., & Schlosser, L. Z. (2007). Becoming psychotherapists: Experiences of novice trainees in a beginning graduate class. *Psychotherapy: Theory, Research, Practice, Training, 44,* 434–449. doi:10.1037/0033-3204.44.4.434

Hill, C. E., Thompson, B. J., & Williams, E. N. (1997). A guide to conducting consensual qualitative research. *The Counseling Psychologist, 25,* 517–572. doi:10.1177/0011000097254001

Hiller, H. H., & DiLuzio, L. (2004). The interviewee and the research interview: Analysing a neglected dimension in research. *Canadian Review of Sociology and Anthropology/Revue Canadienne de Sociologie et d'Anthropologie, 41,* 1–26. doi:10.1111/j.1755-618X.2004.tb02167.x

Kim, B. S. K., Brenner, B. R., Liang, C. T. H., & Asay, P. A. (2003). A qualitative study of adaptation experiences of 1.5-generation Asian Americans. *Cultural Diversity and Ethnic Minority Psychology, 9,* 156–170. doi:10.1037/1099-9809.9.2.156

Knox, S., & Burkard, A. W. (2009). Qualitative research interviews. *Psychotherapy Research, 19,* 566–575. doi:10.1080/10503300802702105

Knox, S., Hess, S. A., Williams, E. N., & Hill, C. E. (2003). "Here's a little something for you": How therapists respond to client gifts. *Journal of Counseling Psychology, 50,* 199–210. doi:10.1037/0022-0167.50.2.199

Kvale, S. (1996). *InterViews: An introduction to qualitative research interviewing.* Thousand Oaks, CA: Sage.

Marcus, A. C., & Crane, L. A. (1986). Telephone surveys in public health research. *Medical Care, 24,* 97–112. doi:10.1097/00005650-198602000-00002

Mishler, E. G. (1986). *Research interviewing.* Cambridge, MA: Harvard University Press.

Musselwhite, K., Cuff, L., McGregor, L., & King, K. M. (2006). The telephone interview is an effective method of data collection in clinical nursing research: A discussion paper. *International Journal of Nursing Studies, 44,* 1064–1070. doi:10.1016/j.ijnurstu.2006.05.014

Patton, M. Q. (1989) *Qualitative evaluation methods.* Beverly Hills, CA: Sage.

Polkinghorne, D. E. (2005). Language and meaning: Data collection in qualitative research. *Journal of Counseling Psychology, 52,* 137–145. doi:10.1037/0022-0167.52.2.137

Rhodes, R., Hill, C. E., Thompson, B. J., & Elliott, R. (1994). Client retrospective recall of resolved and unresolved misunderstanding events. *Journal of Counseling Psychology, 41,* 473–483. doi:10.1037/0022-0167.41.4.473

Schacter, D. L. (1999). The seven sins of memory: Insights from psychology and cognitive neuroscience. *American Psychologist, 54,* 182–203. doi:10.1037/0003-066X.54.3.182

Shuy, R. W. (2003). In-person versus telephone interviewing. In J. A. Holstein & J. F. Gubrium (Eds.), *Inside interviewing: New lenses, new concerns* (pp. 175–193). Thousand Oaks, CA: Sage.

Sturges, J. E., & Hanrahan, K. J. (2004). Comparing telephone and face-to-face qualitative interviewing: A research note. *Qualitative Research, 4,* 107–118. doi:10.1177/1468794104041110

Thomas, S. P., & Pollio, H. R. (2002). *Listening to patients: A phenomenological approach to nursing research and practice.* New York, NY: Springer.

Wampold, B. E., & Bolt, D. M. (2007). The consequences of "anchoring" in longitudinal multilevel models: Bias in the estimation of patient variability and therapist effects. *Psychotherapy Research, 17,* 509–514. doi:10.1080/10503300701250339

*Barbara J. Thompson, Barbara L. Vivino, and Clara E. Hill*

# Coding the Data
## *Domains and Core Ideas*

8

n this chapter we describe the first steps involved in analyzing the data: developing a domain list and constructing core ideas. The goal of developing a *domain list* (i.e., a list of discrete topics) and then assigning the raw data into these domains is to provide an overall structure for understanding and describing each individual participant's experiences. The goal of constructing core ideas is to summarize what the participant has said within each domain in clear and concise terms. Having clear domains and core ideas within the domains facilitates comparisons across cases during the cross-analysis (see Chapter 9, this volume).

We assume that prior to beginning this process researchers will have prepared transcripts of the interviews and checked these transcripts for accuracy (see Chapter 7, this volume). We recommend numbering each line of the transcript consecutively so that team members can refer to specific sections of the transcript with ease (numbering lines is a function available in most word-processing packages). In addition, we assume that the research team members have recorded and discussed their biases and expectations (see Chapter 5, this volume) and are ready to immerse themselves in the experiential world of their participants with open, flexible minds.

# Developing Domains

## CREATING A DOMAIN LIST

The first step is to create a domain list, by which we mean a list of the meaningful and unique topic areas examined in the interview. In previous descriptions of consensual qualitative research (CQR; Hill et al., 2005; Hill, Thompson, & Williams, 1997), two approaches for developing the domain list were discussed. In the first approach, researchers develop a start list or proposed list of domains based on a review of the literature (Miles & Huberman, 1994) and the primary questions in their interview protocol. This method is fine if the data are relatively straightforward and if researchers remain open to modifying the domain list as they become more familiar with the actual interview data. Researchers then apply this start list to several transcripts (similar to the process described below) and modify the domain list to capture the raw data. We used this approach (e.g., Rhodes, Hill, Thompson, & Elliott, 1994) when investigating misunderstanding events within psychotherapy because there was a clear sequential structure of antecedents, events, actions, and consequences to the events (as suggested by Strauss & Corbin, 1990), but we also revised the domains on the basis of the data. Our final domains in that study were Long-Term Background, Immediate Background, Precipitant, Client Experience, Action, Resolution of Event, and Ensuing Process.

The second method for developing a domain list involves reviewing the transcripts themselves to see what topic areas naturally arise from the interview data, bracketing out or not thinking about the interview protocol. This inductive approach to developing a domain list allows researchers to stay close to the data and see what emerges. In this method, each person on the team independently reviews several transcripts, identifying topic areas that represent what the participant said and that reflect the main focus of the research. More concretely, each person goes through an interview and circles or sections off blocks of the narrative that fall under a particular topic area and then identifies a proposed domain name for that topic area (e.g., Client Reactions). When each team member has created a domain list, the team meets to compare notes and consensually create a domain list that best fits the data and the focus of the study. They accomplish this task by going through the chosen transcripts together and explicitly discussing what domains they each pulled from the data, what data fit into that domain, and rationale for each domain (e.g., how the domain structure fits the data and overall purpose of the study). This process requires considerable debate as team members typically focus on different levels of complexity of the data. The team member who conducted the interview often can provide additional insights into the tone of the interview and some of the participant's nonverbal communication that would not be present in a transcript. For example, there have been times when the team member–interviewer has been able to clarify an ambiguous statement. The team might also consider listening to the interviews together so that the participants' tone of voice is heard, enhancing the ability of the team members to really immerse themselves in the data.

Regardless of the method used to develop the domain list, the team then tests the domain list by applying it to new transcripts to ensure that the list continues to "fit" the data. Researchers continue changing the domain list as needed throughout six or seven interviews until the list stabilizes. Stabilization of the domain list tends to occur naturally as the team gains a deeper understanding of the participants' experiences, as more participants are added, as the data become more familiar, and as the focus of the study becomes more clearly defined. Researchers need to remember that whenever changes are made to the domain list, previously coded cases need to be recoded.

One of the concerns that can arise at this stage has to do with how many domains "should" be created. Although the final number of domains will in part be a function of the complexity of the data, we recommend using fairly broad discrete domains at this stage given that categories within the domains are created during the cross-analysis. Too many small and detailed domains can get confusing and can make the analysis more difficult. In a study looking at the experience of trainees having transfer clients during their 1st year (Marmarosh, Thompson, Hollman, Megivern, & Hill, 2010), we initially had more than 20 different domains, some of which were actually subdomains within other domains. After working through a few transcripts, we realized that our domain list was too unwieldy and complicated; with the sage advice of our auditor, we decided to broaden the scope of some of our domains so that we had a list of discrete nonoverlapping domains. For example, we combined Benefits of Transfer Experience and Costs of Transfer Experience to Consequences of the Transfer Experience, recognizing that later we would create categories within this broader domain during the cross-analysis. Although we had to go back and recode several transcripts, the new domain list made the process considerably easier and more reliable.

At the end of this process, researchers should have a relatively finalized domain list (it often continues changing throughout the analysis), with a number assigned for each domain. We cluster the domains so closely related ones are listed near each other on the list (e.g., domains related to the event being studied, such as before, during, and after the event, might be close together on the list whereas domains such as relationship factors might be numbered later). Typically we save the last number for the Other category and the next to last for Reactions to the Research if this was included as a question.

At this point, we give the domain list to the auditor or auditors to review (see Chapter 10 in this volume for greater detail about the auditing process). The auditors provide valuable feedback about the clarity of the domain titles and give an opinion about the adequacy of the level of specificity of the domains. Below are two examples of domain lists.

The domain list created for the misunderstanding study (Rhodes et al., 1994) was as follows:

1. Long-Term Background
2. Immediate Background
3. Precipitant
4. Client Experience
5. Action
6. Resolution of Event
7. Ensuing Process

In contrast, the domain list created for the compassion study (Vivino, Thompson, Hill, & Ladany, 2009) was as follows:

1. Definition of Compassion
2. Comparison of Compassion to Related Constructs
3. Manifestations of Compassion in Therapy
4. Limits to Capacity to Be Compassionate
5. Strategies Therapists Use to Return to Feeling Compassionate
6. Development of Compassion
7. Factors Facilitating Compassion
8. Factors Hindering Compassion

## CODING THE INTERVIEW DATA INTO THE DOMAINS

The team now goes back and assigns each "chunk" or "block" of the interview data into a domain. This task can be done as a team working together until consensus is reached or with each team member "domaining" the data individually and then meeting as a team to review and reach consensus.

### Blocks of Data

Chunks or blocks of data can be phrases, thought units, sentences, and paragraphs that cover the same topic area. It is important to recognize that each of these chunks of data needs to be understood on its own, so researchers must provide enough context of the interview (including the interviewer's questions and comments) for readers to understand what the person is saying. For example, the following block of data would be coded into the domain Reactions to Client (I = interviewer; P = participant):

> *I:* It sounds like you were really feeling conflicted about your client.
>
> *P:* Yes, like, was I going to be able to help him, did I want to really help him, could he be helped? I had very mixed feelings toward the client and the work we were doing.

One caveat here is that the participant, not just the interviewer, has to actually say what is being coded into the domain. Unlike the preceding example, in which the participant describes in his or her own words being conflicted, in the following example, the interviewer puts words on the participant's experience (participant is feeling conflicted) to which the participant minimally agrees but does not elaborate. Hence, it would not be appropriate to place the following block of data into the domain Reactions to Client because the client has not personally stated these reactions.

> *P:* Everything went pretty smoothly in the session except when the client got angry.
>
> *I:* It sounds like you were really feeling conflicted about your client.
>
> *P:* Yeah. So after we talked further about the client's father in that session, it didn't come up again for several weeks.

## Double Coding

By definition, a *domain* is a unique cluster of data that captures one aspect of the focus of the qualitative study. People rarely, however, describe their experiences in unique clusters. Thus, at times the text or narrative seems to fit into more than one domain, calling for *double coding* (putting the same chunk of data into two different domains). There may also be times when it will be necessary to triple code chunks of data. We generally recommend, however, that double or triple coding be done sparingly. If researchers find themselves double and triple coding much of the data, it may suggest that the domains are not as unique as they could be and thus should be combined or modified. For example, the following participant statement related to differences in racial and socioeconomic status was double coded into two domains: Therapist Variables Influencing Transfer Process and Client Variables Influencing Transfer Process:

> I think that we were so different from a racial and socioeconomic perspective made the initial transfer process more difficult—for me it was hard to understand her lifestyle. I think for my client, our differences may have led her to be more wary of me. (Marmarosh et al., 2010)

## Noncoded Data

There will likely be some of what we elegantly refer to as "junk" data in each transcript. Junk data might include greetings, scheduling discussions, reviewing the informed consent, or clearly "sidebar" discussions that have nothing to do with the study and that will not ultimately be included in the data analysis. Data that researchers choose not to code should be clearly defined and agreed on by the team. Because these data will not be coded, researchers can eliminate them from the consensus version of the case (defined below).

## "Other" Domain

Some data do not fit comfortably into the domains. In our experience, participants sometimes go off on tangents that are unrelated to the questions they are asked. For example, in the study on transfer clients mentioned earlier(Marmarosh et al., 2010), the participants sometimes talked about their experiences with clients in general rather than focusing specifically on the transfer experience. Given the richness and complexity of our data, the team consensually agreed to limit the analysis to the data that clearly focused on the transfer process itself, and thus the interview data not directly related to the transfer process was assigned to a domain entitled Other.

Data may also be placed in an Other domain when it seems potentially relevant or interesting but doesn't fit in any of the domains. For example, one participant may spontaneously share valuable information about some aspect of the study focus that might show promise for future research, as when some of the participants in the transfer study mentioned earlier (Marmarosh et al., 2010) talked about transferring their current clients to new trainees even though this question was not part of the interview protocol. We therefore also placed these interview segments into the Other domain and discussed the need to perhaps collect enough data to study this issue in the future. It is important to retain this information throughout the process so that the contents of this domain can later be examined to determine if there is enough information to warrant creation of additional domains.

Once the team has worked together to assign interview data to the domains in several transcripts (e.g., at least four to six), it is often helpful to divide into rotating pairs of judges to code the remaining data from the transcripts into domains (as long as new domains are not emerging and all team members grasp the concepts and feel very confident about the process). Dividing into smaller teams can save time and reduce tedium. When only two judges are used, the other team members review the case, acting as "internal" auditors. Any disagreements are discussed until consensus is reached. When major new domains are created in this final stage of domaining, all team members must be consulted and previous cases revised.

## *Consensus Version*

One person on the team takes responsibility for creating the *consensus version* of each case (i.e., a new file that involves all the raw data cut and pasted and put under the domains). We typically rotate who takes responsibility for the consensus version so that each team member does the consensus version for an equal number of cases. Team members often are responsible for the consensus version for the cases where they were the interviewer.

There are two formats that have been used to create consensus versions. The first method is a narrative format. The case number is listed first, followed by the domain title, followed by the core ideas, and finally the raw data (with an indication of the case number and line numbers). See Exhibit 8.1 for an example.

The second method is to put the data into a table format because this allows for easy sorting later into domains and categories (using the sort function in a word processing program; see Figure 8.1). We typically

---

### EXHIBIT 8.1

Sample Consensus Version Nontable Method From the Transfer Study: Case 1

---

**Domain 1: Influence of Prior Therapist and Therapy**

Core ideas: P noticed that transfer client had a lot that wasn't worked through in the previous therapy. It felt like a lot of issues that the prior therapist and client didn't feel like getting through were dumped on the new therapist. P attributes this to resistance from the prior therapist and client colluding around not wanting to discuss termination fully.
*Raw data (Case 1, lines 45–51)*
*I:* Now that we know more about your overall experience, describe your experience with the transfer clients in the training clinic.
*P:* I've noticed that getting a client that was transferred to me there was a lot about the previous therapist that wasn't worked through. I think that's a natural process but sometimes it seems like also like a dumping of the issues they didn't feel like getting through or didn't have enough time to get through when terminating so they just dump it on the new therapist. And I think that's just resistance from both the therapist and the client and the collusion of not wanting to discuss termination fully. As a new therapist I noticed that a lot. I also noticed that when I transfer to the future therapist that no termination is perfect and regardless of how much I feel like we've processed the termination they are still going to discuss it with the new therapist.

**Domain 7: Consequence of Experience for Participant, Professional Development**

Core ideas: P noticed that when P transferred to new therapists that no termination was perfect, and regardless of how much the termination was processed in the prior therapy, the client is still going to discuss it with the new therapist.
*Raw data (Case 1, lines 53–55)*
*P:* I also noticed that when I transfer to the future therapist that no termination is perfect, and regardless of how much I feel like we've processed the termination they are still going to discuss it with the new therapist.

---

*Note.* The line numbers mentioned here refer to the line numbers in the original transcript. P = participant/interviewee; I = interviewer/researcher.

**FIGURE 8.1**

| Case # | Line # | Raw data from interview | Core ideas | Domain/category |
|---|---|---|---|---|
| 1 | 43–51 | Now that we know more about your overall experience, describe your experience with the transfer clients in the training clinic? I've noticed that getting a client that was transferred to me there was a lot about the previous therapist that wasn't worked through. I think that's a natural process but sometimes it seems like also like a dumping of the issues they didn't feel like getting through or didn't have enough time to get through when terminating so they just dump it on the new therapist. And I think that's just resistance from both the therapist and the client and the collusion of not wanting to discuss termination fully. As a new therapist I noticed that a lot. | P noticed that transfer client had a lot that wasn't worked through in the previous therapy. It felt like a lot of issues that the prior therapist and client didn't feel like getting through were dumped on the new therapist. P attributes this to resistance from the prior therapist and client colluding around not wanting to discuss termination fully. | 1 |
| 1 | 51–53 | I also noticed that when I transfer to the future therapist that no termination is perfect and regardless of how much I feel like we've processed the termination they are still going to discuss it with the new therapist. | P noticed when P transferred to new therapists that no termination was perfect and regardless how much P processes the termination, the client is still going to discuss it with the new therapist. | 7 |

Sample consensus version table method from the transfer study. P = participant.

organize the transcript into a table with five columns. The first column is the case number, and this gets repeated every line (for later sorting across cases). The second column has the line numbers from the original transcript (which is also kept for later reference). The third column includes all the raw interview data from one contiguous chunk of the transcript. The fourth column is for the core ideas (to be described in the next section). The fifth and final column is for the domain number (which will be modified during the cross analysis to include the category and subcategory numbers). If sections of the transcript are double or triple coded for separate domains, each separate chunk must be placed in its own row of the table (to facilitate later sorting) with appropriate line numbers. It is helpful to either highlight the text or in some other way designate when data is double coded (e.g., place "dc" at the end of the raw data).

We do not typically send the consensus version to the auditors at this point. Rather, we wait until the core ideas are added so that the auditors can look at both the domains and core ideas together.

### Use of Software Packages to Code Data

We are often asked if we use specific software packages to process CQR data to avoid the time-intensive administrative type of work involved in cutting and pasting the data from the transcript into the consensus version and then later organizing the data. We have not found or created a software package that accomplishes these tasks. In fact, we probably would not use one if it did exist. There is a certain benefit to keeping close to the data and knowing where each piece goes. So all of the tasks described here are done through word-processing programs. As word processing and software become more sophisticated, CQR researchers may find new methods to manage the data. What is most important for later steps of the analysis is that all units or chunks of data are assigned to at least one domain, that the domain and raw data are placed close together in the consensus version, and that the line numbers from the original transcribed version of the text are maintained in the consensus version to facilitate later checking of the raw data.

# Constructing Core Ideas

The next step in the data analysis is constructing core ideas or summaries of the data that capture the essence of the participant's statement in fewer words. The goal of constructing core ideas is to transform the individual participant's narrative into clear and understandable language that will enable researchers to then compare data across cases. This process of constructing core ideas is necessary because participants often can be confusing, rambling, and contradictory. Participants also often refer back to previous things they have said, making it difficult to understand what they have said without the context. By carefully studying the text, researchers can often make sense of the data and use language that is consistent across cases.

As with developing domains and putting data into the domains, teams can work in either of two ways. They can do all the work together as a team or they can work independently and then come together and compare ideas and arrive at consensus. We have found that it is valuable to at least do the first few cases together to further coalesce the team and to ensure that everyone is "on the same page" in terms of how to arrive at core ideas.

Constructing core ideas is simply the process of summarizing the narrative. Because it is important to remain as close to the data as possible at this stage, team members help one another avoid making assumptions, making inferences about the participant intentions, or using psychological jargon. By talking about their understanding of the narrative within the context of the entire case, team members separate out their beliefs and biases from what the participant is actually saying. It is important to keep the context of the whole case in mind when constructing core ideas because the meaning often is understood by what the person has said elsewhere.

We find it helpful to replace pronouns in the narrative with agreed-on designations (e.g., "he" or "she" becomes "C" for client or "T" for "therapist"; "I" becomes "P" for participant) and to place the narrative in third person. Hesitancies or redundancies are removed, and the team tries to make what the participant has said clearer and more concise.

## PROCESS OF CONSTRUCTING CORE IDEAS

We suggest that judges come to the team meeting having already read through the entire case so that they are familiar with its content. If so desired, the team might then first create a title for the case (e.g., "The Sausage Eater") to remind them of the key features of the case. Then one person reads aloud the chunk of interview data in the domain. That person then gives his or her version of how to best summarize what the participant said, staying as close as possible to his or her actual words while adding context and replacing pronouns as necessary. Team members help the person revise it (adding details, articulating how they may have heard what the participant meant differently, etc.), reaching consensus on each word of the core idea. The person responsible for the consensus version of the case records the final core ideas either onto a sheet of paper or directly into the computer. Once consensus on a core idea has been reached, the process repeats itself as the next team member reads aloud the next chunk of data in the domain and proposes his or her version of the core idea, with team members helping revise the core idea until consensus has been reached.

The stage of developing core ideas is another time when, as mentioned earlier, having team members listen to some portions of the interview together can enhance the process. Listening to the session can allow team members access to nonverbal data not present in the transcript and further encourage immersion in the data.

Team members sometimes differ on decisions about the level of detail to include in the core idea. The purpose of creating core ideas is to capture the content of the interview data in a succinct manner, staying grounded in the data and not interpreting participant intentions. That being said, there may be some aspect of a participant's statement that seems less important or redundant to some team members but not to others. For example, a participant might state that the session ran over by 10 or 15 minutes. One team member might feel that it is important to retain the exact "10 to 15 minutes," whereas another might feel that time frame will not be relevant to the topic and prefer to just say "the session ran over time." Thus, the team needs to come to consensus about how much detail is necessary. As a guideline, however, we suggest that the core ideas should be briefer than the raw data, including only the essential data and not trivial details.

We have found that one of the advantages of having so many people review the core ideas is that if important content is missed by one person, another will catch it. When disagreements during any part of the analysis arise, researchers go back to the interview data and to reach consensus. Because of the need to go back to the data, case and line numbers must be included so that team members can readily find the section to review.

The following is an example of how the raw data from the interview could be transformed into a core idea:

> Raw interview data: I think of empathy as a capacity to really stand in somebody else's shoes and know what it feels like to be, to be with what that person is with. But I think compassion takes it a step further in that for me compassion really entails an active quality, there is a dynamic nature to compassion which is more than just the capacity to feel what it's like to be somebody else but to actually be really engaged with that person in what that place is and to help them move through it, whatever that might look like.

> Core idea: P thinks empathy is a capacity to stand in another's shoes and know what it feels like to be that person. Compassion

takes it a step further and entails an active, dynamic nature, that of being really engaged with and helping the C move.

Another consideration when constructing core ideas is that each core idea needs to make sense on its own so that it can be understood outside of the context of the case. For example, if the interviewer asked a question that provides a context for the participant's answer, this information needs to be included in the core idea, as in this excerpt from the transfer study mentioned earlier (Marmarosh et al., 2010):

I: Okay, um how about anything about the clinic you know again that made it more challenging to work with transfer clients. You mentioned the timing I guess before.

P: Um, yeah, the fact that we started seeing these patients right during our finals week was a little hectic and I think that kind of threw everybody for a loop and stressed people out really more than needed to be.

The core idea for this chunk might be as follows: "P felt the clinic's timing of the transfer process (during semester finals) made it more stressful for students to start working with patients." Thus, we added information ("clinic" and "timing") from the interviewer's question to help make sense out of the participant's comment.

## CORE IDEAS FOR DOUBLE-CODED TEXT

When constructing core ideas for double- or triple-coded text, it is important to remember to construct the core ideas to be relevant to the specific domain. Thus, the core idea will only include the relevant part of the data that fits for the individual domain. For example, "I felt that my positive transference toward my client was both a strength in that I really liked him, but also got in my way because sometimes I failed to acknowledge all of his pathology" was double coded into the two domains of Facilitating Participant Characteristics and Hindering Participant Characteristics. The core idea for the domain of Facilitating Characteristics might be, "P felt positive transference toward C was a strength because P really liked C." The core idea for the Hindering Participant Characteristics domain might be "P felt positive transference toward C was a weakness because P sometimes failed to acknowledge C's pathology."

## SHORTCUTTING THE PROCESS

Once the team has worked through several transcripts together and everyone feels confident in the process, it is possible to shortcut the process somewhat. One person (perhaps the same one who does the consensus version) might draft core ideas that are then reviewed and worked through with the whole team. It is important, however, that all members of the team remain close to the data and reach consensus on the content of each core idea.

## AUDIT

The consensus version of each case, with the domains and core ideas indicated, is sent to the auditor or auditors for review (see Chapter 10, this volume). Once the auditors review the consensus version, the team meets to argue through to consensus whether to make the recommended changes. Typically, the team goes back to the raw interview data repeatedly to check what the data actually say and resolve any conflicts. Once all of the consensus versions are complete and have been audited, the team begins the cross-analysis (see Chapter 9, this volume).

## *Conclusions*

The tasks of creating the domain list, blocking the data into domains and constructing core ideas are central tasks in the data analysis phase of CQR (see Exhibit 8.2). Careful attention to details here provides a strong foundation for comparing data across cases in the cross-analyses. Initial tasks involve developing clear procedures for how the data will be coded. Later tasks involve maintaining attention to detail while not getting bogged down by the details.

---

### EXHIBIT 8.2

**Steps in Developing Domains and Core Ideas**

---

Steps in developing domains
1. Develop domain list from start list or inductively.
2. Verify and update domain list with new transcripts.
3. Assign blocks of interview data into domains.
4. Develop consensus version of interview data and associated core ideas within domains for each case.

Steps in constructing core ideas
1. The interview data in each domain in each case is cored (e.g., "edited") to yield concise and clear wording and then put into the consensus version.
2. The consensus version is audited.
3. The audits are evaluated and changes made based on returning to the raw data to resolve discrepancies.
4. The consensus version of each case is finalized.

---

## *References*

Hill, C. E., Knox, S., Thompson, B. J., Williams, E. N., Hess, S. A., & Ladany, N. (2005). Consensual qualitative research: An update. *Journal of Counseling Psychology, 52,* 196–205. doi:10.1037/0022-0167.52.2.196

Hill, C. E., Thompson, B. J., & Williams, E. N. (1997). A guide to conducting consensual qualitative research. *The Counseling Psychologist, 25,* 517–572. doi:10.1177/0011000097254001

Marmarosh, C. L., Thompson, B. T., Hollman, S. N., Megivern, M. M., & Hill, C. E., (2010). *Trainee experiences of client transfer: A qualitative study.* Manuscript in preparation.

Miles, M. B., & Huberman, A. M. (1994). *Qualitative data analysis: An expanded sourcebook* (2nd ed.). Thousand Oaks, CA: Sage.

Rhodes, R., Hill, C. E., Thompson, B. J., & Elliott, R. (1994). Client retrospective recall of resolved and unresolved misunderstanding events. *Journal of Counseling Psychology, 41,* 473–483. doi:10.1037/0022-0167. 41.4.473

Strauss, A., & Corbin, J. (1990). *Basics of qualitative research: Grounded theory procedures and techniques.* Newbury Park, CA: Sage.

Vivino, B. L., Thompson, B., Hill, C. E., & Ladany, N. (2009). Compassion in psychotherapy: The perspective of psychotherapists nominated as compassionate. *Psychotherapy Research, 19,* 157–171. doi:10.1080/ 10503300802430681

*Nicholas Ladany, Barbara J. Thompson, and Clara E. Hill*

# Cross-Analysis 9

A crucial element of consensual qualitative research (CQR) is the *cross-analysis* —identifying common themes across cases. The research team conducts a cross-analysis after placing the data in domains and constructing core ideas for each case. Cross-analysis is more complicated than these other relatively straightforward tasks of domain placement and core idea development; however, we aim to explain the process in manageable and understandable steps in this chapter.

## Data for the Cross-Analysis

When establishing domains and core ideas, researchers construct a consensus version of the document for each case, using either an outline format or a table format (see Chapter 8, this volume). Before proceeding to the cross-analysis, researchers must compile all of the consensus documents from individual cases into one mega-document (sometimes affectionately referred to as "the beast" or "the monster table"), sorted by domains (i.e., Domain 1, with core ideas from each case; Domain 2, with core ideas from each case; etc.). If an outline format was used, data from each case needs to be inserted sequentially for each domain. If a table format was used, the table can be automatically sorted by domain number such that all core ideas for each domain are next to one another (to do this, use the sort function in your word-processing software). In both the outline and table format, researchers now delete the raw transcript text, but they retain the case number and line numbers associated with each core idea to enable them to go back to the original transcript as needed to clarify or resolve disagreements.

# Categories

## DEVELOPING CATEGORIES

Researchers conduct the cross-analysis one domain at a time. The team begins the process by choosing a domain for analysis. We suggest starting with a relatively small and easy domain so that the team can gain competence with the task of conducting a cross-analysis.

Once a workable domain has been identified, each team member reviews all the core ideas within that domain and clusters similar core ideas by identifying common elements or themes across cases. The goal here is to create a category structure that captures most if not all of the data within the domain. Categories are determined via a discovery-oriented process (Hill, Thompson, & Williams, 1997; Mahrer, 1988). Researchers must remain mindful that category titles should be derived from the data rather than from preconceived notions about what the data should look like.

After each team member has developed categories, the team meets to discuss these preliminary categories and work toward consensus regarding which categories to include and what these categories will be called. To illustrate, consider the relatively circumscribed domain of Emergence of Sexual Attraction from Ladany et al.'s (1997) sexual attraction study (see Table 9.1). After independently identifying possible categories in this domain, the team agreed on two categories that seemed to be common across participants: (a) Sexual Attraction Emerged After Therapy Began and (b) Sexual Attraction at First Sight.

There is no set recommendation for how many categories to develop for each domain. Some domains (such as the one above) will only have two major categories. Other domains might have eight or nine categories. In addition, subcategories are common within larger domains as a way of more adequately describing the data. Referring again to Table 9.1, the domain Client Factors Associated With Therapist Sexual Attraction had several categories. One of these categories (Client Was

| TABLE 9.1 | |
| --- | --- |

**Partial Cross-Analysis for Sexual Attraction Study (Ladany et al., 1997)**

| Domains/Categories | Frequency |
| --- | --- |
| Emergence of Sexual Attraction | |
|   Sexual Attraction Emerged After Therapy Began | Typical |
|   Sexual Attraction at First Sight | Variant |
| Therapist's Experience of Sexual Attraction | |
|   Negative Feelings | Typical |
|   Physical Response Evoked in Therapist | Typical |
|   Positive Feelings | Variant |
| Client Factors Associated With Therapist Sexual Attraction | |
|   Client Was Physically Attractive | Typical |
|   Client Was Interpersonally Attractive | General |
|     Client Was a Good Therapy Client | Typical |
|     Client Seemed Needy or Vulnerable | Variant |
|     Client Was Sexually Provocative or Flirtatious | Variant |
|     Client Had Attractive Personality | Variant |
|   Client Was Similar to Therapist | Variant |
|   Client Similar to Therapist's Previous or Current | |
|     Romantic Partner | Variant |
|   Client Was Not the Usual Type Therapist Finds Attractive | Variant |

*Note.* The frequency labels in this table differ from those in the original publication because we use the new method of labeling frequencies within categories. General is for 12 or 13 cases, typical is for seven to 11 cases, and variant is for three to six cases. Adapted from "Sexual Attraction Toward Clients, Use of Supervision, and Prior Training: A Qualitative Study of Predoctoral Psychology Interns," by N. Ladany, K. M. O'Brien, C. E. Hill, D. S. Melincoff, S. Knox, S., and D. A. Petersen, 1997, *Journal of Counseling Psychology, 44,* pp. 417–418. Copyright 1997 by the American Psychological Association.

Interpersonally Attractive) was further divided into four subcategories: Client Was a Good Therapy Client, Client Seemed Needy or Vulnerable, Client Was Sexually Provocative or Flirtatious, and Client Had an Attractive Personality.

The process of developing categories is creative because it involves organizing and conceptualizing the data to see how it clusters together into themes. This task can only be done effectively by judges who have immersed themselves in all the cases and know the data intimately. Throughout the process of domaining and coring, the team members have been developing hypotheses about the data, and this is the time for them to see how the data fit together.

## PLACING THE CORE IDEAS INTO CATEGORIES

Each core idea may involve a number of separate thoughts, so prior to placing the core ideas into categories, researchers divide the core ideas

---

**EXHIBIT 9.1**

**Core Ideas for Five of the 13 Cases for Client Factors Associated With Therapist Attraction**

---

CASE #3
Therapist attracted to client's mix of emotional strengths and weaknesses, especially her emotional vulnerability, and her difficulties with interpersonal relationships, and to a lesser extent the client's physical attractiveness. On follow-up noted the client's physical attractiveness. Client's primary need and goal of therapy was to develop an emotionally intimate non-sexual relationship. Client was exceptionally good as a client, which may have increased the attraction. Therapist initially attributed the therapist's attraction to the client's manner of interpersonal behavior rather than his own issues.

CASE #6
Client similar to therapist in age and minority status; client was average looking but attractive to therapist; client was sensitive, introspective, and sincere; therapist identified with client's struggles about ways to connect and be more genuine with people.

CASE #10
Therapist attracted to average built and average appearance female who was intriguing, intelligent, therapy savvy, and had little self-esteem and sexualized presentation. Client was rape and incest survivor. Client never did anything overtly sexual, but there was strong transference.

CASE #13
Noted client fit "template," that is, very attractive, similar in age, and from a prominent family. She was very provocative and seductive in her body language, very relaxed, needy, and vulnerable, which made the work challenging. She recently broke up with her husband. Client was someone with whom the therapist had difficulty maintaining boundaries and might have fallen for her in another context.

CASE #14
Client had an attractive personality, and was shy, sensitive, interested in nature, average looking, and insightful. Attraction was to personality more than to physical characteristics. Client was involved in rocky relationship at beginning of therapy that was shortly terminated. Client was not the therapist's usual type.

---

into as many units (i.e., separate ideas) as necessary. Thus, for example, the core ideas for Case 10 (see Exhibit 9.1) were as follows:

> Therapist attracted to average built and average appearance female who was intriguing, intelligent, therapy savvy, and had little self-esteem and sexualized presentation. Client was rape and incest survivor. Client never did anything overtly sexual, but there was strong transference.

We separated these core ideas separated into discrete units as follows:

- Therapist was attracted to client who was intriguing and therapy savvy.
- Client was intelligent.
- Client had little self-esteem.

- Client never did anything overtly sexual, but there was a sexualized presentation and client had a strong love/hate transference to therapist.
- Client was a rape and incest survivor.

Continuing to work with one domain at a time, then, each discrete core idea for each participant is placed within one or more categories or subcategories. In the Emergence of Sexual Attraction domain, core ideas from eight participants were placed into the Sexual Attraction Emerged After Therapy Began category, and core ideas from the remaining five participants were placed within the Sexual Attraction at First Sight category (see Exhibit 9.2). The team can either complete this task together via consensus, or they can individually do it and then meet to consensually decide about placement.

The domain/category list typically changes as the team tries to place the core ideas into categories. Some changes are relatively minor, such as changing the title of a category. Other changes are more significant, such as redefining the categories themselves, increasing or decreasing the number of categories or subcategories, or even collapsing or expanding the domains. Moreover, in the process of categorizing the core ideas, the researchers may notice that a core idea is unclear because it is out of context. In this case, the researchers go back to the raw data and consensually modify the core ideas or the categorization of the core ideas, following each modification with appropriate corrections to the consensus version of the case.

Although researchers try to develop categories and subcategories that fit all of the data, there are inevitably a few core ideas that do not fit any category or subcategory. Sometimes these cores reflect unique experiences that were reported by only one participant. Sometimes they reflect tangents in the data that are not relevant to the study. Core ideas that defy categorization should be put in an Other category. An Other subcategory can also be used for core ideas that fit under a general category but do not fit within any of its subcategories. When the cross-analysis has been completed, the team can go back and examine all the core ideas in the Other category to see if new categories can be developed to accommodate the relevant ideas.

The cross-analysis process (i.e., the development of categories and the placement of core ideas into these categories) is repeated and completed for each domain. Thus, for the sexual attraction study that contained 16 domains, 16 separate cross-analyses were conducted.

## AUDIT OF THE CROSS-ANALYSIS

After completing the cross-analysis process, the primary team submits their work to their auditors. The auditors review these cross-analyses to

EXHIBIT 9.2

**Cross-Analysis for All 13 Cases for Client Factors Associated With Therapist Attraction**

1. Client was physically attractive (10 cases)
     1: Therapist found client physically attractive but stated that the identification was more important than the physical attraction.
     2: Client was physically attractive.
     3: Therapist was attracted, to a lesser extent, to the client's physical attractiveness.
     4: Therapist was attracted to a physically attractive client.
     5: Therapist was mostly attracted to client because of his physical appearance: unique, wide-eyed adoring look, which therapist indicated that in the gay community indicated interest in someone and was not often experienced by the therapist.
     6: Client was average looking but attractive to therapist.
     9: Client was a physically attractive client (i.e., dark hair, brown eyes, and Italian).
     11: Client was physically attractive.
     13: Therapist noted client fit "template" (i.e., his type), that is, very attractive.
     15: Client reminded therapist of a former boyfriend and was strongly attracted by client's looks.
2. Client was attractive in nonphysical attributes (12 cases)
   a. Client was a good therapy client (articulate, bright, insightful) (8 cases)
     2: Client was brilliant, articulate, sophisticated, and richer in attributes than other clients.
     3: Client was exceptionally good as a client, which may have increased the attraction.
     4: Therapist was attracted to an insightful, motivated, and nice client.
     5: Therapist was attracted because client was intelligent and articulate. Client was open to psychological exploration/insight. Therapist felt client was able to use short-term psychotherapy more effectively than many people. Client was reflective and thoughtful.
     6: Client was sensitive, introspective, and sincere.
     9: Client was a YAVIS client.
     10: Therapist was attracted to client who was intriguing and therapy savvy. Client was intelligent.
     14: Client was insightful.
   b. Client seemed needy/vulnerable (5 cases)
     3: Therapist was attracted to client's mix of emotional strengths and weaknesses, especially her emotional vulnerability, her difficulties with interpersonal relationships. Client's primary need and goal of therapy was to develop an emotionally intimate nonsexual relationship.
     4: Therapist saw client as vulnerable because client's fiancé recently broke off the engagement.
     10: Client was needy and had little self-esteem.
     13: Client was needy and vulnerable, which made the work challenging. Client recently broke up with her husband.
     14: Client was involved in a rocky relationship at beginning of therapy that was shortly terminated.
   c. Client was sexually provocative/flirtatious (4 cases)
     10: Client never did anything overtly sexual, but there was a sexualized presentation and client had a strong love/hate transference to therapist.
     11: Client was coy, sexually provocative, childlike, and flirtatious. Flirtatiousness was an integral part of client and not aimed specifically at therapist.

*(continued)*

EXHIBIT 9.2 (*Continued*)

13: Client was very unconsciously provocative and seductive in her body language, very relaxed, which made the work challenging.

15: Client was flirtatious with therapist, which made therapist feel that she was attractive to client.

d. Client had attractive personality (4 cases)

3: Therapist initially attributed attraction to client's manner of interpersonal behavior rather than to his own issues.

12: Therapist was attracted to client's personality (pensiveness, philosophy of life, intellectualism). Client was committed to social justice (Peace Corps), and affiliated with the Baha'i faith. Therapist would have been attracted to client regardless of his presenting problem. Therapist initially thought client was neat, wondered why he didn't have a partner.

14: Client had an attractive personality and was shy, sensitive, interested in nature, average looking. Attraction was to personality more than to physical characteristics.

15: Therapist was strongly attracted to client's personality and problems.

3. Client was similar to therapist (6 cases)

1: Therapist identified with client's loneliness and felt bad for him.

4: Client was close in age to therapist.

5: Therapist identified with reflective/thoughtful attributes of client.

6: Client was similar to therapist in age and minority status. Therapist identified with client's struggles about ways to connect and to be more genuine with people.

12: Client spent time in Latin America (therapist was Latina).

13: Client was similar in age.

4. Client was not the usual type therapist finds attractive (3 cases)

4: Client was not the type to whom therapist usually was physically attracted.

14: Client was not the therapist's usual type.

15: Client was not the type therapist usually finds attractive.

5. Other

1: Client was a recovering substance abuser.

9: Client's personality was not attractive to the therapist (i.e., immature, playful, childlike).

10: Client was a rape and incest survivor.

13: Client was from a prominent family.

15: Client was somewhat older than average college client and younger than therapist. Client appearance was punk/artistic.

*Note.* Numbers are used to indicate categories, and letters are used to indicate subcategories. YAVIS = young attractive verbal intelligent high socioeconomic status.

evaluate their adequacy and offer feedback to the primary team (see also Chapter 10, this volume). Auditors should be particularly attentive to core ideas placed in the Other category so that they can offer guidance to the primary team about whether these ideas fit under existing categories or whether the category structure should be revised to accommodate these ideas.

Typically, we ask the auditors to review each domain as we complete it and then in addition review all the domains at one time at the end to see how they all fit together. In the same manner as was done with the audit of the domains and core ideas, the primary team considers the auditors' suggestions and modifies the cross-analysis accordingly. The primary team and the auditors may need to correspond numerous times until the most elegant solution to the cross-analysis emerges.

## REPRESENTATIVENESS OF THEMES

The categorization process culminates with a determination of the representativeness of the categories to the sample used in the study. To do this, frequency information is calculated for each domain on the basis of the number of participants who have core ideas within each category or subcategory. Although there may be more than one core idea for a given participant in a given category or subcategory, we only count the participant once per category or subcategory (e.g., within a given case, there may be five core ideas that fit into a particular category, but we only count that case once when we consider the frequency for the category).

When a category consists of data from all participants, or all but one of the participants, that category is labeled *general*. Categories that consist of data from more than half of the participants up to the cutoff for general are *typical*. Categories that consist of data from at least two participants up to half of the participants are considered *variant*. When samples are larger than 15, a category would be considered *rare* when it included core ideas from two or three participants (in which case variant categories would contain four or more participants). The category of rare is added with larger samples because these larger samples afford the researcher the opportunity to discover new categories with less risk of overinterpreting anomalies, which might be the case with smaller samples. We believe that narrative frequency labels rather than numerical percentages or frequencies fit better with the qualitative approach, allow for comparison across studies, and provide a meaningful way to communicate findings. Using raw numbers for frequency counts or the calculation of percentages implies greater quantitative precision than we believe we can achieve in this method and makes it difficult to compare results across studies.

It seems important to acknowledge here that the use of the labels of general, typical, and variant do reflect numbers. Traditionally, a hallmark of qualitative research has been the notion that words are better than numbers to characterize data. However, using numbers to help define the words, whether admitted to or not by qualitative researchers, is also part of qualitative inquiry. For example, by definition a theme is the result of the common presence of ideas in a data set. To be common means that it must occur multiple times. The CQR approach explicitly recognizes that numbers are used to reflect the commonality of a theme. Moreover, through the use of numbers, CQR researchers can be systematic and thorough when working with the data.

The frequency labels are placed in the final table, wherein the domains, categories, and subcategories are listed in descending order of frequency with designations next to each regarding whether it was general, typical, variant, or rare. Core ideas in Other categories or subcategories are not reflected in the final table. These core ideas should be retained in the full cross-analysis, however, because they may provide ideas about important avenues for future research (especially in studies with relatively small samples). Again, see Table 9.1 for an example of a table.

## Describing and Comparing Subsamples

Sometimes researchers purposely set forth to compare subsamples of the data, whereas at other times, subsamples emerge as the researchers examine the data. Describing subsamples is useful when researchers recognize that participants differ in some manner that is meaningful and noticeable, and their differentiation helps reduce the variability in the data. For example, in the sexual attraction study, approximately half of the participants disclosed their sexual attraction toward a client to their supervisor and half did not. It seemed fruitful for the researchers to further delve into these findings and compare the subsamples to explore whether there were differences in participants' responses for those who had and had not disclosed their sexual attraction toward a client to their supervisor.

We strongly suggest here that the division into subsamples be done after the cross-analysis has been completed for all the cases. Thus, the categories are developed on the entire sample, making it easier to compare across subsamples. By contrast, if the samples are divided first and then the categories are developed, it is quite likely that different categories will emerge to describe the different subsamples, making it difficult if not impossible to compare the results across subsamples.

The rules described previously apply to the designation of general, typical, and variant frequency labels, but the specific numbers are changed to reflect the number of participants in each of the subsamples. In the sexual attraction study, the variant category was not used because of the small sizes of the subsamples. Also because of the small sample size, general was only used in this case when it applied to the entire subsample.

When comparing samples, the question of what constitutes "different" immediately arises. In some of the first articles comparing samples, CQR researchers used the criterion that samples had to differ by at least one frequency category (typical vs. variant) to be considered different. In Hill et al. (2005), we modified this criterion because the difference between two adjacent frequency categories could be as little as one participant; therefore, we stated that samples had to differ by at least two frequency categories (general vs. variant, typical vs. rare) to ensure that there was indeed a difference. Another way that researchers could determine "difference" is to a priori set a criterion that samples have to differ by at least 30% of cases (given that this difference is fairly large and usually represents a reasonable difference).

Hill et al. (2003) provides an example of a CQR study that examined differences within samples in a study. We asked each of 13 experienced therapists about two different situations: (a) being the target of client anger that was hostile and (b) being the target of client anger that was not asserted but was suspected. Using the old criterion of differing by just one frequency category, we reported differences between hostile and unasserted events for all domains (e.g., hostile events less often involved a good therapy relationship and a disliked therapist intervention). If we now impose the more stringent criteria of differing by two frequency categories, fewer differences emerge. Specifically, for the domain of initial client reactions to therapist interventions, results were more often overtly "hostile" in hostile events and more often "no direct verbal anger" in unasserted events. Likewise, therapists' goals were more often "to decrease or manage client anger" in the hostile events compared with "to help clients express anger appropriately" in the unasserted events.

In working with the data in the Hill et al. (2003) study, we noticed an additional means of dividing the data. Specifically, we noticed by reviewing the cases that the hostile and unasserted events both differed in terms of whether they were resolved or not. Hence, we further analyzed the data to highlight these differences. As an example, for the resolved compared with unresolved unasserted events, there was more often a good therapeutic relationship, therapists raised the topic of anger, and therapists tried to help clients explore the anger and gain insight.

The example of the Hill et al. (2003) study thus illustrates that researchers can set out to collect data about different samples as well as discover different samples to compare once data analysis has started. The idea here is to make results clearer by delineating homogeneous samples and then comparing across samples. However, sample size becomes a major issue when researchers subdivide samples from data that have already been collected. Given that most CQR studies have samples of only 12 to 15 participants, dividing the data can lead to very small samples. We typically recommend that researchers have at least seven participants in each subsample; otherwise the large individual variability within small subsamples can make it difficult for researchers to draw meaningful comparisons.

Another way to compare subsamples and further describe the data is to define pathways for process-oriented data. For example, in a study on misunderstanding events between clients and therapist (Rhodes, Hill, Thompson, & Elliott, 1994), after we had analyzed the data we realized that we had two groups, resolved events and unresolved events, and so we decided to compare categories in each subsample to describe typical pathways that seemed to emerge. As can be seen in Figure 9.1, we started with the domains and then identified the typical responses for resolved versus unresolved cases. The figure shows clearly how the two groups of cases were similar (e.g., clients in both groups experienced negative emotions about self or therapist, and both groups typically went "underground"). From there, the pathways diverged, with one typical pathway for the resolved cases (Mutual Repair Process leading to Resolution of the Event and Client Growth and Enhanced Relationship), and two possible pathways for the unresolved cases (Therapist Maintains Position, Disagreement Continues, Event Not Resolved but Therapy Continues; and Therapist Unaware or Unresponsive, Client Thinks About Quitting, Client Quits). This type of data presentation is particularly helpful when describing sequential processes that have a domain structure that follows a sequential process. We note, however, that not all data lend themselves to graphical display (e.g., attitudes toward help-seeking might not yield data that would easily be traced in pathways).

## Checking for Stability

In the first CQR article, Hill et al. (1997) recommended that researchers analyze all but one or two cases and then examine these additional cases after cross-analysis to determine whether new data emerge or whether the new data fit the final domain/category list. In their 2005 update on CQR, Hill et al. revised this position. After a number of years of experience checking for stability by withholding cases, we discovered that the stability check did not seem to be functioning adequately. We noticed that it was difficult to know exactly what criteria to use to determine whether new information truly emerged, and we noticed a tendency on the part of researchers to minimize the possibility that new data had emerged after the long data analysis process. Because all the interviews are typically conducted at about the same time prior to data analysis in CQR (rather than intertwined with the analysis process as in grounded theory), it would introduce a great deal of uncontrolled data into a study if interviewers were to conduct additional interviews at a later time after data analysis given that the same semistructured interview protocol would be difficult to follow, the research team would have new biases

## FIGURE 9.1

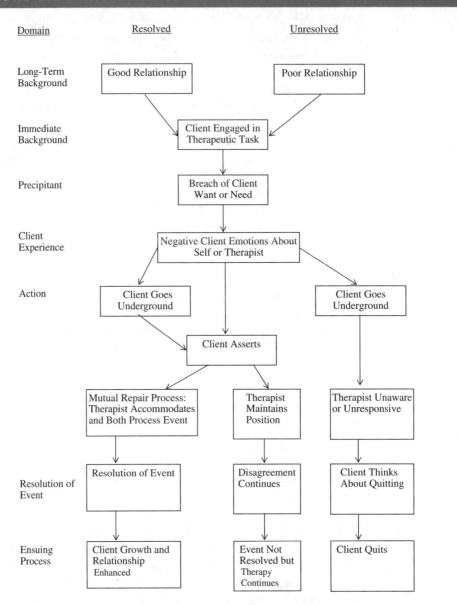

Pathways for retrospective client-recalled resolved and unresolved misunderstanding events. Reprinted from "Client Retrospective Recall of Resolved and Unresolved Misunderstanding Events," by R. Rhodes, C. E. Hill, B. J. Thompson, and R. Elliott, 1994, *Journal of Counseling Psychology, 41,* p. 480. Copyright 1994 by the American Psychological Association.

based on their experiences with the data analysis, and knowledge of the initial results could influence the interview process. Furthermore, we believe that the use of homogeneous samples and semistructured interview protocols lessens the likelihood of obtaining inconsistent data across participants.

For these reasons, Hill et al. (2005) concluded that it was unrealistic and perhaps fruitless to complete stability checks. Instead, CQR has evolved to include more cases than some other qualitative methods use and to include larger teams and more auditors. We argue here that the intensity of the data analysis, the consensual process, and use of external auditors often require substantial modification of domains and categories to better fit the data and thus serve to provide an acceptable level of validity in the qualitative results (see also Chapter 13, this volume). Furthermore, we believe that the best way to achieve adequate trustworthiness in CQR is clearly describing the data analysis process for a given study, indicating changes and decisions that emerge throughout the process, choosing an adequate sample and being mindful along the way about whether the interviews were providing vastly different or some similar findings, and presenting extended examples so readers can confirm the validity of the findings for themselves. In addition, if we find some general and typical categories across samples or within subsamples, we feel more certain that we have obtained representative data. In contrast, if we find only variant categories, we are less certain that we have adequately sampled the population or that the sample is homogeneous.

## *Troubleshooting*

During the cross-analysis process, researchers keep a keen eye on the emerging category structure. In particular, researchers look for category structures that produce either all or no general or typical categories. In either of these cases, the cross-analysis may not represent the data adequately. Cross-analyses that contain primarily variant or rare categories may indicate that the sample was too heterogeneous. In this case, it may be necessary to collect more data.

Poor category structures can also emerge from either poor interviews (e.g., the interviewers did not follow the protocol, failed to probe and ask participants to elaborate or clarify statements, or prompted the participant too much) or from a problematic protocol (e.g., a large number of questions that might have been too broad or too narrow in scope). This outcome can be discouraging given that the researchers have invested quite a bit of time in the study and data analysis. We openly admit that some of our studies have never been published because of critical sampling and/or interview flaws.

## Exemplar Cross-Analysis

In the earlier description of the cross-analysis, we offered a relatively simple example (i.e., Emergence of Sexual Attraction) of the result of a cross analysis. To illustrate the process in more depth, we again look to the Ladany et al. (1997) sexual attraction study but now provide information using the actual core ideas. Exhibit 9.1 provides the core ideas for five of the 13 cases (because of space limitations, we do not provide the data for all of the cases) for the domain Client Factors Associated With Therapist Attraction. As can be seen in Exhibit 9.1, the core ideas for each participant for a domain involve multiple units. The researchers thus divided the core ideas into core idea units each reflecting a single idea (see Exhibit 9.2, where each core idea unit for each participant has been placed under a given category).

## Comparison of Cross-Analyses by Two Teams

Since we first developed CQR, we have been curious about whether two entirely separate teams using CQR on exactly the same data would come up with relatively similar results. We tested this question in a recent study of supervisees' reports of corrective relational experiences in supervision (Ladany et al., in press). In the Ladany et al. (in press) study, a set of graduate student interviewers interviewed other graduate students about their corrective relational experiences in the supervision of their psychotherapy. Two entirely separate teams of judges, each with three judges and two auditors, were formed (all are contributors to this book and are very experienced in conducting CQR). Exhibit 9.3 shows the results of the two cross-analyses side by side. Although there was considerable overlap in the major domains (antecedent, event, consequences), there was a surprising amount of divergence in the cross-analyses. Clearly, the two teams of judges, all of whom had been trained equally well in CQR and who had worked together on many studies, did not see the data in exactly the same way. For example, one team focused on parallel process whereas the other team did not, probably because one of the team members on the first team was especially interested in parallel process. In contrast, the second team had a category for

**EXHIBIT 9.3**

**Results of Cross-Analysis for Two Different Teams**

| Team 1 Domain/Category | No. of cases | Team 2 Parallel Domain/Category | No. of cases |
|---|---|---|---|
| 1. Supervisory relationship prior to event | | 7. Supervisor approach | |
| 1a. Quality of relationship | | | |
| 1ai. Good relationship | 13 | | |
| 1aii. Didn't like some aspect of supervisor's approach | 12 | 7e. Supervisor's approach negative | 8 |
| 1b. Supervisor's Approach | | | |
| 1bi. Teacher, instructional, hierarchical | 11 | | |
| 1bii. Collaborative, supportive, egalitarian, humanistic | 10 | 7b. Supportive, open | 13 |
| 1bviii. Self-disclosing | 3 | | |
| 1biv. Consultant | 5 | 7c. Mentor, collegial, decreased power difference | 10 |
| 1bvii. Mentor | 3 | | |
| 1biii. Flexible | 5 | 7f. Flexible | 3 |
| 1bv. Psychodynamic, focus on countertransference | 5 | | |
| | | 7d. Interpersonal, process-oriented | 9 |
| 1bvi. Focus on multicultural | 4 | | |
| 2. Antecedent | | 1. Antecedent | |
| 2a. Difficult supervision or supervisory relationship | 10 | 1a. Trainee had concerns about supervision or supervisor | 6 |
| 2b. Dealing with a difficult, challenging client situation | 7 | 1b. Trainee discussed clinical concerns | 4 |
| 2c. Dealing with feelings related to self | 5 | 1c. Trainee upset, questioned self regarding clinical issues, pressed to feel competent | 3 |
| | | 1f. Trainee encountered difficulties outside of supervision | 2 |
| | | 1d. Trainee treated by supervisor as colleague | 3 |
| 3. Event | | 3. Supervisor interventions | |
| 3a. Supervisor supported supervisee | 13 | 3a. Supportive and focused on the alliance | 11 |
| 3f. Supervisor gave supervisee feedback about behavior | 5 | 3b. Normalized or validated | 10 |
| | | 2bi. Supervisor normalized, validated, or supported trainee's work or challenge with a client | 8 |
| 3b. Supervisor was open | 10 | 3a. Supportive and focused on the alliance | 11 |
| | | 3f. Supervisor self-discloses | 4 |
| 3c. Supervisor and supervisee processed the supervisory relationship | 10 | 3a. Supportive and focused on the alliance | 5 |
| | | 3g. Processed supervision | 11 |
| | | 3h. Discussed parallel process | |

(*continued*)

**EXHIBIT 9.3** (*Continued*)

**Results of Cross-Analysis for Two Different Teams**

| Team 1<br>Domain/Category | No. of<br>cases | Team 2<br>Parallel Domain/Category | No. of<br>cases |
|---|---|---|---|
| | | 2biii. Discussion of supervision process | 5 |
| 3d. Supervisor and supervisee explored and worked for insight | 9 | 3c. Explored feelings | 7 |
| | | 3d. Focused on the therapeutic process | 5 |
| 3e. Supervisee shared, was open and vulnerable | 8 | 2biv. Trainee became more open, real, or genuine | 4 |
| 3g. Supervisor provided supervisee with specific action ideas | 3 | 3i. Encouraged trainee to trust instincts or find own answers | 3 |
| 3h. Supervisor treated supervisee like a professional or colleague | 3 | | |
| | | 6a. Parallel process from supervision to therapy increased therapy skills/awareness | 9 |
| | | 6b. CRE helped increase comfort and trust, and strengthened relationship from supervision to therapy | 4 |
| | | 6c. Explicitly discussed parallel process in supervision | 3 |
| | | 2bii. Supervisor reacted differently than the trainee expected | 6 |
| | | 2bv. Negative experience with supervisor | 3 |
| 4. Consequence of CRE | | 5. Outcome | |
| 4a. Improvements in supervision | | | |
| 4ai. Improved alliance or felt supported | 15 | 5a. Strengthened or transformed supervisory relationship | 15 |
| 4aii. Improved the work of supervision or less formal boundaries | 14 | 5b. Increased comfort in disclosing issues in supervision | 13 |
| | | 5d. CRE was positive | 12 |
| 4aiii. Supervisor was more available, responsive, or collegial | 7 | 5e. Trainee's expectations or perceptions of supervisor changed or improved | 12 |
| 4aiv. More able to discuss the supervisory relationship | 5 | | |
| 4b. Improvements in supervisee | | | |
| 4bi. Professional gains | 14 | 5g. Positive impact on work with clients | 9 |
| | | 5f. Increased trainee's self-efficacy and confidence as a professional | 11 |
| 4c. Supervisor evaluated supervisee more positively | 13 | 5c. Improved supervisor's perceptions of trainee's evaluation or recommendation | 13 |

(continued)

**EXHIBIT 9.3** *(Continued)*

**Results of Cross-Analysis for Two Different Teams**

| Team 1 Domain/Category | No. of cases | Team 2 Parallel Domain/Category | No. of cases |
|---|---|---|---|
| 5. What supervisee wished could have been done differently | | 4. Wishes | |
| 5a. By supervisor | | | |
| 5ai. No changes | 7 | 4a. No desire to change | 9 |
| 5aii. Had been more sensitive to supervisee's needs | 5 | | |
| 5aiii. Had provided more explanation | 3 | | |
| 5b. By supervisee | | | |
| 5bi. Had been more open, assertive, or proactive | 9 | 4c. Had been more present or open with supervisor | 3 |
| 5bii. No changes | 7 | 4a. No desire to change | |
| | | 4b. Concern had been addressed earlier | 7 |
| 6. Reactions to interview | | 8. Response to research | |
| 6a. Stimulated reflection; helped inte grate, process, or consolidate CRE or supervision experience | 9 | 8a. Stimulated thought about CRE and supervision | 13 |
| 6b. Interview was interesting; had positive reactions | 3 | | |

*Note.* We did not include data from Other categories or categories with only two participants. In addition, the numbers used to identify the categories were based on the order in which each team analyzed the data.

processing the supervisory relationship whereas the first team did not, again probably because of the interest in the second team about immediacy. These findings illustrate that two teams can go in different directions, and so clearly the findings are a reflection of the team. These data suggest strongly that CQR is indeed a subjective approach and that the team matters in terms of the conclusions that will be drawn from the data.

## Conclusions

The cross-analysis process (see Exhibit 9.4) involves a great deal of creative thought, attention to detail, and repetition and revision. The primary team and the auditors need to be up to the task of revisiting the raw data at each step along the way. Although tedious at times, diligence and meticulousness can make the difference between a qualitative study of high quality versus one that is disjointed and does not honor the data at hand. The choice is clear for the qualitative researcher: Rigor precludes rigor mortis!

---

**EXHIBIT 9.4**

**Steps in Cross-Analysis**

1. Combine all participants into one data set organized by domain number.
2. Begin with one domain.
3. Team members independently identify common themes or categories in this domain cases.
4. Team consensually agrees on category list for domain.
5. Repeat steps for all domains.
6. Send cross-analysis to outside auditors, integrate findings.
7. Assign frequency labels within each category (general, typical, variant, rare).
8. If appropriate or indicated, divide sample for further comparisons.
9. Send to auditors for final audit.

---

# *References*

---

Hill, C. E., Kellems, I. S., Kolchakian, M. R., Wonnell, T. L., Davis, T. L., & Nakayama, E. Y. (2003). The therapist experience of being the target of hostile versus suspected-unasserted client anger: Factors associated with resolution. *Psychotherapy Research, 13,* 475–491. doi:10.1093/ptr/kpg040

Hill, C. E., Knox, S., Thompson, B. J., Williams, E. N., Hess, S.A., & Ladany, N. (2005). Consensual qualitative research: An update. *Journal of Counseling Psychology, 52,* 196–205. doi:10.1037/0022-0167.52.2.196

Hill, C. E., Thompson, B. J., & Williams, E. N. (1997). A guide to conducting consensual qualitative research. *The Counseling Psychologist, 25,* 517–572. doi:10.1177/0011000097254001

Ladany, N., Inman, A. G., Hill, C. E., Knox, S., Crook-Lyon, R., Thompson, B. J., Burkard, A., . . . Walker, J. A. (in press). Corrective relational experiences in supervision. In L. G. Castonguay & C. E. Hill (Eds.), *Transformation in psychotherapy: Corrective experiences across cognitive–behavioral, humanistic, and psychodynamic approaches.* Washington, DC: American Psychological Association.

Ladany, N., O'Brien, K. M., Hill, C. E., Melincoff, D. S., Knox, S., & Petersen, D. A. (1997). Sexual attraction toward clients, use of supervision, and prior training: A qualitative study of predoctoral psychology interns. *Journal of Counseling Psychology, 44,* 413–424. doi:10.1037/0022-0167.44.4.413

Mahrer, A. R. (1988). Discovery-oriented psychotherapy research. *American Psychologist, 43,* 694–702. doi:10.1037/0003-066X.43.9.694

Rhodes, R., Hill, C. E., Thompson, B. J., & Elliott, R. (1994). Client retrospective recall of resolved and unresolved misunderstanding events. *Journal of Counseling Psychology, 41,* 473–483. doi:10.1037/0022-0167.41.4.473

*Lewis Z. Schlosser, J. Jane H. Dewey, and Clara E. Hill*

# Auditing 10

Across the life of a consensual qualitative research (CQR) project, auditors play an important role in determining the quality and eventual completion of the research. Like a good editor, the auditors pay close attention to small details as well as big-picture implications. Like a good consultant, the auditors affirm and expand on the primary team's findings. And like a good critic, the auditors disagree with and challenge the primary team to think about the data in new and illuminating ways. Auditor feedback at key points throughout the development and analysis of the study provides the primary team with a very useful system of checks and balances and hopefully enhances the trustworthiness and quality of the results.

Because of the importance of the auditor role, careful consideration must be made with regard to a number of questions: Why have auditors? Who will the auditors be? How many auditors should be employed? How involved will the auditors be with the conceptualization of the study? What exactly do the auditors do? The answers to these and other questions will be discussed in this chapter.

## *Philosophical Foundation*

The nature of the role of the auditor can be historically grounded in the philosophical hermeneutics of Hans-Georg Gadamer. In short, *hermeneutics* is the study of meaning-making; a theoretical framework for the process of interpreting a text or piece of art (Gadamer, 1975). Gadamer and his mentor Martin Heidegger were among the first philosophers to emphasize the critical importance of looking inward to our own biases and the impact that worldview can have on textual analysis. The social sciences in general have been heavily influenced, whether consciously or not, by this philosophical supposition (Butler, 1998).

Most salient to the role of the auditor is Gadamer's notion of the dialectic process inherent in the "hermeneutic circle of understanding" (i.e., the interplay of the individual and contextual factors of both the text and interpreter influencing one another in a circular fashion; Gadamer, 1975). As described by Butler (1998), "interpretation of social phenomena is never a straight-forward activity: ambiguity and conflict characterize interpretations" (p. 289). According to Gadamer, the only reasonable way to resolve ambiguity and conflict in understanding (the product of disparate worldviews and lived experiences) is to enter into a discursive–dialectical process (Butler, 1998; Gadamer, 1975).

The word *dialectic* has roots in the Greek word for the "art of conversation" (Butler, 1998, p. 290). In CQR, this dialectic exists throughout the layers of dialogue unique to each step of the process. The first conversation is between the interviewer and the subject. The next is the intrapersonal dialogue that the members of the primary team and the auditor have as they individually make meaning from the text (i.e., the intrapsychic dialogue between the text and the reader). After this, the interpersonal dialectic begins, and meaning-making among the primary team becomes a group activity. Finally, mapping the auditor's intrapersonal understanding onto the primary team's collective assumptions deepens the analysis and reduces the influence of groupthink on the final interpretation of the data.

In addition to Gadamer's philosophical hermeneutics, the process of auditing can also be grounded theoretically in the work of anthropologist Gregory Bateson (Bateson, 1972, 1980). As described by Brack, Jones, Smith, White and Brack (1993), Bateson is best known for "discussing the benefits of mapping different worldviews onto the same data" (p. 619). Bateson believed that the sum of two or more worldviews is, in essence, greater than the contributions of the constituent parts.

Existing external to the primary team's process, the auditor has a unique vantage point from which to offer an analysis that provides perspective from an additional worldview—one that has not been impacted by the discursive process of the primary team.

## *Why Have Auditors?*

In our experience, using at least one auditor has been a critical component to the success of using CQR. While the primary team meets regularly to discuss, debate, and ultimately arrive at consensus about the placement and meaning of data, the auditor exists outside this process of consensus and acts as a "check for the team" at set points throughout the analysis (Hill, Thompson, & Williams, 1997, p. 548). Although the primary team may make every effort to maintain objectivity, the auditors lend a fresh perspective and, as outsiders in the process, have the ability to reduce the potential impact of primary team groupthink on the results (Hill et al., 2005, p. 196).

Why is this additional perspective so critical? As stated by Hill et al. (1997), "Working with words is extremely difficult, and having many perspectives is crucial for capturing the essence of the data" (p. 548). Rather than increasing the number of researchers on the primary team, one or more auditors are invited into the process. Often these individuals are content area experts and individuals who have previous CQR experience (Hill et al., 2005). Each auditor works intimately with the data from a vantage point that is functionally separate from the primary team and from one another (in cases of multiple auditors). This independent feedback provides the primary team with new perspectives that have not been impacted by the primary team's dialogues.

The process of achieving consensus within the primary team is an evolutionary one in which team members' initial understandings about the meaning of the data differ from one another in meaningful ways. In a similar fashion, the auditor can help the team move closer to a better understanding of the data. A multiperspective approach "yields better decisions and has the potential to reduce individual biases" (Hill et al., 1997, p 524). Additionally, the auditor is instrumental in reducing the impact of group-level bias that may be affecting the objectivity of the analysis. Whether the auditor finds a way to subtly tweak a domain name to be more representative of the data or sheds light on major chunks of data that have not been adequately abstracted, the additional perspective is critical to maintaining a rigorous, scientific process.

## Characteristics of Successful and Unsuccessful Auditors

It has been our experience that the ideal auditor is someone with content area expertise and familiarity with and openness to CQR. That being said, are there specific personality traits that are associated with relative success or failure as an auditor? In our experience, it is helpful for auditors to

- be confident and self-assured,
- have good attention to detail,
- be able to work independently,
- be thorough,
- be timely, and
- be open and flexible.

In fact, timely feedback keeps the primary team's thinking on the content from growing stale (which can occur when a lot of time elapses between the primary team's deliberations and their receipt of a particular audit). Conversely, unhelpful feedback would come from an auditor who

- provides timid, limited, or no feedback;
- provides only superficial comments regarding the primary team's work;
- misses key details of the content being studied; and
- misses the "big picture" of the content being studied.

When an auditor lacks self-confidence, has difficulty working alone, or is not timely in the provision of feedback, then the primary team is likely to be frustrated and the completion of the research delayed.

Because a great many CQR teams involve collaborations from multiple institutions (often from different states and sometimes different countries), it is also essential for auditors to be comfortable using technology, including using conference calls or communicating feedback via software designed to display feedback and edits (e.g., track changes). In addition, the auditors must have a sufficient level of investment in the project. The auditors should not join a team to pad curricula vitae with publications or because they are friends with someone on the primary team. Instead, the auditors should have a genuine interest in and expertise in CQR and the subject matter under investigation; anything less than this may lead to suboptimal auditing.

But going beyond competence, what makes for a *great* auditor? Perhaps what differentiates an exceptional auditor from an adequate one is

- the ability to attend to the details of a CQR analysis (e.g., the proper domain coding of a speaking turn) while simultaneously seeing how the pieces of the data analysis fit in a larger, overall conceptualization of the phenomenon under investigation;

■ the ability to comment on the process of the primary team as it is evidenced in their data analysis work; and

■ an intimate knowledge of CQR along with the ability to be creative in seeking solutions to problems in specific studies.

We would posit that these characteristics are advanced skills and might be a product of innate ability and learned experiences from being a primary team member and an auditor across a number of different CQR projects.

## *Selecting the Auditors*

CQR researchers need to consider how many auditors should be a part of the project and whether the auditors will be internal or external (i.e., serving both primary team and auditor roles or serving only as an auditor outside the consensus process). The first studies using CQR used only one external auditor. Since the 2005 Hill et al. CQR update, however, some researchers have begun to use two auditors, and others have used rotating auditors who also served as primary team members (usually these involved large teams of at least 6 people). Hill et al. (2005) suggested that if only one auditor is used, having that person as an external auditor would reduce the effects of groupthink. Being external allows the auditor to operate independently from the primary team's group dynamics in drawing their conclusions and offering their feedback. If multiple auditors are used, then whether the auditors are internal or external is of less consequence because a larger number of people are contributing views of the data. Having a larger CQR team may also reduce the impact of groupthink.

In terms of the number of auditors, we now suggest having two auditors unless the single auditor is extremely conscientious and experienced. An additional auditor is advantageous given that different auditors typically pick up on different things. The variability in feedback across auditors is likely a combination of differences in background, experiences, biases, and expectations. This, of course, argues in favor of having multiple auditors who have different perspectives, personalities, backgrounds, and worldviews.

As noted above, it has been our experience that the best auditors are those who have worked with CQR before and who have content area expertise pertaining to the phenomenon under study. Hill et al. (2005) stressed the importance of methodological familiarity over and above knowledge of the topic area. We agree with this assessment and would choose an auditor well versed in CQR over a content area expert who had no knowledge of the method. As an evaluator of the work of the primary team, an auditor adept at the CQR method does not have to rely on the primary team for instructions and examples of what is expected. An auditor with no CQR experience might too frequently defer on the basis of an assumption that the primary team "knows better." The primary team may inadvertently bias an inexperienced auditor by using examples from the study itself to educate the auditor about the CQR method.

Finally, it is probably wise for researchers to choose auditors with whom they are familiar and comfortable and whom they trust and respect. Given that auditors are often at some distance from the primary team, it is often important to have a solid relationship built on mutual trust before embarking on a CQR project.

## Roles and Functions of Auditors

Auditors perform a variety of tasks from the start to the finish of a CQR project. The auditor typically takes part in the research process both prior to data gathering and during the data analysis, although it would be rare for the auditor to conduct any of the interviews. Prior to collecting data, the auditor might aid the primary team in conceptualizing the study but should especially be involved in the interview protocol development and refinement. At a minimum, auditors should review the interview protocol (and all the revisions thereof) and share their expectations and biases with the primary team. During the data analysis, the auditor reviews the primary team's work at each major step (i.e., domains, core ideas, cross-analysis). We now examine each of these tasks in greater detail.

When auditors review the interview protocol, they look at the number, order, clarity, and relevance of the questions. They try to imagine being asked the questions and how that would feel.

For the domain list, auditors examine the wording of the titles of the domains. They also think about how the domains fit the data, look for overlap among the domains, and look for domains that are too large and complicated.

When reviewing the core ideas, the auditors look to see if the core ideas are crisp, concise, well articulated, nonredundant, appropriate for the domain, and close to the words of the participants. In reviewing the core ideas, the auditors review all of the raw data, read the core ideas developed by the primary team, and determine if (a) anything is missing and (b) the core ideas could be stated in a better way. By immersing themselves fully in the data, the auditors essentially do an independent data analysis. In the auditing of the core ideas, it is helpful for auditors to be both as picky as possible (even about the specific word choice) and to help the primary team see the big-picture perspective of what the project is about.

When reviewing the cross-analysis, the auditors review the domains one by one as they are completed by the primary team, and they also examine the entire cross-analysis (i.e., all domains at once) to look for areas of overlap and completeness. The auditors determine whether the categories fit the data and assess whether the core ideas are placed in the correct categories. When examining the whole cross-analysis, the auditors are looking for concise elegance of the hierarchical structure of the data. They want to see whether there are too many general categories that could be subdivided or too many variant categories that are too small and meager (and could be combined with other categories). Across the analysis, the auditors check to see whether data placed in the "Other" domains and categories could go elsewhere or whether new categories could be created.

When two auditors are used, the data can either be sent to both auditors at the same time or sent first to one and then to the other after the feedback from the first is processed, thereby getting a complete new audit after revisions have been made. We have been using the sequential model more often recently because it provides the maximum input from the two auditors when the second auditor reviews the revised consensus version.

Feedback from the auditor is generally presented in writing. The auditor might provide comments directly on the document using something like track changes, summarize the changes in an e-mail carefully noting the page and line numbers, or write the comments legibly on a hard copy of the document.

Finally, auditors should also read the manuscript and provide feedback to the primary team. In this way, they can provide the critical commentary of an external reviewer while simultaneously having intimate working knowledge of the study.

## *The Feedback Loop*

### GENERAL RESEARCH PROJECT (NOT A THESIS OR DISSERTATION)

The check on the power of the auditors is the primary team's right to disagree with and ultimately disregard comments (except in the situation of a master's thesis or doctoral dissertation; see the following section). In practice, most primary teams accept some of the auditor's recommendations and refute others through a cyclical feedback process. First, the team considers the feedback and returns to the raw data before making a decision regarding the validity of the feedback. In the event that there is considerable disagreement between the team and an auditor, the team may choose to return the data to the auditor for commentary and further thinking about the decision to dismiss or accept the feedback and then continue the whole process until agreement evolves.

In theory, a primary team may decide to dismiss all of the auditor's feedback and to keep their original data analysis intact. As outlined by Hill et al. (1997), however,

> If the team is ignoring everything the auditor says or the auditor makes no suggestions, there is some basis for concern about the process. In such cases, the team might need to meet with the auditor to resolve disagreements or misunderstandings and clarify thinking. (pp. 548–549)

The primary team's dialogue surrounding a decision to ignore a recommendation made by the auditor should be thorough and thoughtful, and their rationale should be clear and compelling.

## STUDENT RESEARCH (PAPER, THESIS, OR DISSERTATION)

Somewhat different guidelines apply to students using CQR for the first time for a master's thesis or doctoral dissertation. We have found that the advisor, who is usually an auditor, is very involved at all stages of the process in guiding the student and preventing unnecessary confusion while the student is learning the method. We have found that despite clarity in the published descriptions of CQR, novice CQR researchers often get confused and need help working through each stage. Hence, the advisor often asks the team for evidence of how they are processing the audits and asks for progress notes on how the team is functioning, often intervening when disputes erupt. Close contact with the primary team is beneficial to prevent major problems along the way, especially at the beginning as the team is learning the process. Clara E. Hill recalls a painful time when a thesis student she was advising thought she was doing things right and did not show Hill her work until several consensus versions had been done; they were done incorrectly, and the team had to go back and do them all over again.

# Negotiating Relationships Between the Primary Team and Auditors

Respect and egalitarianism are prerequisites for successful CQR analysis, but problems inevitably arise on both sides. The primary team might feel that the auditor is dismissing all their hard work and is not "getting it." In contrast, the auditor may understandably struggle with the idea that the primary team has the final say regarding the incorporation of feedback. If the feedback loop is complete and the primary team or auditor continues to feel very strongly about an idea, we suggest further dialogue. At this stage, a phone conference or face-to-face meeting may be beneficial to help resolve differences.

Before requesting this dialogue, all parties involved should spend some time considering their reactions. If there is a legitimate concern that the primary team or auditor has dismissed something inappropriately (e.g., because of biases that the team may hold of which the auditor is aware, because one member of the primary team is being highly domineering, because of the perceived impact of groupthink), this meeting is warranted. If the reaction comes more from a personal place (e.g., the auditor has difficulty with rejection, the auditor feels personally slighted), he or she should reconsider the need for this meeting. Another advantage of working with an experienced auditor is that the person will have had the experience of accepting and rejecting another auditor's feedback when serving as a member of a primary team. Recalling this experience can help the auditor take the current team's decision less personally.

## Conclusions

The role of the auditors is crucial in terms of ensuring the quality of the analyses. Just as it takes a village to raise a child, it takes a community to understand the complexity and richness of qualitative data and to bring them to life in the analyses. Given that there are so many ways to view data, we encourage CQR researchers to view the role of auditor as an opportunity to get preliminary feedback about the data and thus enhance the validity of the conclusions regarding them.

## References

Bateson, G. (1972). *Steps to an ecology of mind.* New York, NY: Ballantine Books.

Bateson, G. (1980). *Mind and nature.* New York, NY: Bantam Books.

Brack, G., Jones, E. G., Smith, R. M., White, J., & Brack, C. (1993). A primer on consultation theory: Building a flexible worldview. *Journal of Counseling and Development, 71,* 619–628.

Butler, T. (1998). Towards a hermeneutic method for interpretive research in information systems. *Journal of Information Technology, 13,* 285–300. doi:10.1057/jit.1998.7

Gadamer, H. G. (1975). *Truth and method.* New York, NY: Seabury Press.

Hill, C. E., Thompson, B. J., & Williams, E. N. (1997). A guide to conducting consensual qualitative research. *The Counseling Psychologist, 25,* 517–572. doi:10.1177/0011000097254001

Hill, C. E., Knox, S., Thompson, B. J., Williams, E. N., Hess, S.A., & Ladany, N. (2005). Consensual qualitative research: An update. *Journal of Counseling Psychology, 52,* 196–205. doi:10.1037/0022-0167.52.2.196

*Sarah Knox, Lewis Z. Schlosser, and Clara E. Hill*

# Writing the Manuscript

11

From the introduction to the Method section, as well as in the Results and Discussion sections, authors of consensual qualitative research (CQR) manuscripts confront several difficult decisions. In this chapter, we first describe some of these challenges and then provide recommendations. We note at the start, however, that there are no tried-and-true "rules" for writing such manuscripts, and different topics may require different presentation formats. Thus, our goal in this chapter is to help readers with the many important decisions they must make in preparing a manuscript involving CQR data. We have divided the chapter into sections that correspond to those of a manuscript, and we conclude with some general recommendations to authors.

## The Introduction

In qualitative methods, the key tasks in the introduction are to provide a context for why the area of study is important, briefly review the relevant literature, justify the unique aspects of the design, and state the purposes and research questions. CQR authors must also assert why they have chosen to use CQR, thereby ensuring that readers accept their premises and do not evaluate the study using a quantitative paradigm or another qualitative approach (e.g., grounded theory, phenomenology).

The process of accomplishing these tasks has changed as CQR has gained acceptance among journal editors as a rigorous qualitative method. Our initial attempts to publish CQR studies were met with varying degrees of skepticism. Such hesitation about CQR manifested in journal editors requiring greater justification for the choice of CQR over other qualitative approaches (e.g., grounded theory) and demanding lengthy descriptions of the CQR method itself (see below). As CQR has become more widely accepted, these demands have lessened. The challenge for authors continues to be deciding how much to articulate the justification for selecting CQR. Our recommendation is to provide a clear rationale for the choice of a qualitative approach in general and CQR specifically, the latter of which can highlight the strengths of CQR vis-à-vis other qualitative methods (e.g., multiple judges to arrive at consensus; external auditors).

## The Method Section

As noted above, one salient challenge of the CQR method section is determining the degree to which authors need to describe CQR itself. We recommend including a brief paragraph highlighting the four key steps of CQR (i.e., interview, domains, core ideas, cross-analysis) and referencing the seminal CQR writings (this volume; Hill et al., 2005; Hill, Thompson, & Williams, 1997). If authors deviate substantively from the CQR method described in these sources, they should provide additional description of and justification for those changes.

Another issue worth mentioning is context and bias. Specifically, CQR researchers usually describe themselves (e.g., age, gender, race–ethnicity, experiences related to the topic of study) and their biases and expectations in the Method section so that readers can understand the context that may influence the results. For example, if a CQR team is examining the inclusion of religion and spirituality in psychotherapy (as was done by Knox, Catlin, Casper, & Schlosser, 2005), then it would be relevant to provide descriptions of the research team members' religious and spiritual self-identification and their biases and expectations: Doing so informs readers of the researchers' backgrounds, illuminating the potential impact of the researchers on data collection and analysis. Hence, we recommend that relevant cultural identities and biases and expectations be included in a description of the research team (typically along with a description of the interviewees and interviewers in the Participants section of the Method section).

# The Results Section

Next is the Results section, where we share the findings of our research with readers. Here, too, authors must make important decisions regarding how best to present their work.

## THE CHALLENGE OF DECIDING WHAT RESULTS TO REPORT

Researchers using CQR often collect and analyze more data than they can reasonably present in a manuscript, given the tight space limitations in journals. Thus, they have to decide which findings to report to answer their research questions and which are more peripheral and could be omitted from the manuscript. Given the labor that goes into such research, these are neither easy, nor often happy, decisions, but they are indeed necessary decisions.

Authors are best guided by the question noted above: What findings most directly address the research questions on which the project was based? Findings that speak to those questions should clearly be included in the manuscript; those with only an indirect link to the research questions may well be excluded. For example, many researchers using CQR begin their data-gathering interview with warm-up questions that gently facilitate interviewee comfort and set the stage for the major questions—for example, "Please tell me about your experience of this therapy" in a study examining clients' experiences of therapy termination (Knox, Adrians, et al., in press); or "Please describe your individual supervision experiences as a supervisee thus far" in a study of supervisees' experiences of supervisor self-disclosure (Knox, Edwards, Hess, & Hill, in press). Data yielded by such questions are not likely, nor are they really intended, to address the central questions of the particular study, so researchers may decide not to report these results. In addition, researchers often ask questions at the end of an interview that are similarly, and purposefully, not closely wedded to the foundational questions (e.g., "How did this interview affect you?"; "Why did you choose to participate in this interview?"). The answers to such queries may be important to the investigators but seldom answer the research questions undergirding the whole study and so often can be dropped from the manuscript.

Furthermore, even seemingly substantive data may not find its way into the manuscript. In a recent study examining clients' experiences of giving gifts to their therapist (Knox, Dubois, Smith, Hess, & Hill, 2009), one question asked participants to describe how their experience of giving a gift to the therapist compared with any prior therapy gift-giving experiences. This question yielded data from some, but not all, participants; more important, the data failed to tell the researchers much new about the topic beyond that which had been already gained by asking about one specific gift-giving event. These data, then, were not reported in the published manuscript.

As another example of a challenging decision regarding what data to report, in a study on therapist self-disclosure (Knox, Hess, Petersen, & Hill, 1997), the authors chose on the basis of a comment from the manuscript's prepublication reviewers not to report data about unhelpful disclosures. In retrospect, the authors felt that they should not have deleted those data because they were, in fact, valuable: Although not all participants could recall unhelpful disclosures, the lack of such disclosures was illuminating; furthermore, the few instances in which participants found self-disclosures to be unhelpful were important and might have been a valuable contribution to the literature.

Decisions regarding what findings to include may also be influenced by the "juiciness" of the findings (though the pursuit of such "juice" should certainly not lead authors to overemphasize outliers). For instance, results that are surprising, that are of substantial theoretical or practical significance, that are new and exciting, or that call into question previously held ideas may well be worthy of inclusion in the manuscript (Landrum, 2008). For instance, in the previously cited study on gifts (Knox, Dubois, et al., 2009), the authors separately presented the data from one case that involved multiple gifts, even though this case was an outlier from the sample, because it demonstrated the significant problems that can arise from such circumstances.

We recommend, then, that authors use the precious space of their Results section to focus on findings that directly speak to the research questions guiding the study. Beyond that consideration, findings that are novel, contain practical or theoretical implications, or challenge existing ideas may also be included. Finally, we suggest that authors briefly inform readers what findings they have chosen not to report and their reasons for doing so.

## ORGANIZATIONAL CHALLENGES

Another decision authors face involves the structure and organization not only of the Results section, but also of the Discussion section. In publications using CQR as the primary data-gathering method, most authors have presented these two sections separately, though a few have combined them into an integrated Results and Discussion section. The former structure is certainly more traditional and may thus be more familiar to and comfortable for readers, especially those new to CQR or to qualitative research in general. This structure may be simpler for authors as well because it clearly defines the content that is to appear in each area. The purpose of the Results section is thus solely to state the findings of the research: On the basis of the prior Method section ("here's what we studied and how we studied it . . . "), the authors now simply state " . . . and here's what we found and the evidence for it." Left to the Discussion section is the authors' wrangling with what the findings mean in terms of import, significance, and implications.

A few authors (e.g., Knox, Burkard, Jackson, Schaack, & Hess, 2006), however, have integrated the Results and Discussion sections because of the substantial overlap between the sections and the desire not to be repetitive. Doing so need not short-change either section and in fact may render the whole paper more potent because readers see immediately not only what the findings are but what sense the researchers make of them. As a reader, it may be quite gratifying to see the authors' understanding and interpretation of their data alongside the data themselves. The greater immediacy and integration afforded by such a structure is certainly worthy of consideration when determining how best to present and explain the findings. Our recommendation, then, is that authors carefully consider what structure for the Results and Discussion sections will most compellingly present the findings and the meaning thereof. We particularly recommend combining the Results and Discussion sections when authors find themselves repeating their results in the Discussion section (i.e., such as when the results are so lengthy or complex that the reader has to be reminded of them in the Discussion section). Thus far, journal reviewers and editors have shown no consistent preference for either of the organizational structures.

## WHERE BEST TO INCLUDE CORE IDEAS OR QUOTES?

Some authors of CQR-based manuscripts include illustrative core ideas or participant quotes in the body of the Results section, whereas others include them in tables at the end of the manuscript. Wherever it appears, such content is vital because it brings vigor to the manuscript by using researchers' abstracts of actual interview content (core ideas), or even more immediately uses participants' own words in the form of relevant quotes to substantiate the researchers' findings. The decision regarding where such material should appear is likely driven by author preference and by the nature of the core ideas or quotes themselves.

As noted earlier, some authors prefer to include such content in the body of the Results, fearing that this section will be dry and boring without this material. This approach also ensures that readers encounter the complete findings (domains, categories, and core ideas and quotes) in this one important section of the manuscript, as was done in an examination of novice therapists' experiences in a beginning graduate class (Hill, Sullivan, Knox, & Schlosser, 2007).

Other authors prefer that the body of the Results briefly note the domains and categories of the study's findings as more of an overview and then direct readers to a table at the end of the manuscript, deeming this a more efficient presentation of the findings given the scarcity of manuscript space. In this approach, the table includes the same content as the earlier style (domains, categories, and core ideas and quotes) but presents this material with visual efficiency in what is often a single-page table, as was done in a study of supervisees' experiences of supervisor self-disclosure (Knox, Edwards, et al., in press).

An important consideration in deciding where to place this illustrative content is, as mentioned above, the nature of the core ideas and quotes themselves. If longer quotations are required to illustrate the findings vividly and clearly, they may well be best presented in the body of the Results section. If, on the other hand, the findings can be illustrated via fairly brief core ideas and quotes, they may be effectively presented in a table. Thus, we again recommend that authors include the core ideas and quotes where they may most powerfully contribute to the manuscript.

In addition to the usual core ideas and quotes we have described, some authors also present whole-case illustrative examples in the Results section to integrate the study's main findings and serve as a springboard for the ensuing Discussion section (see the following section). In a recent investigation of supervisees' experiences of supervisor self-disclosure (Knox, Edwards, et al., in press), for example, we presented two illustrative examples, one describing supervisees' positive experiences of supervisor self-disclosure and the other exemplifying more problematic supervisor self-disclosure experiences. Each example was a composite based on the prevailing findings of each type of event, and each example vividly captured the nature of participants' experiences. An alternative and equally effective approach to such composite examples is to use the actual findings from a single case (appropriately de-identified—e.g., using pseudonyms, altering demographic information). Whether composite or based on a single case, such content is frequently presented at the end of the Results section to highlight and integrate the findings just described but may also prove helpful at the beginning of the Results to provide readers a sense of the phenomenon before they enter into the specific findings. Either approach may be successful, and we again counsel authors to choose the style of presentation that most effectively conveys their findings.

Finally, occasionally researchers present a figure to illustrate the results graphically (e.g., Rhodes, Hill, Thompson, & Elliott, 1994, whose figure is reprinted as Figure 9.1 in this volume). Although not all studies lend themselves to such graphic depictions, it can be useful as a way of integrating the findings.

# The Discussion Section

As is true of each of the preceding sections, authors also wrestle with important decisions in the Discussion section of a CQR-based manuscript. These decisions directly affect the quality and interest of the "story" told by the researchers' findings.

## HOW TO TELL THE MOST COMPELLING STORY

A challenge that regularly besets CQR researchers is how to craft a Discussion section that does more than simply repeat the findings and instead weaves those findings into a compelling story. An effective Results section clearly describes what the study has discovered—what answers it has found to its guiding research questions. The Discussion section, then, must move beyond the "trees" of the Results and now speak of the "forest" that those trees create. This is no easy feat.

One strategy we have used is to identify the three to five essential "take-away" messages that we hope readers learn from a manuscript, which Landrum (2008) called the "big bang" (p. 118). Paring down months of effort and many pages of data into the three to five juiciest nuggets is a daunting challenge, but it is one that forces researchers to distill their findings to the most fundamental essence, an essence that should of course be linked to the research questions guiding the study and also to the extant literature. Once identified, these foundational nuggets form the backbone of the Discussion section, in that all Discussion content leads directly or indirectly back to these ideas. For instance, in a manuscript on supervisees' experience of supervisor self-disclosure (Knox, Edwards, et al., in press), the components that appeared to contribute most to the positive or problematic effects of such disclosures were the supervisory relationship, supervisors' responsiveness to supervisees' needs or concerns, and appropriate and clear intentions for the disclosure. The Discussion section, then, was structured to discuss the meaning of these components and tie them into the existing literature. Such an approach has proven successful in fostering the vital "big picture" thinking that characterizes the Discussion section.

Another approach we have used is to structure the Discussion section around the whole-case illustrative examples presented in the Results section (see previous section). From those more "tree"-focused illustrative examples, we move out to a broader level of abstraction in the Discussion to describe the "forest" they depict, incorporating the extant literature where appropriate. So instead of focusing on such details as the different antecedents to supervisors' self-disclosures or the different types of disclosures, we could speak in the Discussion section about the discovery that there was no particular antecedent pattern or predominant type of disclosure. Supervisors, in fact, appeared to notice and respond to a range of supervisee needs in deciding to disclose, and they revealed both clinical and personal information (e.g., Knox, Edwards, et al., in press).

Yet a third approach is to overtly frame the Discussion section around the extant literature and use that existing knowledge base to understand the current data. For example, Schlosser, Knox, Moskovitz, and Hill (2003) examined doctoral students' views of their advising relationships. In that study, two dimensions from Gelso's (1979, 1993) theory of research training environments (i.e., instructional and interpersonal components) were used to frame the discussion of the findings. Not all of the data fit neatly into one of these two clusters, however, so the remaining data were discussed separately. Regardless of the specific approach followed, situating the results within current theory and research helps authors understand the degree to which their findings are similar to or different from previous research and contextualizes the current data in the larger body of existing knowledge.

## LIMITATIONS SECTION

CQR authors must address the limitations of their research to enable readers to consider potential shortcomings in the study and thus know to whom the results may translate. We recommend, for instance, that authors acknowledge anything unusual about the sample, especially if that sample was heterogeneous or anomalous in some way (e.g., age, sex, race–ethnicity, experience related to topic of study), and also caution their audience about generalizing the findings to the larger specific population. In addition, authors may prevent against unwarranted criticisms by reminding readers that small samples are the norm in this method.

Authors also need to address particular features of the research team and/or the participant sample (e.g., minimal racial–ethnic diversity) and posit the possible effects of such differences. Authors need to speak here about the potential impact of their identities, experiences, and biases and expectations on their understanding and analysis of the data. For example, different research teams, with different characteristics, might well come up with slightly different results. In a recent study of advisors' positive and problematic dissertation experiences (Knox, Burkard, et al., in press), for instance, we noted that the faculty on the primary team had had relatively few experiences as dissertation advisors at the time of the research, and the students were at the time preparing for or engaged in their dissertations. Furthermore, one of the faculty had had a uniformly positive dissertation experience as a dissertator, whereas the other faculty member's experiences as a dissertator were more mixed. We acknowledged that these experiences could have biased our interpretation of the data but also noted that we hoped the use of external auditors reduced the likelihood of flagrant misperceptions. We thus strongly recommend that writers of CQR manuscripts engage in similar self-reflection regarding the potential impact of their own background and experiences on their understanding of the data.

## IMPLICATIONS SECTION

Here, authors offer a glimpse of the larger import and meaning of the findings, both in terms of theory, practice, and research. Given that many readers are unfamiliar with qualitative research, and thus also with CQR, it is important that authors clearly assert how their findings may increase our understanding of the studied phenomenon. In an investigation of client gifts to therapists (Knox, Dubois, et al., 2009), the first study to closely examine clients' perspectives on this experience, for instance, the authors spoke in this section of how powerful it was for many of the participants to give their therapists a gift as well as of the effects of this exchange on the participants and their therapy, suggesting that such interactions can have potent effects on the therapy process and thus must be managed with great sensitivity. The authors also reminded readers of the alarmingly troubling experiences that one participant had with a therapist who appeared to solicit gifts, further strengthening the need for extreme care in such interactions.

Authors should conclude this section by reflecting on possible avenues for future research. Given that no one study answers all questions, and indeed usually raises additional questions, this section allows authors to describe fertile future directions in the hope that doing so will spark the imagination of other researchers for further explorations.

## *General Considerations*

CQR researchers face other decisions in progressing toward and preparing a manuscript. These decisions are equally important as those noted above.

## WRITING AND THE RESEARCH TEAM

Many important decisions must be made when assembling a CQR research team (see Chapter 4, this volume); we limit our discussion here, however, to those that affect the writing of the manuscript. In our experience, implicit assumptions among the team members about the responsibilities for manuscript writing tend to be the norm. These assumptions are that the first author writes the manuscript and the other team members provide feedback on drafts prior to submission for publication. Occasionally, however, other authors have written sections (e.g., Method) of the paper.

Although first authors writing the bulk of a manuscript may be standard for collaborative scholarship, we advise researchers to discuss and clarify the roles and responsibilities of all team members at the outset of the project, including who will write what parts of the eventual manuscript. This discussion, which should also include designating order of authorship among team members, reduces the likelihood of painful feelings about the amount of recognition (i.e., authorship order) relative to the amount of work invested. To that end, the principal investigator (PI) typically is the first author, with the members of the primary team coming next in the order of authorship, and the auditor or auditors last. We also frequently comment in the author notes section on the relative contributions of the team members if the order of authorship does not adequately reflect the contributions. For example, if the first author (of a three-person primary team) has essentially written the manuscript, then we might comment that "the second and third authors contributed equally to this project." Such a statement acknowledges that the level of involvement by the primary team is substantial and was equal among primary team members other than the first author.

Whatever decision is reached regarding writing the manuscript, the authors should consider the effects, positive and negative, of having the first author write the entire manuscript versus having team members write sections of the manuscript. Employing a model where the first author writes the entire manuscript yields a paper with one clear voice and writing style. It may also, however, place a significant burden on the first author and could contribute to an idiosyncratic presentation of the findings, which can be tempered by team members reviewing drafts of the paper. The alternative approach of sharing the writing can be beneficial in that work is more evenly distributed among team members, ideally on the basis of team members' strengths and interests. However, the first author eventually still must synthesize the various contributions into one coherent voice for the manuscript.

## USE OF EXTERNAL READERS

An additional consideration is the use of external readers. Speaking personally, we often rely on at least one external reader to review a manuscript prior to submission for publication. This external reader is not part of the research team, nor is she or he an author of the paper; this position as an independent "outsider" allows for a more impartial, critical review of the manuscript, more like what will be received from reviewers of journals. A primary consideration regarding the decision of whether to use an external reader is the experience level of the team members (who review manuscript drafts prior to the external reader). That is, critical feedback on a manuscript is often hard to obtain from more novice graduate student coauthors, especially when the first author also serves as students' advisor, supervisor, and/or course instructor. In such cases, the critical commentary from an external reviewer can highlight areas in need of attention prior to journal submission. If an external reader (or readers) is used, she or he should be selected for content area expertise and openness to, and preferably familiarity with, CQR; such readers should be noted in the acknowledgments section of the paper.

## PRESENTING CQR RESEARCH AT CONFERENCES

Finally, it can be very beneficial to present CQR research at appropriate professional meetings before publication. In addition to the general dissemination of research knowledge, presenting CQR data at a conference forces authors to focus on the essential findings that would be most compelling for the audience. An additional benefit from such presentations is receiving feedback, which might facilitate the generation of new ideas and perspectives. The effort to focus on the most primary and compelling findings, as well as the opportunity to receive helpful feedback, may both contribute to a stronger CQR manuscript.

## *Conclusions*

Many, then, are the challenges of writing an effective CQR-based manuscript. As we have faced these challenges, we have certainly learned and grown as researchers and as authors, and we are confident that others will do the same. We hope that what we have offered here proves helpful for those who wish to follow in this path. In Table 11.1, we summarize the recommendations made throughout this chapter.

**TABLE 11.1**

**Writing the Manuscript**

| Step | Recommendations |
|---|---|
| Introduction | Provide a clear rationale for choosing a qualitative approach in general, and also for specifically choosing CQR (i.e., highlight CQR strengths). |
| Method | Include a brief paragraph highlighting the four key steps (interview, domains, core ideas, cross-analysis) of CQR. |
| | Reference seminal CQR method writings. |
| | Describe the research team and their expectations and biases. |
| Results | Focus on findings that answer the research questions guiding the study. |
| | Include novel findings, those that yield practical or theoretical implications, or those that challenge existing ideas. |
| | Inform readers what findings have not been reported and why. |
| | Determine whether separate or combined Results and Discussion sections will most compellingly present the findings and the meaning thereof. |
| | Include core ideas, quotations, and whole-case illustrative examples where they most powerfully contribute. |
| | Include illustrative figures where possible. |
| Discussion | Determine how to tell the most compelling story and connect that story to the literature (e.g., focus on three to five essential "take-away" messages; structure Discussion around whole-case illustrative examples; or overtly frame Discussion around extant literature). |
| | Acknowledge anything unusual about the sample or researchers and the effects thereof. |
| | Caution readers about generalizations. |
| | Remind readers that small samples are the norm for CQR. |
| | Clearly state how the findings may increase understanding of the studied phenomenon. |
| | Suggest implications for theory, practice, research, teaching, and supervision, as appropriate. |
| Writing and the team | Discuss authorship order and responsibilities early. |
| External readers | Consider use of external readers for manuscript drafts. |
| Conference presentations | Consider presenting at conferences to disseminate results, focus on essential findings, and receive feedback. |

*Note.* CQR = consensual qualitative research.

# References

Gelso, C. J. (1979). Research in counseling: Methodological and professional issues. *The Counseling Psychologist, 8,* 7–36. doi:10.1177/001100 007900800303

Gelso, C. J. (1993). On the making of a scientist–practitioner: A theory of research training in professional psychology. *Professional Psychology, Research and Practice, 24,* 468–476. doi:10.1037/0735-7028.24.4.468

Hill, C. E., Knox, S., Thompson, B. J., Williams, E. N., Hess, S.A., & Ladany, N. (2005). Consensual qualitative research: An update. *Journal of Counseling Psychology, 52,* 196–205. doi:10.1037/0022-0167.52.2.196

Hill, C. E., Sullivan, C., Knox, S., & Schlosser, L. Z. (2007). Becoming psychotherapists: Experiences of novice trainees in a beginning graduate class. *Psychotherapy: Theory, Research, Practice, Training, 44,* 434–449. doi:10.1037/0033-3204.44.4.434

Hill, C. E., Thompson, B. J., & Williams, E. N. (1997). A guide to conducting consensual qualitative research. *The Counseling Psychologist, 25,* 517–572. doi:10.1177/0011000097254001

Knox, S., Adrians, N., Everson, E., Hess, S. A., Crook-Lyon, R., & Hill, C. E. (in press). Clients' experiences of termination in psychotherapy. *Psychotherapy Research.*

Knox, S., Burkard, A. W., Jackson, J. A., Schaack, A., & Hess, S. A. (2006). Therapists-in-training who experience a client suicide: Implications for supervision. *Professional Psychology: Research and Practice, 37,* 547–557. doi:10.1037/0735-7028.37.5.547

Knox, S., Burkard, A. W., Janecek, J., Pruitt, N. T., Fuller, S., & Hill, C. E. (in press). Positive and problematic dissertation experiences: The faculty perspective. *Counselling Psychology Quarterly.*

Knox, S., Catlin, L., Casper, M., & Schlosser, L. Z. (2005). Addressing religion and spirituality in psychotherapy: Clients' perspectives. *Psychotherapy Research, 15,* 287–303. doi:10.1080/10503300500090894.

Knox, S., Dubois, R., Smith, J., Hess, S. A., & Hill, C. E. (2009). Clients' experiences giving gifts to therapists. *Psychotherapy: Theory, Research, Practice, Training, 46,* 350–361. doi:10.1037/a0017001

Knox, S., Edwards, L. M., Hess, S. A., & Hill, C. E. (in press). Supervisees' experiences of supervisor self-disclosure. *Psychotherapy: Theory, Research, Practice, Training.*

Knox, S., Hess, S., Petersen, D., & Hill, C. E. (1997). A qualitative analysis of client perceptions of the effects of helpful therapist self-disclosure in long-term therapy. *Journal of Counseling Psychology, 44,* 274–283. doi:10.1037/0022-0167.44.3.274

Landrum, R. E. (2008). *Undergraduate writing in psychology: Learning to tell the scientific story.* Washington, DC: American Psychological Association.

Rhodes, R., Hill, C. E., Thompson, B. J., & Elliott, R. (1994). Client retrospective recall of resolved and unresolved misunderstanding events. *Journal of Counseling Psychology, 41,* 473–483. doi:10.1037/0022-0167.41.4.473

Schlosser, L. Z., Knox, S., Moskovitz, A. R., & Hill, C. E. (2003). A qualitative examination of graduate advising relationships: The advisee perspective. *Journal of Counseling Psychology, 50,* 178–188. doi:10.1037/0022-0167.50.2.178

*Clara E. Hill, Sarah Knox, and Shirley A. Hess*

# Qualitative Meta-Analyses of Consensual Qualitative Research Studies

**12**

Any single consensual qualitative research (CQR) study can be informative and important. For example, learning more about Filipino American identity development (Tuason, Taylor, Rollings, Harris, & Martin, 2007), adaptation experiences of 1.5 generation Asian Americans (Kim, Brenner, Liang, & Asay, 2003), or ethical values of master therapists (Jennings, Sovereign, Bottorff, Mussell, & Vye, 2005) is fascinating and helps us better understand these phenomena. Despite the potential contributions of individual studies, however, we cannot neglect questions about the representativeness of findings beyond the specific sample. Was the sample unusual in some unknown way? Did the interviewers obtain rich information? Did the research team's biases unduly influence the data analysis? Given such questions, the opportunity to replicate findings across a series of studies exploring similar phenomena seems likely to yield more trustworthy results. Similarly, in their seminal article describing CQR, Hill, Thompson, and Williams (1997) noted that results would be stronger and more believable if there were replications of findings across several studies. They lamented, however, that there were no existing methods for such comparisons at that time.

Fortunately, progress has been made since 1997 in aggregating results across qualitative studies. Specifically, Timulak

(2009) presented guidelines for performing qualitative meta-analysis (QMA), which he defined as "a precise and comprehensive picture of findings across qualitative studies that investigate the same research topic" (p. 591). Just as quantitative meta-analysis (see Berkeljon & Baldwin, 2009) first looks at overall effects (e.g., is there an overall effect for psychotherapy?) and then explores particular features of subsamples (e.g., do the effects sizes differ by therapy approach or client diagnosis?), Timulak noted that the aims of QMA are to summarize overall findings and then to explore possible differences among samples.

Out first goal in conducting QMA on CQR studies, then, involves aggregating results across studies investigating the same phenomenon. Here, researchers examine a set of studies and determine how many report the same or similar findings. Recall that in CQR we label findings as *general* if they represent all or all but one of the participants, *typical* if they apply to more than half up to the cutoff for general, and *variant* if they apply to two or three up to the cutoff for typical. Thus, if out of a hypothetical set of 20 studies, 15 reported typical findings for a particular category (e.g., insight was a helpful aspect of the therapy), three reported this category as variant, and two did not have a related category, we suggest that 18 out of 20 studies reporting the same category as at least variant (i.e., variant, typical, or general) provides strong support for believing that this category is descriptive of the phenomenon under investigation. In contrast, if out of a same hypothetical set of 20 studies, only two reported typical findings for a particular category, three reported this category as variant, and 15 did not have a related category, we would not have as much confidence that this category is descriptive of the phenomenon under investigation. We suggest that the majority of studies (which in the above example would be 11 of the 20 studies) need to report a category as at least variant to consider the category as representative of the phenomenon under investigation.

Our second goal involves exploring differences among samples to assess the effects of specific aspects of samples (e.g., therapist vs. client participants) or data collection (e.g., data collected via face-to-face vs. telephone interviews). In this second goal, researchers seek to determine whether such differences among samples influence the overall results. By comparing results across studies exploring a phenomenon from both therapist and client perspectives, for example, we could determine the possible influence of perspective on the results. Thus, if eight of 10 hypothetical studies from the therapist perspective indicated that the category of "insight was a helpful aspect of therapy" occurred typically or variantly, whereas only one out of 10 hypothetical studies from the client perspective found this category to be typical or variant, then we would have some preliminary evidence that insight may be more important to therapists than to clients.

In this chapter, we first provide an example of a QMA. We then outline the specific steps researchers might follow to conduct a QMA.

## *Example of a QMA*

In this section, we demonstrate QMA of CQR data by examining findings for 10 investigations in which researchers asked participants why they chose to participate in the project. These data were never published because of journal space limitations and because the results were not directly tied to the studies' central questions of interest. Given the similarity of questions across studies, however, they were ideal for a first foray into a QMA of CQR data.

We had access to the core ideas from all of the cross-analyses, so the three authors of this chapter read over the category labels and the core ideas for each category for all 10 studies. We quickly noted that codings into categories were not consistent across studies, and we felt a bit uncertain about what each of the categories meant. To become clearer, we reexamined the original category labels and their underlying core ideas and then developed six broad categories that seemed to capture the findings across studies regarding why participants chose to take part in the research. Next, we went back to each individual study and determined by consensus into which of our six new categories each individual core idea fit (again, regardless of into which original category it had been placed by the researchers). On the basis of which coding predominated, we then placed the original category, as a whole, into one of the six new categories (again, regardless of the original label given by the authors of the study). As an example, let's say that an original category was supported by 30 core ideas across participants and that 20 of those core ideas best fit new category A, seven best fit new category B, and three best fit new category C. Because the vast majority of the core ideas from this original category best fit new category A, the entire original category and its 30 core ideas were placed under new category A. On the basis of this work, we then created a table that showed where each of the original categories from each study (using their original labels) fit into our six new QMA categories (see Table 12.1).

Our first goal in this QMA, then, was to determine how many of the 10 studies found similar categories explaining why participants took part in the project. The reasons that were cited at least variantly were as follows:

- The most frequent reason cited was a desire to help, emerging at least variantly in 90% of the studies, indicating that participants most often agreed to participate because they had a desire to be altruistic or helpful.
- The second most common reason cited was that the topic was interesting or important to the participants (emerged as at least variant in 80% of the studies).

| TABLE 12.1 |
| :-- |

**Comparison of Reasons for Participation in 10 Consensual Qualitative Research (CQR) Studies**

| Study | Participants | Reason | |
| :-- | :-- | :-- | :-- |
| | | **To help** | **Topic is interesting or important** |
| Knox, Burkard, Jackson, Schaack, and Hess, 2006 | Graduate students | To support research (typical) | Important /touching topic (variant) |
| Hess et al., 2008 | Graduate students | Wanted to be helpful (typical) | Interested in topic (typical) |
| Burkard et al., 2009 | Graduate students | Research karma/help researchers (typical) | |
| Knox, Edwards, Hess, and Hill, in press | Graduate students | To advance knowledge/ contribute to or help research (typical) | Interesting topic/had relevant experience (typical) |
| Knox, Schlosser, Pruitt,and Hill, 2006 | Postgraduate professionals | Support research/ researchers (typical) | Topic important/ interesting (typical) |
| Knox Burkard, Edwards, Smith, and Schlosser, 2008 | Postgraduate professionals | To help (variant) | |
| Knox, Burkard, et al., in press | Postgraduate professionals | | Interesting topic (typical) |
| Knox, Dubois, Smith, Hess, and Hill, 2009 | Clients | To help (typical) | Interested in topic (variant) |
| Knox, Hess, Hill, Burkard, and Crook-Lyon, in press | Clients | Research karma (variant) Altruism/be helpful to researchers (variant) | Stimulating/interesting topic (typical) |
| Knox et al., 2011 | Clients | To contribute to or help research/research karma (general) | Interesting topic/had relevant termination experience (variant) To contribute to or help research/research karma (general) |
| Summary[a] | | | |
| Total sample (N = 10) | | 90% | 80% |
| Graduate students (n = 4) | | 100% | 75% |
| Postgraduates (n = 3) | | 66% | 66% |

*Note.* The categories in each column were judged as assessing the same construct. Empty cells indicate that this reason was not mentioned in the data for this study. general = all or all but one participant in study; typical = more than half of the participants; variant = two to at least half of the participants; LGB = lesbian/gay/bisexual; CRE = corrective relational experiences.
[a]Percentages shown indicate number of studies in which the results were at least variant.

| Had a meaningful related experience | Desire to educate or contribute to literature | Likes qualitative research | Invited by colleague or advisor | Miscellaneous |
|---|---|---|---|---|
| | To educate future therapists (typical) | | | |
| Worked on LGB issues (variant) Interesting topic/ had relevant experience (typical) | Advance LGB research (typical) | Likes or has done CQR or qualitative research (variant) | | |
| | Increase knowledge/ skills about topic (typical) Interest in topic/thinks topic important (typical) Nothing in literature on topic (variant) | | Connection to researchers (typical) Help colleague (typical) | Facilitate participant's own research (variant) |
| Had meaningful experience (variant) Interesting/powerful CRE to share (variant) Interesting topic/ had relevant termination experience (variant) | | Has done/is doing/ wants to do qualitative research (variant) Likes/has done CQR/ qualitative research (variant) | Advisor/researcher invited to participate (variant) | Topic not invasive or exploitive (variant) Wanted experience as interviewee (variant) |
| | | Summary[a] | | |
| 50% | 50% | 30% | 30% | |
| 50% | 50% | 25% | 0% | |
| 0% | 100% | 0% | 66% | |

- Other reasons that were mentioned less frequently were having had a meaningful related experience (at least variant in 50% of the studies), wanting to educate or contribute to the literature (at least variant in 50% of the studies), liking qualitative research (at least variant in 30% of the studies), and being invited by a colleague or advisor (at least variant in 30% of the studies).
- Three reasons (to facilitate participant's own research, topic was not invasive or exploitative, participant wanted experience as an interviewee) were mentioned in single studies but were not replicated in any other studies.

On the basis of the findings of this QMA, then, researchers might consider targeting their recruiting efforts to appeal to the wish to be helpful and to be involved in an important, interesting topic.

Our second goal in this QMA was to determine whether there were any consistent differences among the samples that might explain some of the variation in the findings. An examination of the details of various studies (e.g., demographic data about the participants, methodological features) revealed only one noticeable difference in the samples: Four studies involved graduate students as participants, three involved practicing postgraduate professionals (e.g., postgraduate therapists or faculty members), and three involved clients. However, because the three studies involving clients included both therapists in training and practicing therapists as participants, we did not include these in the comparison. Hence, we next compared the four studies involving graduate students and the three studies involving postgraduate professionals.

We a priori arbitrarily decided that we would consider a difference between the two samples to be important if they differed by at least 30% in number of studies (because a difference that large seemed unlikely to have occurred just by chance). We also decided that the category had to have occurred at least variantly (i.e., occurred variantly, typically, or generally). Differences were found for four categories:

- Professionals more often than graduate students mentioned participating because they were invited by a colleague (66% were at least variant for professionals vs. 0% for graduate students).
- Professionals more often than graduate students mentioned participating because they had a desire to educate or contribute to the literature (100% were at least variant for professionals vs. 50% for graduate students).
- Graduate students more often than professionals mentioned participating because they had a relevant meaningful experience (50% were at least variant for graduate students vs. 0% for professionals).
- Graduate students more often than professionals mentioned participating because they wanted to help (100% were at least variant for graduate students vs. 66% for professionals).

On the basis of these QMA findings, researchers might consider tailoring their recruitment of graduate students to those who have had relevant meaningful experiences and who want to be helpful (emphasizing research karma), whereas they might personally ask colleagues and appeal to their desire to contribute to knowledge when recruiting postgraduate professionals.

# Steps for Conducting QMA on CQR Data

Stepping back now from the specific example, we offer the following guidelines for conducting QMA with CQR data. These guidelines are based on Timulak's (2009) description of QMA, which we modified on the basis of our experiences (described above) applying QMA to existing CQR data. Table 12.2 provides a summary of these guidelines.

## CHOOSING A TEAM

We recommend having three to four people on a QMA research team to allow for a variety of opinions. It could also be useful to have one or

### TABLE 12.2

**Summary of Steps for Conducting Qualitative Meta-Analysis on Consensual Qualitative Research (CQR) Data**

| Step | Recommendation |
| --- | --- |
| Choosing a team | Select 3 to 4 experienced CQR researchers. |
| Choosing the studies | Select studies that address the same topic. |
| | Set inclusion and exclusion criteria for studies. |
| | Search literature thoroughly. |
| Choosing the evidence | Need categories and supporting core ideas or quotes. |
| Comparing categories across studies | Determine equivalence of categories based on data. |
| Summarize the findings | State frequency of categories across studies. |
| | Summarize percentage occurring at least variantly or typically. |
| | Consider important if in more than half the samples. |
| | If using, send to auditors. |
| Exploring differences among samples | Note relevant features of studies. |
| | Set criterion for differences between samples. |

two auditors to provide feedback on the team's analysis, although at this point it does not seem to be absolutely necessary if enough people are included in the research team. In terms of qualifications for the team and any auditors, experience with CQR seems most relevant, along with expertise in the topic being studied.

## CHOOSING THE STUDIES

To facilitate fair comparisons across studies, researchers need to select studies that address the same or similar topics (i.e., at least some portion of each study must address the same topic). For example, all selected studies might address helpful aspects of therapy, or some part of the chosen studies might address why participants agreed to participate in the study.

Researchers need to determine inclusion and exclusion criteria to indicate what kinds of studies they will and will not include in their review. For example, they might decide to include only studies that faithfully followed CQR and might exclude studies that did not report quotes or core ideas to illustrate categories (because it would be very difficult to determine what categories meant without such supporting information). Researchers then exhaustively search the literature to make sure that they include all possible studies that fit their criteria. Given that not all studies include the term *consensual qualitative research* in the abstract, this search might entail more examination of paper copies of journals than is usually done and following up on references in published studies on the topic.

With regard to numbers of studies needed for a QMA, this decision depends on the reason for conducting the QMA. If the intent is to feel confident about the findings in a particular area, then many studies are needed (Patterson, Thorne, Canam, & Jillings, 2001, recommended at least a dozen studies) because the stability of the results emerges only when multiple samples are examined. Similarly, if the purpose is to investigate the effects of specific features of the studies (e.g., type of sample), many studies would be needed so that potential differences among examined features emerge with some stability. If the purpose is to perform a preliminary comparison of findings across studies in an area where few studies exist, however, as few as two studies could be included in the QMA because two studies can provide preliminary evidence about stability of findings across samples. Given the current paucity of CQR studies examining the same topic, we may need to rely on fewer CQR studies than might be ideal in these early stages of QMA.

## CHOOSING THE EVIDENCE

Typically, researchers will have available to them only the evidence that has been published, which usually consists of the category labels and either representative core ideas or quotes for each category or subcategory. It is crucial to have at least the exemplar core ideas or quotes to obtain a clear understanding of what category labels mean within the individual studies. In ideal circumstances, researchers would also have access to each project's cross-analysis so that they could actually see the core ideas for each category, but we recognize that QMA researchers may not always have access to such data. If the cross-analyses are available for some of the studies but not others, QMA researchers must decide whether to include unequal levels of data (e.g., category labels and core ideas for some studies vs. entire cross-analyses for other studies) in their QMA. If, from an examination of the exemplar core ideas and quotes, the category labels seem clear and discrete, researchers may include studies for which not all the core ideas are available; on the other hand, if researchers are not sure about what the category labels really mean, it is probably wiser not to include such studies in the QMA (and note this in the paper).

## COMPARING CATEGORIES ACROSS STUDIES

In this step, the primary team (i.e., all those except auditors) examines the categories within parallel domains across studies and determines if there are similarities. Specifically, they look at the category labels and exemplar quotes and core ideas (and all of the core ideas if the cross-analyses are available) and determine whether the categories across studies convey sufficiently similar meaning such that regardless of category title they represent the same construct. For example, by examining such evidence (i.e., the category label, the exemplar core ideas), the team might determine that for a domain capturing participants' reasons for taking part in a study, the category "wanted to help" in one study is equivalent to the category "to help out a colleague" in another study but that both of these categories differ from the category "had the time" (see example above). Determination of equivalence between categories is made by consensus among the research team members based on considerable discussion and examination of all the available data.

## SUMMARIZING THE FINDINGS

Once it is determined that the categories represent the same construct, the next decision is how to summarize the findings. We suggest here that researchers indicate which categories occurred generally, typically, and variantly across studies. For example, let us suppose that researchers in a hypothetical QMA of 10 studies about helpful components of psychotherapy indicate that the category "insight" was general in four studies, typical in three, variant in one, and did not emerge at all in two studies, whereas the category of "action ideas" was not general in any studies, was typical in one, variant in three, and nonexistent in six. They could then summarize these results and say that "insight" occurred at least variantly in 80% of the studies, whereas "action ideas" occurred at least variantly in only 40%. Researchers could be more stringent and consider only those categories that occurred at least typically in order to represent findings that held for at least half of the samples. Thus, in our hypothetical example, "insight" occurred at least typically in 70% of the studies, whereas "action ideas" occurred at least typically in only 10%.

The next decision is what to make of the above findings regarding how often each category occurred. Here, then, we need to decide how often the category had to occur to consider it a key component of the phenomenon. We tentatively suggest that more than half of the studies must include the chosen category at least variantly (or if researchers wish to be more stringent, the category must occur at least typically) for the category to be considered representative of the phenomenon. Thus, if six out of 10 studies found "achieving insight" at least variantly to be a helpful component of therapy, we would have confidence that insight is indeed helpful; in contrast, if only two of 10 studies found "developing action ideas" at least variantly to be helpful, we would have less confidence that this is a valued component of therapy.

If auditors are used, the results would now be sent to them. Auditors would examine all of the evidence and comment on the results. The primary team would then consider the auditors' comments and make needed adjustments.

## EXPLORING DIFFERENCES AMONG SAMPLES

As a follow-up to the main analyses of overall effects, researchers may decide to continue even further in their analysis (if they have enough studies) to determine whether results differed across samples. Differences based on characteristics of the samples might have muddied the overall results, and thus a more micro level of examination might clarify that variation was due to something related to the samples. For example, minimal consistency might be found across studies if samples differed in terms of the theoretical orientation of therapists. If we could identify such differences among samples, and if we had enough studies in each subgroup, we might be able to account for variation across studies. Continuing the hypothetical example from the previous section, if clients in studies involving psychodynamic therapy often cited "achieving insight" as a helpful component, whereas clients in studies involving cognitive–behavioral therapy often cited "developing action ideas" as helpful, we would consider this to be an "important" difference (note that we cannot call it a "significant" difference because we did not do statistical tests of significance).

In order to investigate the influence of various features of the studies on the obtained results, researchers first must note the relevant features of the chosen studies. For example, researchers might record the stated theoretical orientation and stated expectations and biases of the research team, the size and characteristics of the sample, the procedures for collecting and analyzing data, any deviations from standard CQR procedures, and any concerns about the trustworthiness of the data and data analysis. For instance, if it appears from an examination of the findings that there was considerable variation with regard to therapists' experience level, researchers might note which samples used postgraduate therapists and which used therapists in training as participants. Researchers are constrained, of course, by what is available about the studies in the published records, unless they contact the authors for more detail.

Assuming that the researchers have enough studies for each of the subgroups of interest (we suggest at least three studies in each subgroup), they can then investigate whether different results emerged for the different subgroups. For example, researchers could explore whether the results differed on the basis of how the data were gathered (e.g., face-to-face interviews, telephone interviews, written questionnaires) and whether the sample reflected different cultural backgrounds (e.g., China vs. the United States) or experience levels (e.g., doctoral students vs. experienced therapists as participants). In another example, researchers might find that two of 10 studies reported at least typical results for the category of sexual fantasies in dreams about clients on the basis of telephone interviews compared with eight of 10 studies reporting typical or variant results for this category when face-to-face interviews were used.

Researchers must then decide how much difference needs to be present to consider the samples as having responded differently. We recommend that there be a difference of at least 30% between subsamples (e.g., eight of 10 studies vs. five of 10 studies would be a 30% difference). Although the 30% criterion is admittedly arbitrary, it seems relatively large and thus likely to reflect true differences between subsamples (and seemed to reflect meaningful differences when we examined some data and yet was not overly restrictive). We advise researchers to set their criteria for important differences prior to data analyses (otherwise researchers are likely to set criteria to support their biases) and to state them clearly in the manuscript. Thus, researchers might determine that in speaking of helpful aspects of therapy, clients of postgraduate therapists more often yielded an "insight" category than did clients of therapists in training, basing this conclusion on the evidence that eight of 10 hypothetical studies with postgraduate therapists included the "insight" category as general or typical, whereas only two of 10 hypothetical studies with therapists in training yielded "insight" as a general or typical category (a 60% difference clearly exceeds the 30% criterion set a priori for differences to be considered important).

## Conclusions

By presenting a clear description of an approach to conducting QMA, we hope to encourage researchers to engage in this type of analysis. We also encourage researchers to replicate studies so that there will be enough data to conduct additional QMA. We hope that the results of such efforts will provide greater confidence in the findings across a body of research. In contrast, if similarities are not found across studies, even when different features of studies are accounted for, researchers might lose confidence in the utility of CQR and need to modify the approach.

Finally, we acknowledge again that these qualitative meta-analytic procedures are very new. We fully expect the methods to change as researchers gain more experience with them. We thus eagerly await further extensions of the method.

## References

Berkeljon, A., & Baldwin, S. A. (2009). An introduction to meta-analysis for psychotherapy outcome research. *Psychotherapy Research, 19,* 511–518. doi:10.1080/10503300802621172

Hess, S., Knox, S., Schultz, J. M., Hill, C. E., Sloan, L., Brandt, S., . . . Hoffman, M. A. (2008). Predoctoral interns' nondisclosure in supervision. *Psychotherapy Research, 18,* 400–411. doi:10.1080/1050330070 1697505

Hill, C. E., Thompson, B. J., & Williams, E. N. (1997). A guide to conducting consensual qualitative research. *The Counseling Psychologist, 25,* 517–572. doi:10.1177/0011000097254001

Jennings, L., Sovereign, A., Bottorff, N., Mussell, M., & Vye, C. (2005). Nine ethical values of master therapists. *Journal of Mental Health Counseling, 27*(1), 32–47.

Kim, B. S. K., Brenner, B. R., Liang, C. T. H., & Asay, P. A. (2003). A qualitative study of adaptation experiences of 1.5-generation Asian Americans. *Cultural Diversity & Ethnic Minority Psychology, 9,* 156–170. doi:10.1037/1099-9809.9.2.156

Knox, S., Adrians, N., Everson, E., Hess, S. A., Hill, C. E., & Crook-Lyon, R. (2011). Clients' perspectives on therapy termination. *Psychotherapy Research, 21,* 154–167. doi:10.1080/10503307.2010.534509

Knox, S., Burkard, A. W., Jackson, J. A., Schaack, A., & Hess, S. A. (2006). Therapists-in-training who experience a client suicide: Implications for supervision. *Professional Psychology: Research and Practice, 37,* 547–557.

Knox, S., Burkard, A. W., Edwards, L., Smith, J., & Schlosser, L. Z. (2008). Supervisors' reports of the effects of supervisor self-disclosure on supervisees. *Psychotherapy Research, 18,* 543–559. doi:10.1080/ 10503300801982781

Knox, S., Burkard, A. W., Janecek, J., Pruitt, N. T., Fuller, S., & Hill, C. E.(in press). Positive and problematic dissertation experiences: The faculty perspective. *Counselling Psychology Quarterly.*

Knox, S., Dubois, R., Smith, J., Hess, S. A., & Hill, C. E. (2009). Clients' experiences giving gifts to therapists. *Psychotherapy: Theory, Research, Practice, Training, 46,* 350–361. doi:10.1037/a0017001

Knox, S., Edwards, L. M., Hess, S. A., & Hill, C. E. (in press). Supervisees' experiences of supervisor self-disclosure. *Psychotherapy: Theory, Research, Practice, Training.*

Knox, S., Hess, S. A., Hill, C. E., Burkard, A. W., & Crook-Lyon, R. E. (in press). Corrective relational experiences of therapists or therapists-in-training. In L. G. Castonguay & C. E. Hill (Eds.), *Transformation in psychotherapy: Corrective experiences across cognitive behavioral, humanistic, and psychodynamic approaches.* Washington, DC: American Psychological Association.

Knox, S., Schlosser, L. Z., Pruitt, N. T., & Hill, C. E. (2006). A qualitative examination of graduate advising relationships: The advisor perspective. *The Counseling Psychologist, 34,* 489–518. doi:10.1177/ 0011000006290249

Patterson, B. L., Thorne, S. E., Canam, C., & Jillings, C. (2001). *Meta-study of qualitative health research: A practical guide to meta-analysis and meta-synthesis.* Thousand Oaks, CA: Sage.

Timulak, L. (2009). Meta-analysis of qualitative studies: A tool for reviewing qualitative research findings in psychotherapy. *Psychotherapy Research, 19,* 591–600. doi:10.1080/10503300802477989

Tuason, M. T. G., Taylor, A. R., Rollings, L., Harris, T., & Martin, C. (2007). On both sides of the hyphen: Exploring the Filipino-American identity. *Journal of Counseling Psychology, 54,* 362–372. doi:10.1037/ 0022-0167.54.4.362

# OVERALL CONSIDERATIONS

*Elizabeth Nutt Williams and Clara E. Hill*

# Establishing Trustworthiness in Consensual Qualitative Research Studies

## 13

E stablishing the validity of any empirical research study is crucial (Choudhuri, Glauser, & Peregoy, 2004; Stiles, 1993). In qualitative research, the meaning and operationalization of "validity" has been more difficult to determine than in the quantitative studies that have traditionally dominated in psychology. First, qualitative researchers have no shared "shorthand," such as $p$ values, estimates of interrater reliability, and error variance on which to rely (Williams & Morrow, 2009). Thus, thinking about and assessing the construct of validity is difficult. Second, qualitative researchers have struggled against simply adopting the language and approaches of quantitative research (Arminio & Hultgren, 2002). Merely applying standards (e.g., the use of a kappa statistic) from quantitative research does not make sense given that the two types of research are based on different underlying paradigms (see Chapter 2 in this volume).

Instead of using the term *validity*, then, some qualitative researchers have begun to use the term *trustworthiness* (e.g., Elliott, Fischer, & Rennie, 1999), referring to the researchers' claim to have used appropriate, adequate, and replicable methods and to have correctly reported the findings. In 1981, Guba suggested that qualitative researchers should use credibility, transferability, dependability, and confirmability to evaluate trustworthiness. Indeed, many have adopted these criteria as a way to address challenges to methodological rigor leveled at qualitative research (Hoyt & Bhati, 2007). Others (e.g., Morrow, 2005) have used these criteria to further define trustworthiness. For this chapter, we rely on the three criteria that were initially presented by Morrow (2005) and then refined by Williams and Morrow (2009):

1. Establishing the integrity of the data,
2. Balancing the tension between subjectivity and reflexivity, and
3. Clearly communicating the findings and their applicability to research and practice.

In this chapter, we review these three criteria, paying particular attention to the specific strategies that consensual qualitative researchers can use to establish the trustworthiness of their data.

## Integrity of the Data

Researchers can use several strategies to substantiate the integrity of the data. Among these are providing details about the methods, triangulating methods, looking for saturation, and thinking about generalizability.

### PROVIDING DETAILS ABOUT THE METHODS

The integrity, or dependability (Patton, 2002), of the data refers to the clear description of both the methods and the results (e.g., do the results answer the research questions and do they provide sufficient detail?). A first critical step in establishing the integrity of the data is to provide enough methodological detail in the research report to allow for replication of the study's procedures (though not necessarily its results). In a consensual qualitative research (CQR) study, authors should describe

- the research team members in detail,
- the research team's biases and expectations,
- evidence regarding the adequacy of the sample,
- the interview protocol (and consider providing a copy in the appendix of the report),
- the recruitment strategy used (and its success rate),
- the interview process itself (by whom, where, how long, how recorded),
- the transcription process,
- the specific process followed in the data analysis (and how clearly the procedures followed the CQR approach in particular),
- attempts at establishing stability of the data (e.g., that new cases do not add significant new categories to the findings), and

■ any other details of the study that other researchers would need to know to replicate the study.

An excellent example of a CQR study that describes these factors is Knox, Burkard, Edwards, Smith, and Schlosser (2008). These authors provided a full description of the research team, including providing an overview of their biases as an appendix. Also in an appendix is the full interview protocol, and the authors provided a good deal of information about the interview process itself (including the piloting of the protocol) and about the recruitment strategy used for the sample.

## TRIANGULATING METHODS

Williams and Morrow (2009) also noted the use of triangulation as a strategy for establishing the integrity of qualitative data. *Triangulation* is the use of multiple (mixed) methods for collecting data (e.g., written surveys, interviews, physiological measures) and the collection of different participant perspectives (e.g., asking clients and therapists to respond to the same interview questions about a session). If results are not consistent, then researchers need to conduct further research to determine if discrepancies are due to the methods or perspectives. As an example from CQR research, Williams, Judge, Hill and Hoffman (1997) studied novice therapists' attempts to manage their reactions in counseling sessions. They collected data from the clients, the therapists themselves, and the therapists' supervisors. They also used both quantitative surveys (e.g., ratings of anxiety and self-efficacy) and written, open-ended interview questions. Such triangulation ensured a more complete representation of the therapists' strategies over the course of a prepracticum course in graduate school. If results are consistent across methods and perspectives, researchers can begin to feel more confident about the data.

## CHECKING FOR SATURATION

Williams and Morrow (2009) also recommended the use of theoretical saturation for establishing trustworthiness. Glaser and Strauss (1967) described *theoretical saturation* as the point where no new data emerge in the study, where the "researcher becomes empirically confident" (p. 65) in the findings. Thus, saturation demands that researchers have collected enough data to ensure stability in the domains and categories that emerged in their data sets and have linked the data to the research questions and theoretical underpinnings of the research. In CQR, this type of saturation has usually been referred to as *stability of findings* (Hill, Thompson, & Williams, 1997, p. 552). To establish stability, CQR researchers have sometimes withheld one or two cases from the cross-analysis; when those cases are added into the analysis, the researchers can check to determine whether there are any "substantial changes" (defined by Hill et al., 1997, as creating a change in category designation, such as moving a category from variant to typical). Although this procedure for establishing stability has merit, it has not often been very helpful for CQR studies in particular. Because all the interviews in a CQR study are typically collected prior to data analysis to ensure consistency across cases, it is not usually feasible for researchers to collect new data if the analysis indicates that the results are not stable. Furthermore, there are no clear standards for what constitutes stability—how much the withheld cases need to add for the results to be considered unstable. Given these concerns, Hill et al. (2005) suggested that researchers no longer attempt to use stability checks in this way.

Rather than a stability check, researchers can use other methods to establish integrity. First, researchers generally try to include a relatively large sample (about 13 to 15 participants) that is relatively homogeneous so that they are more likely to obtain consistent findings (see Chapter 6 in this volume). Second, researchers work hard to connect the individual results to the overarching categories determined by the cross-analysis. This task is usually done by presenting exemplar core ideas or using quotes from the data. A good example can be found in Hayes et al.'s (1998) study on therapist countertransference. The authors presented information within and across cases about the frequency of categories found in the cross-analysis, included numerous quotes in the results, and provided summaries of their eight cases. Their connection of the individual cases to the overall findings gave a strong sense of the applicability of the emerging categories as well as good documentation of the integrity of the data.

## DETERMINING THE GENERALIZABILITY OF THE FINDINGS

CQR researchers often struggle with the issue of generalizability as it applies to trustworthiness in qualitative research. Given that CQR studies use small samples that may not perfectly represent the population and rely on rich, descriptive data, it is often hard to generalize results beyond the specific sample of participants and researchers. In fact, some qualitative researchers use the term *transferability* instead of *generalizability*. Transferability is fostered when researchers provide detailed information about the participants and the research process so that readers can judge whether findings might transfer to other settings. In pursuing transferability, we try to select participants randomly from a well-defined and fairly homogenous population, and we use relatively large samples (relative to other qualitative approaches). We note, as well, that participants for a CQR study are selected not because they fulfill the representative requirements of statistical inference, and thus generalizability, but because they can speak in detail about the experience under investigation (Polkinghorne, 2005). We also resolve seeming contradictions in the data, account for all data from each participant, provide examples to illustrate the findings, and respond to questions about the fit of findings with the data (Fischer, 2006). In addition, the strength of qualitative inquiry is more linked with the information richness of the cases selected and the observational and analytical capabilities of the researchers than with sample size (Patton, 1990).

Moreover, although generalizability in a more strictly quantitative sense has referred to generalizing findings beyond a sample to the population, CQR researchers find it is important to establish the typicality of the findings within a study. We demonstrate typicality by indicating the frequency with which categories emerge in the study: *general* (applies to all or all but one case in the sample), *typical* (applies to more than half of the cases), and *variant* (applies to less than half of the cases). It would be difficult to defend the trustworthiness of a study that had only variant categories in a CQR study because those categories are not reflective of even the sample used in that particular study. Given that the presence of only variant categories sometimes reflects variability within the sample, researchers might try dividing the sample (if it is large enough) and see whether more general or typical results emerge. Though not all studies find general categories, the existence of typical categories also argues for the existence of some theoretical saturation of the data.

## *Reflexivity and Subjectivity*

Once the integrity of the data has been established, CQR researchers can turn their attention to balancing the tension between what the participants say and how the researchers interpret their responses. Qualitative research, indeed any research, is inherently subjective (i.e., never truly objective). Subjectivity enters into the research questions we decide to ask (or not ask), the responses of the participants (and their non-responses), and the researchers' attempts at accurately representing the participants' views. Because of this inherent subjectivity, CQR researchers must be careful to explore and manage (where possible) their biases and expectations (see also Chapter 5, this volume). Rennie (2004) labeled this process of exploring and managing biases and expectations as *reflexivity*, or an awareness of self. Thus, researchers must remain aware of their own biases, interpretive lenses, and expectational sets and attempt to differentiate between what the participants really "mean" and how the researchers perceive that information. This process is akin to therapists' attempts to keep a clear perspective on what the client brings to a session and what the therapist must "own" as his or her own issues.

To manage these threats to our ability to clearly represent our participants' voices, CQR researchers have typically used the strategy of *bracketing* (or being aware of and setting aside) their biases and expectations (Hill et al., 2005). As an example of how CQR researchers have attempted to manage this balance between subjectivity and reflexivity, Knox, Hess, Williams and Hill (2003) grappled with the difficulties of protecting participants' confidentiality (in terms of balancing how much detail to present in the research paper) and with the complexities of understanding the meaning to therapists of their clients' gifts with the overlying reactions of the research team to particular gifts and therapists responses. The sheer volume of the data obtained in this study necessitated a clear and dynamic exploration of the research team's understanding of the various therapists' perceptions of and feelings about the gifts they received. Because some of the gifts were quite large and sometimes surprising, the research team had to work to ensure that their own reactions (whether a gift was "too" large or expensive, whether a gift was "inappropriate" or "out there") were separated from the therapists' perceptions of the gifts they had received from their clients. With such a charged topic, the researchers found an even greater need, and therefore responsibility, to identify their own subjective responses and stay true to the participants' voices, meanings, and interpretations.

One way that CQR researchers have addressed this need to balance reflexivity and subjectivity is by having multiple team members and auditors. CQR is built on the concept of consensus and the idea that multiple perspectives will help ensure a truer representation of the participants' meanings. As Hill et al. (1997) stated, "The assumption is that multiple perspectives increase our approximation of the 'truth' and are more likely to be free from researcher bias" (p. 523; see also Marshall & Rossman, 1989). Not only do group members on the primary research team help individuals clarify their own perceptions and interpretations of the data, but having external auditors provides an additional layer of review. In the event that a research team has developed groupthink (Janis, 1982) related to some aspect of the study, the auditors may be able to raise that issue and ask the research team to reconsider whether they have clearly and correctly represented the participants' voices in the analysis.

## Clear Communication of Findings

Williams and Morrow (2009) emphasized that researchers must present their results and the meaning of those results clearly and with purpose. Clarity goes beyond the strictly grammatical level of the writing (though such clarity is indeed important). Communicating the findings with clarity includes ensuring that the readers have enough information to know what was found and what relationship the findings have to broader theoretical issues, past research, and implications of the findings.

One way that researchers can clearly present the implications of their findings is to tie their results explicitly to the purpose for conducting the study. Williams and Morrow (2009) noted several specific purposes that qualitative researchers might emphasize particularly in psychotherapy research. First, researchers could describe how their findings could be used to improve psychotherapy process or outcome, including psychotherapy, training, and supervision processes. For example, Hill, Sullivan, Knox, and Schlosser (2007) examined the developmental experiences of novice therapists in their process of training to be psychotherapists. The reason for the study and the conclusions drawn were based on the desire to provide ideas for enhancements to clinical supervision and training. On the basis of their findings, they suggested four implications for training: to continue a focus on helping skills training beyond an initial semester of practicum work; the continued use of intensive supervision; specific training, including experiential exercises, for helping novice therapists learn to manage their internal processes (such as anxieties and self-talk); and specific skills training for helping novice therapists process emotional reactions in therapy.

Second, CQR researchers could establish the limitations of a particular therapeutic or methodological approach. For example, Ladany et al. (in press) tested whether two different teams working on the same data would arrive at the same conclusions. Specifically, they studied the topic of corrective emotional experiences of supervisees in supervision. Results (shown in more depth in Chapter 9 of this volume) indicated that there was both considerable overlap and considerable divergence in the findings between the two teams. These results suggest to us that CQR is indeed a subjective process and that different teams will indeed view data in different ways. Given that these two teams were all trained together and shared relatively similar backgrounds (i.e., all were White and from the United States), we would expect even bigger differences in the results between research teams that come from different cultures or have team members with widely different worldviews.

Third, the research findings could be used to encourage a further dialogue, such as between researchers and practitioners. For example, Castonguay et al. (2010) described the use of a practice research network (PRN) and interviewed the participants of the network to determine what researchers and practitioners could learn from each other. They were able to identify difficulties that psychotherapists experience when participating in research (such as added time and effort) but also the benefits of doing so (such as gaining new knowledge, the utility of the findings for clinical practice, and feeling good about collaborations and contributions made). What is perhaps most exciting about this study is that it provided a venue in which this important dialogue could occur and in which psychotherapists could give researchers advice on conducting future PRN studies.

Finally, the research could be used to suggest a new course of action (such as a change to research procedures or psychotherapeutic methods). For example, Tuason, Taylor, Rollings, Harris, and Martin (2007) used CQR methodology to explore an understudied group, Filipino Americans. They investigated the different experiences of Filipino immigrants to the United States and U.S.-born Filipino Americans. They summarized the impact of their findings in the following way: "This study's relevance lies in its understanding of Filipino Americans in an empowering way— these definitions of ethnic identity are shaped *by* them instead of *for* them" (p. 370). Such constructivist approaches to understanding personal identities can help facilitate better understanding of different cultural groups and can assist researchers in the exploration of cultural issues in ways that allow the participants to lead and contribute extensively to the findings.

Whatever the research purpose, we encourage CQR researchers to clearly tie their findings to theory (where possible) and to the previous literature. Above all, CQR researchers should address the context of their findings (the particular strengths and limitations of the sample, the setting, the researchers, the procedures). Because qualitative research relies on the full and detailed description of individual perspectives, such understanding of context is a critical element to understanding the complexity of the findings. Such an understanding is aided by the "thick descriptions" (Ponterotto & Grieger, 2007) usually found in qualitative research and by a clear establishing of the trustworthiness of the study.

## Conclusions

Establishing the trustworthiness of CQR data is important to convince readers that the researchers have valiantly and honorably tried to collect, analyze, and report the data. Given that readers cannot be present to look over researchers' shoulders during each step of the process, readers need to be able to trust that what the researchers did was reasonable and appropriate.

We encourage further dialogue about the issue of trustworthiness. Finding innovative ways to demonstrate trustworthiness could advance the credibility of the CQR method in the scientific community. For example, new methods such as qualitative meta-analysis (see Chapter 12), which enable us to summarize results across studies, could help establish the trustworthiness of individual studies. If consistent results are found across studies, we can feel more certain that individual studies were conducted in a trustworthy manner. In contrast, if inconsistent results are found, we might suspect that either a given study was not conducted in a trustworthy manner or that characteristics of the samples or data collection varied across studies. If we find specific practices that lead to untrustworthy results, we can begin to clarify those aspects of the method.

## *References*

Arminio, J. L., & Hultgren, F. H. (2002). Breaking out of the shadow: The question of criteria in qualitative research. *Journal of College Student Development, 43*, 446–460.

Castonguay, L. G., Nelson, D. L., Boutselis, M. A., Chiswick, N. R., Damer, D. D., Hemmelstein, N. A., . . . Borkovec, T. D. (2010). Psychotherapists, researchers, or both? A qualitative analysis of psychotherapists' experiences in a practice research network. *Psychotherapy: Theory, Research, Practice, Training, 47*, 345–354. doi:10.1037/a0021165

Choudhuri, D., Glauser, A., & Peregoy, J. (2004). Guidelines for writing a qualitative manuscript for the *Journal of Counseling & Development. Journal of Counseling and Development, 82*, 443–446.

Elliott, R., Fischer, C. T., & Rennie, D. L. (1999). Evolving guidelines for publication of qualitative research studies in psychology and related fields. *British Journal of Clinical Psychology, 38*, 215–229. doi:10.1348/014466599162782

Fischer, C. T. (2006). *Qualitative research methods for psychologists: Introduction through empirical case studies.* San Diego, CA: Academic Press.

Glaser, B., & Strauss, A. L. (1967). *The discovery of grounded theory: Strategies for qualitative research.* Hawthorne, NY: Aldine de Gruyter.

Guba, E. (1981). Criteria for assessing the trustworthiness of naturalistic inquiries. *Educational Communication and Technology Journal, 29*, 75–91. doi:10.1007/BF02766777

Hayes, J. A., McCracken, J. E., McClanahan, M. K., Hill, C. E., Harp, J. S., & Carozzoni, P. (1998). Therapist perspectives on countertransference: Qualitative data in search of a theory. *Journal of Counseling Psychology, 45*, 468–482. doi:10.1037/0022-0167.45.4.468

Hill, C. E., Knox, S., Thompson, B. J., Williams, E. N., Hess, S.A., & Ladany, N. (2005). Consensual Qualitative Research: An update. *Journal of Counseling Psychology, 52*, 196-205. doi:10.1037/0022-0167.52.2.196

Hill, C. E., Sullivan, C., Knox, S., & Schlosser, L. Z. (2007). Becoming psychotherapists: Experiences of novice trainees in a beginning graduate class. *Psychotherapy: Theory, Research, Practice, Training, 44,* 434–449. doi:10.1037/0033-3204.44.4.434

Hill, C. E., Thompson, B. J., & Williams, E. N. (1997). A guide to conducting consensual qualitative research. *The Counseling Psychologist, 25,* 517–572. doi:10.1177/0011000097254001

Hoyt, W. T., & Bhati, K. S. (2007). Principles and practices: An empirical examination of qualitative research in the *Journal of Counseling Psychology. Journal of Counseling Psychology, 54,* 201–210. doi:10.1037/0022-0167.54.2.201

Janis, I. L. (1982). *Groupthink* (2nd ed.). Boston, MA: Houghton-Mifflin.

Knox, S., Burkard, A. W., Edwards, L., Smith, J., & Schlosser, L. Z. (2008). Supervisors' reports of the effects of supervisor self-disclosure on supervisees. *Psychotherapy Research, 18,* 543–559. doi:10.1080/10503300801982781

Knox, S., Hess, S. A., Williams, E. N., & Hill, C. E. (2003). "Here's a little something for you": How therapists respond to client gifts. *Journal of Counseling Psychology, 50,* 199–210. doi:10.1037/0022-0167.50.2.199

Ladany, N., Inman, A., Burkard, A. W., Crook-Lyon, R., Hess, S. A., Hill, C. E., . . . Williams, E. N. (in press). Corrective relational experiences in supervision: Tests of differences between research teams. In L. G. Castonguay & C. E. Hill (Eds.), *Transformation in psychotherapy: Corrective experiences across cognitive behavioral, humanistic, and psychodynamic approaches.* Washington, DC: American Psychological Association.

Morrow, S. L. (2005). Quality and trustworthiness in qualitative research in counseling psychology. *Journal of Counseling Psychology, 52,* 250–260. doi:10.1037/0022-0167.52.2.250

Patton, M. Q. (1990). *Qualitative evaluation and research methods* (2nd ed.). Thousand Oaks, CA: Sage.

Patton, M. Q. (2002). *Qualitative evaluation and research methods* (3rd ed.). Thousand Oaks, CA: Sage.

Polkinghorne, D. E. (2005). Language and meaning: Data collection in qualitative research. *Journal of Counseling Psychology, 52,* 137–145. doi:10.1037/0022-0167.52.2.137

Ponterotto, J. G., & Grieger, I. (2007). Effectively communicating qualitative research. *The Counseling Psychologist, 35,* 404–430. doi:10.1177/0011000006287443

Rennie, D. L. (2004). Reflexivity and person-centered counseling. *Journal of Humanistic Psychology, 44,* 182–203. doi:10.1177/0022167804263066

Stiles, W. B. (1993). Quality control in qualitative research. *Clinical Psychology Review, 13,* 593–618. doi:10.1016/0272-7358(93)90048-Q

Tuason, M. T. G., Taylor, A. R., Rollings, L., Harris, T., & Martin, C. (2007). On both sides of the hyphen: Exploring the Filipino-American identity. *Journal of Counseling Psychology, 54,* 362–372. doi:10.1037/0022-0167.54.4.362

Williams, E. N., Judge, A. B., Hill, C. E., & Hoffman, M. A. (1997). Experiences of novice therapists in prepracticum: Trainees', clients', and supervisors' perceptions of therapists' personal reactions and management strategies. *Journal of Counseling Psychology, 44,* 390–399. doi:10.1037/0022-0167.44.4.390

Williams, E. N., & Morrow, S. L. (2009). Achieving trustworthiness in qualitative research: A pan-paradigmatic perspective. *Psychotherapy Research, 19,* 576–582. doi:10.1080/10503300802702113

*Arpana G. Inman, Erin E. Howard, and Clara E. Hill*

# Considerations Related to Culture in Consensual Qualitative Research

14

G iven the focus on languaged data in qualitative research (Polkinghorne, 2005) and the constructivist emphasis of consensual qualitative research (CQR; Hill et al., 2005), the culture of the individual participants and researchers is central in understanding data yielded by CQR. The major goal of this chapter is thus to explore CQR through a cultural lens and, in particular, to offer some considerations for implementing CQR in light of cultural issues. To begin, we highlight the importance of situating research within a cultural context. We then address cultural issues relevant to the construction and functioning of the research team, the development of research questions, sampling and data collection, interpretation of data, and data validity and trustworthiness.

## Context

The choice of an etic (e.g., nomothetic) or an emic (idiographic) framework has typically guided researchers with regard to their beliefs about the world, the specific area of study, the choice of participants, the method of data analysis, and interpretation used in the study (Denzin & Lincoln, 2000; Ponterotto, 2005). An etic perspective highlights universal behaviors with a view that there is one external objective reality, whereas an emic perspective emphasizes a culture-specific approach. Thus, an etic approach has been associated with quantitative research, whereas an emic perspective has been connected with qualitative research. We would assert, however, that although researchers may begin with an etic perspective, in fact all research is grounded in a cultural or emic context (Inman, 2008) given that culture is central to our work as researchers. Culture structures and orients our personal experiences and interpretation of reality (Ani, 1994). The assumptions and values that evolve from our cultural experiences influence how communication is given and received (Hardy & Laszloffy, 1992).

An important assumption that flows from this perspective is that of *constructivism*, that "people not only construct their own realities but that there are multiple and equally valid socially constructed versions of 'the truth'" (Hill et al., 2005, p. 197). A unique feature of a constructivist paradigm is that the researchers are an inherent part of the data analytic process, and the meaning that is created from the data is a function of a dialectical interaction between the researchers and participants (Ponterotto, 2005). In essence, the researcher and the participant cocreate and interpret the experience from an emic perspective and through an idiographic lens (Ponterotto, 2005).

Recognizing how one's own personal experiences (e.g., biases) as well as conceptual and theoretical assumptions or beliefs (e.g., expectations) influence research topics and questions, participant selection, interpretation of data, and subsequent development of theories (Hill et al., 2005; LeCompte & Preissle, 2003) is critical in CQR. In light of this, practicing cultural self-reflexivity or self-awareness (e.g., situating oneself in terms of one's gendered, ethnic, and other cultural identities) can increase awareness of how the researcher's own culture, personal agendas, and blind spots influence how research questions are developed, presented, and probed. Thus, whether engaged in studies on cultural phenonema or research in general, efforts need to be made by the research team to stay aware of these contextual influences and discuss them throughout data analysis (see Table 14.1).

## Construction and Functioning of the Research Team

A central aspect of CQR is the selection as well as the functioning of the research team. Specifically, CQR calls for multiple judges along with an auditor or auditors. Such multimember teams help to reflect both common and minority viewpoints (Miller, 1989) and thus, it is hoped, yield

## TABLE 14.1

**Recommendations for Taking Culture Into Consideration in Consensual Qualitative Research**

| Step | Recommendations |
| --- | --- |
| Context | Frame research within a cultural context. |
| | Acknowledge that both participants and researchers present multiple and equally valid socially-constructed realities. |
| | Practice cultural self-reflexivity or self-awareness by situating selves on multiple cultural axes. |
| | Demonstrate in manuscript how awareness of researchers' culture, personal agendas, and blind spots influenced how research questions were developed, presented, and probed. |
| Research team | Include members from diverse educational, methodological experience, and cultural backgrounds. |
| | Identify benefits and challenges of how team's cultural makeup informed various processes. |
| | Attend to power dynamics related to culture. |
| Research questions | Ascertain how research questions reflect community being studied. |
| | Pilot research questions with participant sample to determine cultural applicability of constructs. |
| Sampling | Be purposeful and theoretical. |
| | Consider cultural values/norms that may influence entry into community. |
| Data collection | Clarify logistics with participants. |
| | Be attuned to voice inflections, when to allow silences, and when to probe. |
| Understanding the data | Produce accurately translated data. |
| | Consider how language may inform data analysis. |
| | Be aware of the multiple meanings of words in language. |
| Trustworthiness | Identify ethical responsibility in relation to participants. |
| | Establish rapport through immersion into participant's culture. |
| | Explore in depth if an issue or term is unclear to a participant. |
| | Clarify how participant or participant's community will be involved in assessing trustworthiness of data. |
| | Stay close to the data by using participants' quotes. |

better quality decision making (Michaelsen, Watson, & Black, 1989; Sundstrom, Busby, & Bobrow, 1997). In addition, the ability to view data from varying perspectives can bring to the forefront the subtle meanings, complexities, and ambiguities that exist in data (Hill et al., 2005). Although the potential implications of having members diverse in educational level and methodological experience have been noted within CQR (Hill et al., 2005), minimal attention has been paid to how the cultural composition of the research team influences the research process.

Recent CQR studies investigating cultural phenomena have highlighted the need to question how cultural demographics of the research team may inform the various processes in research (e.g., Inman, Howard, Beaumont, & Walker, 2007). This concern has come about because of queries such as how a member's cultural identification influences the team as a whole and how it influences the analytic process, what the benefits of personal familiarity or identification with the topic of study are, and how cultures influence research expectations and biases. When culturally heterogeneous teams have one team member who identifies with participants' culture or with the cultural phenomenon of study, is it important to consider the differences in power dynamics that might exist, especially when assumptions are made about team members' "expert status" regarding what is being studied.

Incorporating research team members who have some level of cultural immersion in the topic or research community promotes "using the self as an instrument of inquiry" (McCracken, 1988, p. 32). Having lived within the culture under study provides familiarity with the topic, creates an advantage in that the researcher has an intimate knowledge of the subject matter, and allows the researcher to identify issues or concepts not identified by the literature (McCracken, 1988). For example, in studies examining the experience of Asian Americans post-9/11 (Inman, Yeh, Madan-Bahel, & Nath, 2007; Yeh, Inman, Kim, & Okubo, 2006), efforts were made to have a team that had not only conducted research in the area of Asian American issues but that was also representative of the different Asian American communities. This representation allowed for an authentic discussion of Asian American experiences from different generational as well as cultural perspectives.

Conversely, having members from different cultural backgrounds might allow for greater exposure, increased knowledge, and a healthy dialogue about potential biases and blind spots than would occur if all the researchers were immersed in the same culture. For instance, in Inman, Howard, et al.'s (2007) study of ethnic identity transmission in Asian Indian immigrant parents, the primary research team included an Asian Indian female who had immigrated to the United States as an adult and two U.S.-born Caucasian females who identified with Irish and German Irish heritage. This heterogeneous nature of the team forced the Asian Indian researcher to actively examine her own cultural biases and understanding of her culture, whereas it required the two non-Asian Indian team members to familiarize themselves with participants' accents and produce more accurate verbatim transcripts, understand the role of circuitous response tendencies (e.g., storytelling), and learn the meanings of some unique culture-specific language used by participants (e.g., *pujas,* or religious services; *stotras,* or prayers and hymns). In addition, the influence of gender (given that it was an all-female research team) on the interview and research process was also a point of discussion. Approaching analysis from these different perspectives meant that team members often varied in their initial interpretations of the data, which contributed to a healthy amount of disagreement and a rich consensus-building process. This variety of perspectives required ongoing discussion about how team members' own cultural values and differences in familiarity with Asian Indian culture and gender issues affected interpretations of the data, and shaped power dynamics in the consensus process.

Given the emphasis on the consensual process in CQR, managing power dynamics is an important element in building a strong research team. To address issues of power, it helps to have team members take turns leading the discussion and to include time in team meetings for members to talk about their perceptions of the consensual analytic process (see also Chapter 4, this volume). Furthermore, when culturally heterogeneous teams have one team member who identifies with participants' culture or with the cultural phenomenon of study, it is important to consider how the differences in power dynamics can affect the consensus-building process within a team. When team members hold varying positions of power (e.g., faculty members vs. graduate students, people from cultural backgrounds that traditionally differ in deference to authority, or people from cultures that differ in valuing a collective vs. an individualistic orientation), a truly egalitarian consensus-building process may not be automatic! Rather, certain assumptions may exist about team members' expert status that can impact the analytic process and, ultimately, how data are interpreted.

In sum, we assert that cultural issues influence the functioning of the research team. Thus, CQR researchers, regardless of the topic of study, should be conscious of the possible contributions or hindrances that can evolve from cultural assumptions (Juntunen et al., 2001).

# Development of Research Questions

Research questions need to be assessed for their cultural applicability to the community being researched to ensure that they are reflective of the experience of that community (Yeh & Inman, 2007). For instance, in a current investigation examining the experience of racism among first- and second-generation Asian Indians conducted by Inman and her colleagues, interviews were piloted with both generations. One particular research question related to participants' socialization to racism. The researchers were interested in how issues of racism were dealt with at home in the upbringing of both first- and second-generation Asian Indians. Through the piloting of the interview, the authors realized that because first-generation participants grew up in India, their responses to this question may have been constricted. On the basis of feedback, the idea of asking both groups about messages in the family while growing up in India and in their family postimmigration was explored. The ensuing discussion brought to the forefront an important cohort–generational distinction that may have been lost had authors not piloted the interview and received feedback.

Similarly, in a study on international advisee perspectives in advising relationships conducted by Inman and her colleagues, the semistructured interview was piloted to assess the cultural relevance of the questions. Within the piloted sample, one student was from Canada and a second was from India. Despite both identifying as international students, the cultural similarity between Canada and the United States and the differences between India and the United States highlighted the significant differences in the acculturation and adjustment processes for the two students. In particular, the international student from Canada noted fewer challenges because of the student's familiarity with the education system compared with the student from India. These cultural nuances helped the research team define and reevaluate the criteria for sample selection as well as phrase the questions used in the study.

## *Sampling and Data Collection*

In CQR, the selection of a sample should be purposeful (i.e., specific to the population being studied) as well as theoretical (i.e., grounded in conceptually relevant constructs; Strauss & Corbin, 1990). However, when conducting research that is culturally congruent, issues related to recruitment, confidentiality, and anonymity are also critical. As such, the relationship that develops between the interviewer and participant in qualitative research is very important and not unlike the working alliance needed in working within clinical practice (Heppner, Kivlighan, & Wampold, 1999; Yeh & Inman, 2007). We have found that recruiting participants from a minority community must be based on developing an emotional bond with the participant. For example, in researching the experience of 9/11 in the South Asian community (e.g., Inman, Yeh, et al., 2007), it became apparent that the Asian Indian cultural norm against sharing sensitive information with strangers influenced the recruitment process. Specifically, caregivers, service providers, and researchers who were not immersed in the culture or well versed in its cultural values were viewed as being insensitive to the cultural norms. For instance, one participant spoke about the insensitivity on the part of a caregiver who suggested that the participant was still young and could remarry. Although a comment such as this so early in the grieving process is insensitive irrespective of the culture one comes from, the idea of remarriage is not something easily ventured into in the Asian Indian community. Not being aware of this cultural nuance made this participant reticent about seeking additional assistance or being open to speaking with other non-Indian personnel. Thus, beyond understanding cultural values, developing a relationship prior to conducting research or providing a service was important in that it allowed for greater trust and access into the community. Understanding this cultural norm was an important aspect of recruitment and continuation of the study.

Similarly, the relationship between the interviewer and interviewee is important when conducting interviews over the telephone (Heppner et al., 1999). Without access to nonverbal information, the potential for increased misunderstandings due to cultural differences can be great. For example, when interviewing participants for the 9/11 study (Inman, Yeh, et al., 2007), telephone interviews were conducted within the United States and across continents. Apart from being clear about the logistics of the interview (e.g., how long it would last, what steps would be taken if the interviewer and caller became disconnected), managing the potentially awkward issues related to informed consent and audio recording (e.g., verbalizing when the recording is beginning and ending), given the sensitive nature of the topic, was important in orienting the participants and preventing potential misunderstandings. Furthermore, being attuned to voice inflections or pace of speech, especially when topics are emotionally charged and culture specific, is an important consideration when nonverbal cues are absent or not easily accessible. Focusing on such paralanguage can further help guide when to use or allow silence and when to seek clarification in the interview process.

A final consideration is that of interviewing in the native language of the participant. Being able to express one's thoughts in one's own language can be powerful and more meaningful for the participant. When the language of the interview is the participant's second language, grammatical errors, intended meanings, or lack of access to words in the new language may create challenges not only for the participant but also for later examination of the data. Having a research team member who is bilingual and well versed in both the native language and the language into which the interview is to be translated is very important. Not only does the process allow for a greater emotional connection between participant and researcher but also promotes more in-depth and accurate probing of participants. Such clarity in communication and "relational interconnectedness between researcher and participant can contribute to shared understandings and perspectives that foster [more] accurate interpretations" (Yeh & Inman, 2007, p. 381).

## *Understanding the Data*

Cultural contexts provide a window into how people perceive, internalize, and project their experiences. In particular, expression of experiences is intricately tied to patterns of communication (e.g., direct or indirect) and language (e.g., word choices, phrases) and thus become important considerations when interpreting and analyzing culturally informed data (Denzin & Lincoln, 2000; Yeh & Inman, 2007). For instance, in studies exploring how Asians and South Asians coped with the 9/11 tragedy (Inman, Yeh, et al., 2007; Yeh et al., 2006) and how Asian Indians transmitted cultural values and cultural identity to their children (Inman, Howard et al., 2007), participants tended to be circuitous in their responses and to share their thoughts through cultural metaphors and stories. In Inman, Howard, et al.'s (2007) study about cultural transmission of Asian Indian ethnic identity, participants were asked to describe factors that contributed to their sense of ethnic identity. Many participants shared specific experiences and stories about food (e.g., trying cheese for the first time, looking for Indian food grocery stores) to convey how central the value of vegetarianism was to their ethnic identity. The process of condensing these stories and extracting their critical meaning (e.g., the novelty of eating in a new country, challenges in retaining cultural identity in a new society) required careful line-by-line examination of the data as well as consideration of the meaning of the story as a whole.

Furthermore, accurately translating culture-specific language is critical in data analysis. For instance, in Inman, Yeh, et al.'s (2007) study on the 9/11 experience of South Asians, one of the participants used the word *mann*. In Hindi, *mann* can refer to the mind, heart, soul, and/or consciousness. Thus, the phrase "Mann nahi karta" can mean "My heart is not in it because of feeling sad," "[I] don't feel like it because I am not interested," or "I am bored because I have nothing to do" (Yeh & Inman, 2007, p. 380). As is evident in these examples, language "can illuminate or conceal narrative realities that have personal and political implications" (Hoshmand, 2005, p. 184) and thus pose significant challenges in the translation and interpretation processes. Having at least one team member who was fluent with the language, being aware of the multiple meanings that this phrase can have, and probing further for clarification during the interview were all critical factors in connecting with the participants and in picking up on the contextual nature of these data.

The importance of translating culturally based data can be seen especially when words in other languages have no direct translation in English. For example, in our research on the cultural transmission of

Asian Indian ethnic identity (Inman, Howard, et al., 2007), one of our participants used the term *madi*, referring to a religiously based practice. This term has no exact English counterpart, which affected our ability to fully reflect this participant's experiences. At the simplest level, in the Kannada language, *madi* refers to elders in the family not allowing anybody to enter the kitchen without bathing. However, this concept can also extend to prohibiting menstruating women from entering religious spaces, having sexual relations during menstruation, and eating certain types of foods. Although these connotations stem from long-held cultural beliefs and anecdotes rather than scientific study, the research team's understanding of *madi* and its varied implications was important in being able to provide an insider's perspective about the meaning. In addition, translating words or metaphors (e.g., "hitting a home run from third base") from their original language can decrease the potency that such phrases have in their original forms. Within this context, language is not merely a mode of communication but a critical conduit for expressing cultural beliefs, emotions, and deeper meanings underlying participants' experiences (Santiago-Rivera & Altarriba, 2002). Thus, researchers might struggle with whether to retain the original language, translate to clarify the meaning, or consolidate the wording to distill the essential meaning of the data. Having bilingual research team members who can translate and back-translate (Brislin, 1980) as well as address appropriate semantics and construct validity of the concepts is important in addressing cultural nuances inherent in such research (Yeh & Inman, 2007).

## *Validity and Trustworthiness*

Issues of trustworthiness, representativeness, and coherence are particularly relevant in qualitative studies. Because methods of ensuring validity and trustworthiness in CQR are described in Chapter 13 in this volume, we focus here on issues of credibility, data display, and consequential validity within a cultural context.

As is the case in CQR and other kinds of qualitative studies, the most relevant and methodologically sound studies are those in which the participants' experiences are deeply explored, thoroughly and accurately interpreted, well-documented, and verified by the participants themselves. Researchers' ability to tap into and portray participants' phenomenological experiences, especially when the focus is on cultural-specific phenomena, can be quite challenging.

As we alluded to in our earlier discussion of language and translation issues, the establishment of rapport between the interviewer and participant is essential in obtaining credible data. Because participants are unlikely to engage in deep reflection and share personal matters (especially as related to cultural practices and identity) without feeling comfortable with the interviewer, we recommend that researchers think about issues of rapport from the point of initial contact. Apart from beginning each interview with at least two warm-up questions to help ease into a dialogue that more directly relates to the phenomena of study, we argue that some level of cultural immersion is required for valid data to both emerge and be construed accurately. Such intimacy is not only developed throughout the investigation but also by working directly with those members as an active participant.

During the interview, interviewers can work hard to clarify the meaning behind participants' statements, especially in the case of ambiguously described or very nuanced experiences. It is important that interviewers ask participants to expand on their responses or to "say a little more" about what they mean so that the research team does not have to "stretch" (e.g., speculate or interpret) to accurately code and organize the data.

Beyond this, we also emphasize the relevance of incorporating member checks (Hill, Thompson, & Williams, 1997; Lincoln & Guba, 1985) to ensure that the meaning participants intended to convey was accurately understood and translated by researchers. Thus, we routinely invite participants to review the transcripts of their interviews as well as the interpreted data, which not only serves to verify that participants' words were accurately heard and captured but also offers participants an opportunity to reflect on the interview content and clarify culturally nuanced responses. Furthermore, we recommend incorporating feedback from presentations to research professionals and to focus groups from the community being studied. By presenting the data to multiple audiences, the research team is forced to look deeper into the data to make sure they have understood it and are reflecting participant voices.

Relatedly, we strongly concur with Hill et al.'s (1997) original recommendation to integrate verbatim quotations in order to showcase participants' voices and stay "close to the data" (Hill et al., 1997, p. 197). Thus, maintaining culture-specific words can be critical; for instance, using the word *stotras* in our study on Asian Indian ethnic identity transmission (Inman, Howard, et al., 2007) allowed us to stay close to the data without distorting the voices of participants. Similarly, highlighting phrases and quoting participants (e.g., "I was blaming my own destiny. . . . It was not my age to become a widow at 27"; Inman, Yeh, et al., 2007, p. 106) not only portrayed the depth of the sentiment expressed by the participant but also stressed the potency of the data that would otherwise have been lost with just reporting core ideas.

In addition, the notion of consequential validity is also relevant when considering cultural phenomena. *Consequential validity* refers to a standard of validity that assesses the extent to which research can be a catalyst for social change and political action (Denzin & Lincoln, 2000,

p. 181). For example, in our studies on 9/11 (Inman, Yeh, et al., 2007; Yeh et al., 2006), we not only highlighted family experiences within the context of the 9/11 tragedy but also advocated for culturally relevant mental health and immigration policy changes through press conferences. It is with a focus on consequential validity that constructivist inquiry, an inherent aspect of CQR, starts to embody the cooperative or participative nature of research and present validity as an ethical relationship between participant and researcher (Lincoln & Guba, 2000).

# Conclusions

Because all communication (verbal or nonverbal, direct or indirect) is culturally situated, understanding research through a cultural lens is an important means of shedding light on the meanings behind voiced and unvoiced emotions, thoughts, and actions. We encourage researchers to make special efforts to maintain awareness of the interactive cultural dynamics among the research team and participants while keeping in mind the steps inherent to the research method itself throughout the investigative process. Cultural information can be so deeply embedded in one's experiences that team members may not talk about it, may not be consciously aware of it, and may take it for granted. Figuring out ways to study these dynamics in CQR presents new and exciting challenges for researchers.

# References

Ani, M. (1994). *Yurugu: An African centered critique of European cultural thought and behavior*. Trenton, NJ: African World Press.

Brislin, R. W. (1980). Translation and content analysis of oral and written materials. In H. Triandis & J. W. Berry (Eds.), *Handbook of cross-cultural psychology* (Vol. 2, pp. 389–444). Boston, MA: Allyn & Bacon.

Denzin, N. K., & Lincoln, Y. S. (2000). Introduction: The discipline and practice of qualitative research. In N. K. Denzin & Y. S. Lincoln (Eds.), *Handbook of qualitative research* (2nd ed., pp. 1–28). Thousand Oaks, CA: Sage.

Hardy, K., & Laszloffy, T. A. (1992). Training racially sensitive family therapists: Context, content, and contact. *Families in Society, 73*, 364–370. doi:10.1606/1044-3894.1711

Heppner, P. P., Kivlighan, D. M., & Wampold, B. E. (1999). *Research design in counseling* (2nd ed.). Belmont, CA: Wadsworth.

Hill, C. E., Knox, S., Thompson, B. J., Williams, E. N., Hess, S.A., & Ladany, N. (2005). Consensual qualitative research: An update. *Journal of Counseling Psychology, 52,* 196–205. doi:10.1037/0022-0167.52.2.196

Hill, C. E., Thompson, B. J., & Williams, E. N. (1997). A guide to conducting consensual qualitative research. *The Counseling Psychologist, 25,* 517–572. doi:10.1177/0011000097254001

Hoshmand, L. T. (2005). Narratology, cultural psychology, and counseling research. *Journal of Counseling Psychology, 52,* 178–186. doi:10.1037/0022-0167.52.2.178

Inman, A. G. (2008). Cross-cultural counseling: Etic–emic distinctions. In F. T. Leong (Ed.), *Encyclopedia of counseling* (Vol. 4, pp. 1144–1147). Thousand Oaks, CA: Sage.

Inman, A., Howard, E., Beaumont, R., & Walker, J. (2007). Cultural transmission: Influence of contextual factors in Asian Indian immigrant parents' experiences. *Journal of Counseling Psychology, 54*(1), 93–100. doi:10.1037/0022-0167.54.1.93

Inman, A., Yeh, C., Madan-Bahel, A., & Nath, S. (2007). Bereavement and coping of South Asian families post 9/11. *Journal of Multicultural Counseling and Development, 35*(2), 101–115.

Juntunen, C. L., Barraclough, D. J., Broneck, C. L., Seibel, G. A., Winrow, S. A., & Morin, P. M. (2001). American Indian perspectives on the career journey. *Journal of Counseling Psychology, 48,* 274–285. doi:10.1037/0022-0167.48.3.274

LeCompte, M. D., & Preissle, J. (2003). *Ethnography and qualitative design in educational research* (2nd ed.). New York, NY: Academic Press.

Lincoln, Y., & Guba, E. (1985). *Naturalistic inquiry.* New York, NY: Sage.

Lincoln, Y. S., & Guba, E. G. (2000). Paradigmatic controversies, contradictions, and emerging confluences. In N. K. Denzin & Y. S. Lincoln (Eds.), *Handbook of qualitative research* (2nd ed., pp. 163–188). Thousand Oaks, CA: Sage.

McCracken, G. (1988). *The long interview: Quantitative research methods* (Vol. 13). New Delhi, India: Sage.

Michaelsen, L. K., Watson, W. E., & Black, R. H. (1989). A realistic test of individual versus group consensus decision making. *Journal of Applied Psychology, 74,* 834–839. doi:10.1037/0021-9010.74.5.834

Miller, C. E. (1989). The social psychological effects of group decision rules. In P. Paulus (Ed.), *Psychology of group influence* (2nd ed., pp. 327–355). Hillsdale, NJ: Erlbaum.

Polkinghorne, D. E. (2005). Language and meaning: Data collection in qualitative research. *Journal of Counseling Psychology, 52,* 137–145. doi:10.1037/0022-0167.52.2.137

Ponterotto, J. G. (2005). Qualitative research in counseling psychology: A primer on research paradigms and philosophy of science. *Journal of Counseling Psychology, 52,* 126–136. doi:10.1037/0022-0167.52.2.126

Santiago-Rivera, A. L., & Altarriba, J. (2002). The role of language in therapy with the Spanish–English bilingual client. *Professional Psychology: Research and Practice, 33,* 30–38. doi:10.1037/0735-7028.33.1.30

Strauss, A., & Corbin, J. (1990). *Basics of qualitative research: Grounded theory procedures and techniques.* Newbury Park, CA: Sage.

Sundstrom, E., Busby, P. L., & Bobrow, W. S. (1997). Group process and performance: Interpersonal behaviors and decision quality in group problem solving by consensus. *Group Dynamics, 1,* 241–253. doi:10.1037/1089-2699.1.3.241

Yeh, C. J., & Inman, A. G. (2007). Qualitative data analysis and interpretations in counseling psychology: Strategies for best practices. *The Counseling Psychologist, 35,* 369–403. doi:10.1177/0011000006292596

Yeh, C. J., Inman, A., Kim, A. B., & Okubo, Y. (2006). Asian American families' collectivistic coping strategies in response to 9/11. *Cultural Diversity & Ethnic Minority Psychology, 12,* 134–148. doi:10.1037/1099-9809.12.1.134

*Alan W. Burkard, Sarah Knox, and Clara E. Hill*

# Ethical Considerations in Consensual Qualitative Research

15

T he American Psychological Association's (APA's) *Ethical Principles of Psychologists and Code of Conduct* (APA, 2010) provides psychotherapy researchers a foundation for ethical research practice and decision making. This ethical code is founded on five general principles (i.e., beneficence and non-maleficence, fidelity and responsibility, integrity, justice, and respect for people's rights and dignity) that our profession uses to uphold our ethical ideals and to protect the public. In addition, institutional review boards (IRBs) monitor ethical guidelines about research and now most require researchers to complete IRB and ethics training. Although the APA ethical code and IRBs offer specific guidelines for researchers, there are often additional challenges of specific concern to those engaged in consensual qualitative research (CQR). Thus, a discussion of the ethical considerations related to CQR is pertinent.

The unique features of CQR require researchers to familiarize themselves with ethical concerns that may not arise as much in other research methods. We have consistently found in our studies, for instance, that protecting participants' confidentiality as well as the confidentiality of others they may discuss takes on new meaning given the intimate experiences and details disclosed by participants. In the current chapter, we review some of the ethical considerations faced by CQR researchers in terms of the focus of the study, the research team, data collection, and presentation of the study's results. We also offer practical suggestions for how to address these concerns.

## The Focus of the Study

Some topics, by definition, are likely to raise ethical considerations (e.g., clients discussing a history of abuse; supervisors or therapists discussing boundary violations in which they have engaged); other topics, in contrast, may seem less vulnerable to ethical challenges but may nonetheless elicit them (e.g., clients giving gifts in therapy; students' dissertation experiences). In a study of doctoral students' perspectives on their dissertation experiences (Burkard et al., 2010), for example, one participant reported being sexually harassed by the participant's dissertation advisor. We discussed our concerns as a team and also consulted with the Ethics Office at APA. Although our team found the situation personally challenging, we recognized that the participant had the right to choose how, or whether, she or he wanted to address or proceed with the situation. We did, however, encourage the participant to pursue making an ethical complaint to APA. In addition, in a recently published investigation of clients' experiences of giving gifts to their therapists (Knox, Dubois, Smith, Hess, & Hill, 2009), one participant (i.e., therapy client) recalled giving hundreds of thousands of dollars' worth of gifts to her or his therapist, some of which the client felt had actually been solicited by the therapist and many of which were not returned when the client asked for them. Here, too, we discussed our concerns as a team, consulted with our university's IRB and also with APA's Ethics Office, and again found ourselves in the uncomfortable position of not being able to intervene on behalf of this client.

Some research topics may pose risks for participants—for example, when those participants are interviewed about their professional activities. In a study about supervisees' sexual attraction to their clients (Ladany et al., 1997), the researchers would have had to intervene if any participant disclosed unethical behavior toward a client. Although none reported such behavior, there may well have been a level of discomfort among them about discussing attraction with the researchers: They may have been concerned that the researchers would consider their treatment of the client compromised, thus possibly warranting intervention. Similarly, in a study of graduate students' experiences of becoming therapists (Hill, Sullivan, Knox, & Schlosser, 2007), the graduate-student participants, all from the same doctoral program, described in detail their perceptions of their first-semester training in basic therapy skills. In doing so, they likely realized that some of the researchers (i.e., those from the same doctoral program) would be able to identify them, and thus their anonymity was not assured. Furthermore, when they discussed elements of the training that they did not like or that they found ineffective, they may have feared repercussions from the faculty member involved because that faculty member not only taught the helping skills class but was also a researcher on the study. Although nothing untoward occurred as a result of the students' participation in this study, the risks were nevertheless present and needed to be considered carefully by the research team.

Given such incidents, which are quite typical in illustrating the potential for a research topic to elicit ethical concerns, our recommendations are not that researchers avoid such topics but rather that they carefully consider how to design studies to minimize potential problems and also how they will respond when inevitable concerns arise. Researchers thus should discuss early in the course of the study what ethical considerations might arise and how they will be addressed. And, when concerns do emerge, we recommend that researchers consult appropriate resources (e.g., their IRB, APA, attorneys) and document these consultations.

## *Research Team Considerations*

Researchers also need to consider the ethics of forming and developing a productive CQR team. We address several of these concerns in this section.

### RESEARCHER COMPETENCE

Developing CQR research competence (see the APA Ethics Code, 2.01a, Boundaries of Competence) may be challenging because CQR is somewhat difficult to learn without mentoring and training. In our own experience learning CQR, we found that we really only understood the process once we actually engaged in CQR studies. In addition, there are a number of skills that novice researchers must learn to become competent CQR researchers, such as conceptualizing a discovery-based qualitative study, developing an interview protocol, interviewing participants, learning how to respond to interview difficulties or distressed participants, analyzing and making sense of the data, and writing a manuscript. Because of space considerations, we cannot address each of these areas and thus focus on those most salient for a discussion of CQR-related ethics: qualitative interviews and data analysis.

## Competence in Interviewing

The interview process presents several challenges because of the close interpersonal contact between participant and researcher and the potential for errors that could be hurtful to participants. In a study of trainees' experiences of client suicide (Knox, Burkard, Jackson, Schaack, & Hess, 2006), for instance, one participant appeared to become anxious during the interview and took control of the interview by stating the interview questions, providing her or his answers, and not allowing the interviewer time to interject with follow-up probes for clarification. Without proper training, the interviewer could have made a number of errors, such as trying to interrupt the participant, confronting the participant, or changing to a therapeutic interview style rather than maintaining appropriate interview boundaries. In this example, we see the importance of developing competence to respond to such situations; the interviewer needs to maintain her or his focus on the interview topic, keep notes on areas for further exploration and probe those areas later in the interview, and remain patient with the participant. As another illustration of the potential ethical challenges of CQR interviewing, a participant disclosed a challenging and difficult supervision experience with a clinical supervisor (Burkard, Knox, Hess, & Schultz, 2009). During the discussion, the participant acknowledged the name of the supervisor, who happened to be an acquaintance of the interviewer, thus creating a dual-role relationship. Here, the interviewer stopped and informed the participant of the relationship, and the participant and interviewer discussed the appropriateness of proceeding with the interview. This situation highlights the interpersonal flexibility that is necessary to accommodate to changing circumstances during an interview.

Given the challenges of interviewing, we carefully screen potential interviewers for competency in interviewing skills, usually requiring considerable training as a therapist and excellent evaluations from supervisors. We have not set minimal levels of training that potential researchers must have prior to joining our teams. We have discovered, however, that some topics are less appropriate for inexperienced interviewers and then elected to work with experienced researchers on those research topics. For example, in a current study of the high school experiences of youth who identify as lesbian, gay, bisexual, or questioning (LGBQ; Burkard, Reynolds, Wurl, & Schultz, 2011), the two senior researchers determined that it would be important that interviewers have significant clinical experience working with LGBQ-identified youth to ensure their sensitivity and responsiveness to the life experiences and potential discrimination that participants may have experienced. Similarly, senior investigators of research teams may want to consider whether their topic or population of interest is appropriate for inexperienced interviewers.

We use a number of training methods to develop interview skills to minimize ethical concerns (see also Chapter 7, this volume). As a team, we review the research protocol, discuss the goals of the interview, and review effective interview strategies. Perhaps most important, we practice the interview process through role-plays, conducting practice and pilot interviews while under supervision, listening to recordings of more experienced interviewers, and debriefing after actual interviews (also see Fassinger, 2005, for additional ideas). We also anticipate the potential emotionality of some interviews and discuss participants' possible reactions as a team, role-play how to respond to these reactions and emotions, and identify how novice researchers can reach principal investigators during and following an interview when concerns do arise. Finally, we assess readiness and ability to interact with participants throughout the training phase of the study and prior to any interviews with actual participants. The assessment should focus on ability to maintain a focus on the research interview (vs. therapeutic interviewing), respond empathically to participants' emotions and experiences, follow up on distressed feelings, and facilitate appropriate referrals (if necessary) at the end of the interview. If a team member is not demonstrating competency after training, it may be necessary to provide additional training or remove the person from doing interviews.

## Competence in Data Analysis

Novice researchers often need guidance in learning the steps of CQR (domains, core ideas, and cross-analysis). As an example of a common difficulty experienced at this stage, novice researchers often make unsubstantiated inferences from the data, thus misrepresenting the participant's experience. Ethically, then, researchers need to learn how to transform participant-reported events into meaningful results that accurately depict participant experiences (see also Chapters 8 and 9, this volume). For instance, in a recent study on supervisee perception of clinical supervisor self-disclosure (Knox, Edwards, Hess, & Hill, in press), the team struggled to avoid inferring a negative bias toward supervisory styles that were authoritarian and that focused on technique or case management and inferring a positive bias toward supervisory styles that were collaborative, supportive, or empowering. Attributing a negative or positive value to participants' experiences could be misleading, potentially misrepresenting participants' supervision experiences.

An approach that we use to reduce such difficulties is to didactically review the concepts behind developing domains, core ideas, category titles, and the cross-analysis and provide instruction about these processes. For example, in developing core ideas, we discuss the importance of staying close to the participant's actual words, not interpreting the meaning of the participant's experience, and making sure each core idea conveys a meaningful idea. We also model these strategies for novice researchers by developing the first sets of core ideas from our own cases and then lead the group review and consensus process for finalizing the core ideas. Relatedly, when a novice researcher develops core ideas for her or his first case, we often write core ideas for a specific domain during a team meeting to demonstrate how to generate clear and comprehensive core ideas. These training and modeling methods seem to have been effective in helping novice researchers develop competence in transforming raw data into domain titles, core ideas, and category titles that do not overstate, understate, or misrepresent participants' disclosed experiences.

## MANAGEMENT OF POWER ON THE TEAM

As a qualitative research method, CQR relies on collaboration among team members, where communication is free of interpersonal difficulties and based on trust (see also Chapter 4, this volume). In essence, a positive group process is necessary for the successful completion of a study. The importance of this group process is probably most evident during the data analysis phase, when team members are actively discussing the coding of data in domains and developing core ideas and cross-analysis categories. Given that research teams are often made up of students and faculty, or of tenured and untenured faculty, there is an inherent imbalance of power. These power differentials can have a detrimental effect on the data analysis because students or untenured faculty may not be as forthcoming with feedback to more senior faculty members for fear of negative repercussions in other contexts. Ethically, senior members of the team who hold positions of power (e.g., professors, tenured faculty) may want to acknowledge the dual-role relationships and be open to discussing these dual roles and the related concerns about management of power, and the team could discuss how to manage any potential influence on data analysis (see also Chapters 4 and 7, this volume).

To facilitate open communication and reduce the influence of power and dual role relationships during a CQR project, we actively seek to develop rapport and group cohesion among members early in the research process. As senior faculty members, for example, we self-disclose about our own experiences with events related to the study. We also talk as a team about the importance of contributing equally to the discussion of the data, and we intentionally provide positive support to students and new researchers as they are developing their research skills. Often this feedback helps novice researchers build confidence and feel more able to offer feedback during team meetings. For instance, during a study of supervisee experiences with client suicide (Knox et al., 2006), one of the senior researchers shared his experience, thoughts, and feelings about a client's attempted suicide. This disclosure normalized the reactions of the less experienced team members, who then became less anxious about sharing their own reactions. We also address group dynamics, often debriefing at the end of meetings to ensure that all members feel able to contribute to the research. If we notice that team members are not contributing in expected ways, we take time during team meetings to discuss concerns and resolve any difficulties in the group process. Finally, we try to have fun during our research meetings and use humor to break up the seriousness and intensity of the work. These strategies seem to have been effective in helping team members feel connected and empowered, and they have helped to reduce the potential influence of power on teams as well as manage dual-role relationships within the research team.

# Participants and Data Collection

In any data collection, the researcher needs to ensure that participants do not feel coerced to participate. Beyond avoiding coercion of participants, however, CQR researchers also need to consider the ethical treatment of participants during data collection procedures. We attend to these concerns in the following sections.

## ONGOING NATURE OF INFORMED CONSENT

A qualitative researcher intrudes on a participant's world by probing and examining in detail the participant's intimate thoughts, feelings, and experiences (Stacey, 1988). Therefore, participants need to have the autonomy to choose whether they want to participate in any given study. Obtaining initial informed consent from participants for involvement in research is a fundamental ethical principle for any project, including CQR investigations, but given the potential intrusiveness of CQR, it is especially important to attend to issues of informed consent throughout the study. Perhaps as a further complication, participants may not have fully anticipated the level of self-disclosure required during the interview or the intensity of emotion they may experience when discussing some topics. For instance, in a recent study of students' dissertation experiences, several participants talked about a difficult relationship between themselves and their advisors and subsequently expressed surprise at the intensity of their emotions and the feelings of vulnerability they experienced when discussing their dissertation experience (Burkard et al., 2010). During the interviews, these participants raised questions about the confidentiality of their responses, and some wondered if their advisors would recognize their stories.

Because of this ongoing need for informed consent throughout a study, we use several strategies to keep participants apprised of their rights. In the opening phase of a study, we prepare participants for the interview by sending protocols (i.e., interview questions) in advance to let them review the types of questions we will ask. We also acknowledge in letters of introduction and informed consent materials that participants may experience intense emotions when discussing their experiences. During the opening of each interview, we review the informed consent procedures and offer participants opportunities to ask any questions about the study or interview process. In moments of intense emotions during interviews, we respond to participant distress, offer support and referrals, and reassess their desire to continue in the project. Finally, we ask specifically about participants' reactions at the end of the interview. These procedures seem to have been effective, given that participants typically have commented that they enjoyed the interview process and the opportunity to reflect on their experiences.

## DE-IDENTIFYING INTERVIEWS AND TRANSCRIPTS

During the course of an interview, interviewers may refer to participants by name, and participants may refer to other individuals relevant to their experiences by name or by position. Similarly, participants may also identify settings, locations, or other attributes. For example, in a current study on marginalized youths' experiences of discrimination during high school (Burkard et al., 2011), one participant discussed the attention she or he had drawn in national media a few years earlier and identified the specific outlets for this coverage. Other individuals identified school administrators by name who contributed to their difficult experiences.

We take some fairly simple steps to protect the identity of participants and any individuals to whom they may refer during the interview. First, we assign each case a code number. During the study, we maintain a copy of participant names and code numbers in a password-protected computer file to which only the first author has access. At the completion of the study, this code list is deleted. Second, prior to any data analysis we de-identify all transcriptions by removing names, geographical references, or any other personally identifying information. Hence, no names are associated with a particular case at any level of data analysis. Additionally, if a participant is known to a member of the research team, her or his interview may be conducted by a different researcher, and her or his data are not reviewed by the team until they have been completely de-identified.

Finally, it can be a good idea to send the transcript of the interview to the participants, asking them to ensure that they are comfortable with what they have disclosed and that the transcript is an accurate reflection of their experiences. This "member checking" allows the participant to have a feeling of control over the process. In our experience, few participants offer any revisions but feel respected by having been given the opportunity to review the transcript.

## PARTICIPANT READINESS FOR OR DISCOMFORT WITH DISCLOSURE

CQR researchers typically assess and respond to participants' readiness for and/or discomfort with self-disclosure. Interviewers will commonly not press forward with an interview if they believe a participant is uncomfortable about disclosing information or is clearly distressed. Recall the earlier example of a participant who disclosed the sexual harassment he or she experienced from her or his dissertation chair (Burkard et al., 2010). If the interviewer had not recognized the participant's discomfort (i.e., the participant seemed hesitant to respond to questions, became vague and tangential in responses, wondered aloud about the appropriateness of her or his dissertation chair's behavior) and pushed forward with the interview, the interview experience itself could have become traumatic. Thus, recounting some experiences can increase participants' sense of vulnerability because of disclosure of events or feelings that are embarrassing or anxiety or fear provoking (Birch & Miller, 2000; Sinding & Aronson, 2003).

When strong emotions are elicited during interviews, the interview experience itself may also exacerbate a participant's fears that an interviewer is evaluating her or him (Adler & Adler, 2002). For instance, in the dissertation study example noted previously, the participant queried the interviewer about her or his immediate reactions to the participant's disclosure of sexual harassment by the dissertation chair and commented that the interviewer must think that the participant was abnormal. These emotional states may directly affect a participant's comfort with disclosure during the interview, and pressing forward could potentially be exploitive of the participant and a breach of ethics.

Many of our recommendations (e.g., informed consent procedures, responding supportively to distress, offering a break, debriefing participants at the end of an emotional interview) are effective strategies in addressing these concerns. We also urge investigators to ensure that participants are emotionally in a good place before ending the interview. To date, we have not had a participant request to withdraw from a study, but stress that this option needs to be provided. Our primary goal in such situations is to help participants make the best possible choice for themselves, to respect their concerns, and to make sure that we as researchers are able to help participants maintain their integrity and dignity.

## Writing the Results and Discussion Sections

### TELLING A POWERFUL STORY WITHOUT IDENTIFYING PARTICIPANTS

In many CQR manuscripts, authors include core ideas and/or illustrative examples to bring the results to life (see Chapter 11, this volume). In doing so, they seek to tell the story of the study's findings in the most compelling way. They must ensure, however, that they do not breach confidentiality in this effort.

Our practice has often been to include core ideas or participant quotes as illustrative examples in the Results section or related tables. The core ideas are less likely to evoke concerns about confidentiality because we keep them brief and succinct, intending them only to illustrate the category from which they come. The illustrative examples, however, do require careful steps to ensure that participants' or others' identities are not revealed. Toward this end, we frequently alter some of the demographic data (e.g., age, sex, geographic location) but are careful not to distort the findings' meaning or integrity. In the study on client gifts (Knox et al., 2009), for example, the illustrative example included gifts that were similar but not identical to those actually disclosed by the participant. Likewise, in a study of therapist self-disclosure, (Knox, Hess, Petersen, & Hill, 1997), the actual disclosures were slightly altered, though their general nature was retained. As a further precaution, we send the final draft of the manuscript to all participants, asking them to ensure that their confidentiality has been maintained.

## Conclusions

Because of the complex nature of CQR research, ethical considerations deserve special attention. We have offered here a review of the common issues we and other CQR researchers have had to address. Our recommendations as outlined in this chapter and as summarized in Table 15.1 provide practical solutions that have been helpful in advancing the training of novice researchers while maintaining respect for the rights of participants and protecting them from harm. Good research practices arise from good ethical practices. Researchers planning a CQR project need not think of ethics as an external set of rules and regulations, but rather as an important means for conducting sound research.

## TABLE 15.1

**Ethics in Consensual Qualitative Research**

| Step | Recommendations |
| --- | --- |
| Planning the study | Consider and address potential ethical concerns and risks for participants prior to interviews. |
| | Consult with university institutional review board and/or the American Psychological Association Ethics Office when difficult concerns or risks arise; document consultation and decisions. |
| Research team | Nurture rapport and cohesion on research team. |
| | Encourage team members to disclose biases and expectations about topic. |
| | Train team members in how to use consensual qualitative research. |
| Interviewer competence | Select interviewers with adequate interviewing skills and knowledge of topic area. |
| | Provide adequate interview training. |
| | Discuss how to address difficult interview situations. |
| | Consider requiring a course in interviewing (e.g., basic counseling skills) for all team members. |
| Participant contact | Send interview protocol to participants before interview. |
| | Inform participants about possibility of intense emotions during interview. |
| | Invite participant to ask questions about research procedures. |
| | Be supportive and offer referrals if participant experiences distress; discontinue interview if necessary. |
| | Check in and debrief participant at the end of interview. |
| Data analysis | De-identify transcripts and assign code numbers. |
| | Model initial development of domains, core ideas, and cross-analysis during team meetings. |
| | Discuss power dynamics and facilitate open communication. |
| | Send transcripts to participants for review, clarification, and comment. |
| Manuscript | Send manuscript to participants for review, clarification, and comment. |

# *References*

Adler, P. A., & Adler, P. (2002). The reluctant respondent. In J. F. Gubrium & J. A. Holstein (Eds.), *Handbook of interview research: Context and method* (pp. 515–536). Thousand Oaks, CA: Sage.

American Psychological Association. (2010). *Ethical principles of psychologists and code of conduct (2002, Amended June 1, 2010).* Retrieved from http://www.apa.org/ethics/code/index.aspx

Birch, M., & Miller, T. (2000). Inviting intimacy: The interview as therapeutic opportunity. *International Journal of Social Research Methodology, 3*, 189–202. doi:10.1080/13645570050083689

Burkard, A. W., Knox, S., DeWalt, T., Downs, J., Fuller, S., Hill, C. E., & Schlosser, L. Z. (2010). *Dissertation experiences of doctoral graduates from professional psychology programs.* Manuscript submitted for publication.

Burkard, A. W., Knox, S., Hess, S., & Schultz, J. (2009). Lesbian, gay, and bisexual affirmative and non-affirmative supervision. *Journal of Counseling Psychology, 56*, 176–188. doi:10.1037/0022-0167.56.1.176

Burkard, A. W., Reynolds, A. R., Wurl, A., & Schultz, J. (2011). *Perceptions of lesbian, gay, and bisexual affirming and hostile high school experiences.* Manuscript in preparation.

Fassinger, R. E. (2005). Paradigms, praxis, problems, and promise: Grounded theory in counseling psychology research. *Journal of Counseling Psychology, 52*, 156–166. doi:10.1037/0022-0167.52.2.156

Hill, C. E., Sullivan, C., Knox, S., & Schlosser, L. Z. (2007). Becoming psychotherapists: Experiences of novice trainees in a beginning graduate class. *Psychotherapy: Theory, Research, Practice, Training, 44*, 434–449. doi:10.1037/0033-3204.44.4.434

Knox, S., Burkard, A. W., Jackson, J. A., Schaack, A. M., & Hess, S. A. (2006). Therapists-in-training who experience a client suicide: Implications for supervision. *Professional Psychology: Research and Practice, 37*, 547–557. doi:10.1037/0735-7028.37.5.547

Knox, S., Dubois, R., Smith, J., Hess, S. A., & Hill, C. E. (2009). Clients' experiences giving gifts to therapists. *Psychotherapy: Theory, Research, Practice, Training, 46*, 350–361. doi:10.1037/a0017001

Knox, S., Edwards, L. M., Hess, S. A., & Hill, C. E. (in press). Supervisees' experiences of supervisor self-disclosure. *Psychotherapy: Theory, Research, Practice, Training.*

Knox, S., Hess, S., Petersen, D., & Hill, C. E. (1997). A qualitative analysis of client perceptions of the effects of helpful therapist self-disclosure in long-term therapy. *Journal of Counseling Psychology, 44*, 274–283. doi:10.1037/0022-0167.44.3.274

Ladany, N., O'Brien, K. M., Hill, C. E., Melincoff, D. S., Knox, S., & Petersen, D. A. (1997). Sexual attraction toward clients, use of supervision, and prior training: A qualitative study of predoctoral psychology interns. *Journal of Counseling Psychology, 44*, 413–424. doi:10.1037/0022-0167.44.4.413

Sinding, C., & Aronson, J. (2003). Exposing failures, unsettling accommodations: Tensions in interview practice. *Qualitative Research, 3*, 95–117. doi:10.1177/1468794103003001770

Stacey, J. (1988). Can there be a feminist ethnography? *Women's Studies International Forum, 11*, 21–27. doi:10.1016/0277-5395(88)90004-0

*Harold T. Chui, John L. Jackson, Jingqing Liu, and Clara E. Hill*

# Annotated Bibliography of Studies Using Consensual Qualitative Research

16

I n this chapter, we provide an annotated bibliography (see Table 16.1) of the studies that have used consensual qualitative research (CQR) so that readers can see the types of topics that have been covered, the types of samples, the compositions of teams, how data have been collected, and a brief idea about the results obtained. We hope that this bibliography will also serve a networking function so that researchers can identify other researchers who are doing similar research.

To determine the corpus of studies, we included the 27 studies reviewed in the CQR update (Hill et al., 2005) as well as studies that we knew about. We then conducted a search in PsycINFO using the search term *consensual qualitative research*. We thus identified 120 studies that had been published in peer-reviewed journals prior to January 2010.

We reviewed these studies for fidelity to the CQR method. Studies that were judged via consensus of all the authors of this chapter as having mixed CQR with other qualitative methods or as not having strictly followed all the steps of the CQR method were excluded, leaving a final tally of 99 studies. We do not claim that this search was exhaustive, given that researchers may have used CQR but not mentioned the method in their abstract (which is what gets searched in PsycINFO), but we hope that this search provides some initial ideas about the use of CQR.

The four authors who conducted this review were three (2 male, 1 female; 2 Asian, 1 White) doctoral students (28 to 29 years of age) in counseling psychology and a 61-year-old White female counseling psychology professor at the University of Maryland. All authors have conducted studies using CQR and believe that the method allows researchers to gain a deep understanding of the phenomenon of interest. In addition, all authors have conducted research using quantitative methods and feel that both quantitative and qualitative methods can be useful depending on the research question.

We organized this bibliography by clustering articles into the seven topics that have received the most attention: (a) psychotherapy, (b) psychotherapist/counselor training or supervision, (c) multiculturalism, (d) career development, (e) trauma, (f) medical and health-related topics, and (g) same-sex relationships. Within each topic, studies were grouped by the CQR method used: traditional CQR, consensual qualitative research—modified (CQR-M), and consensual qualitative research—case study (CQR-C). Articles were ordered chronologically and alphabetically within topic area and CQR format. For each article, we provide information about the topic, method, sample, team, data collection, and brief results. In the next section of the chapter, we provide a brief summary of the trends in the data in each of these categories.

# Summary of Trends in CQR Data

We reviewed this corpus of 99 studies to look for consistencies in authorship, publication outlets, topics studied, types of CQR used, samples, research team compositions, and data collection formats. Figure 16.1 shows the steady increase in the number of published studies using CQR since its inception.

## AUTHORSHIP AND INSTITUTIONAL AFFILIATION

To investigate trends in authorship and institution affiliation, we followed the method used by Buboltz, Miller, and Williams (1999) for assigning credit weighted for author–affiliation contribution. Single authors (and their institutions) received the full credit for a study. If there were two authors, the first and second authors (and their institutions) were given 0.6 and 0.4 points, respectively. Three authors–institutions were given 0.47, 0.32, and 0.21, respectively; four authors–institutions: 0.42, 0.28, 0.18, and 0.12; five authors–institutions: 0.38, 0.26, 0.17, 0.11, 0.08; and six authors–institutions: 0.37, 0.24, 0.16, 0.11, 0.07, and 0.05. No credit

**FIGURE 16.1**

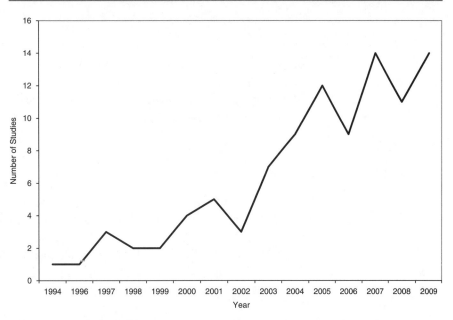

Number of published consensual qualitative research studies by year (1994 to 2009).

was assigned beyond the sixth author–institution. The sum of points equals 1.0 for each article.

According to this analysis, the most prolific CQR authors are Clara E. Hill (6.59; 28 studies), Sarah Knox (5.21; 16 studies), Rachel Cinamon (2.20; 4 studies), Elizabeth Nutt Williams (2.01; 6 studies), Nicholas Ladany (1.83, 7 studies), Madonna Constantine (1.78, 5 studies), Shirley A. Hess (1.71, 9 studies), and Alan W. Burkard (1.69, 5 studies). The institutional affiliations of these authors, in descending order, are the University of Maryland, College Park (19.62; 30 studies); Marquette University, Milwaukee, Wisconsin (8.36; 13 studies); Columbia University, New York, New York (5.63; 9 studies); Lehigh University, Bethlehem, Pennsylvania (4.43; 9 studies); and Shippensburg University, Shippensburg, Pennsylvania (0.99, 6 studies).

It is not surprising that the originators and elaborators of CQR (all contributors to this book) have been quite prolific. But what is surprising and gratifying is that many researchers who have used CQR are not even remotely connected with the institutions associated with these authors, and many of them were not trained in CQR by these authors; thus, researchers seem to have been able to learn the approach just by reading the published materials (Hill, Thompson, & Williams, 1997; Hill et al.,

2005). The ability of others to learn and use CQR speaks well to the portability of CQR.

## PUBLICATION OUTLETS

The leading journals that have published CQR studies are the *Journal of Counseling Psychology* (34 studies), *Psychotherapy Research* (10 studies), *Cultural Diversity and Ethnic Minority Psychology* (six studies), *The Counseling Psychologist* (five studies), and *Psychotherapy: Theory, Research, Practice, Training* (five studies).

## TOPICS STUDIED

In terms of topics, 34 studies investigated psychotherapy, 20 involved psychotherapy training and supervision, 14 were on multiculturalism and immigration issues, 14 studied career development, seven were on trauma, six involved medical and health-related topics, and four focused on same-sex relationships. Thus, although CQR was initially used for psychotherapy studies, it has been widely applied to a variety of topics.

## TYPES OF CQR USED

Of the 99 studies reviewed, 90 used traditional interview-based CQR, six used CQR-C, and three used CQR-M. The number of studies using the different methods reflects the history of development of CQR, with traditional CQR having been developed first and the two modifications having been developed more recently.

## SAMPLES

A total of 2,074 (1,084 male, 940 female, 50 unspecified gender; 1,105 White, 194 African/African American, 194 Asian/Asian American, 113 Latino/a, 31 Native American, 42 Israeli, and 395 other or unspecified race–ethnicity) individuals (9 to 88 years of age) have contributed data to studies using CQR. In traditional CQR studies, sample size has ranged from three to 97 ($M = 15.7$, $SD = 11.5$). In CQR-M, sample size has ranged from 22 to 547 ($M = 206.0$, $SD = 295.6$). In CQR-C, sample size has ranged from two to 16 ($M = 6.7$, $SD = 6.5$). Of the total sample of 99 studies, seven collected data from male participants only, 15 studies from female participants only, 76 from both male and female participants, and one did not report the sex of participants. In terms of race–ethnicity, most (55) involved mixed samples, but many focused on only one group (White = 19, African/African American = 4, Asian/Asian American = 9, Latino/a = 1, Native American/American Indians = 1, Israeli = 3); four did not report race–ethnicity of participants. In terms of age of participants, most (53) involved a mixed age range, but many focused on a narrower range of ages (children and adolescents < 18 years $N = 4$, young adults 18 to 29 years $N = 11$, adults > 30 years $N = 24$); seven did not report age of participants. These samples demonstrate that CQR may be used broadly to conduct research in homogeneous or more diverse populations across the life span.

## RESEARCH TEAM COMPOSITION

A range of people, in terms of educational level, have served as primary team members. Of the total of 395 judges listed in studies (note that some of these are repeats because they were involved in more than one study), there were 33 (8.4%) undergraduate students (in nine studies), 12 (3.0%) master's students (in seven studies), 168 (42.5%) doctoral students (in 67 studies), 33 (8.4%) graduate students unspecified (10 studies), 117 (29.6%) PhD researchers (in 70 studies), 8 (2.0%) professionals working in the field of study (four social workers, two correction officers, one genetic counselor, and one senior clinical supervisor), and 24 (6.1%) whose education level was not specified.

Auditors tended to be more senior and had a higher level of education. Among 121 auditors (again some of these people are repeats because they audited more than one study), there were no (0.0%) undergraduate students, one (0.8%) master's student, 28 (23.1%) doctoral students (in 21 studies), six (5.0%) graduate student unspecified (four studies), 74 (61.2%) PhD (in 61 studies), three (2.5%) counselors with unspecified education level (two studies), and nine (7.4%) auditors whose education level was not specified.

## DATA COLLECTION METHODS

Traditional CQR data have been collected in numerous ways, including in-person interviews (34 studies; 37.8% of traditional CQR studies), phone interviews (29 studies; 32.2%), in-person focus groups (four studies; 4.4%), paper-and-pencil questionnaires (three studies; 3.3%), video-taped conversations (two studies; 2.2%), online focus groups (one study; 1.1%), email questionnaires (one study; 1.1%), journal entries (one study; 1.1%), written case studies (one study; 1.1%), and mixed methods (14 studies; 15.6%; e.g., in-person interview and online messaging). CQR-M studies have collected data via paper-and-pencil questionnaires (two studies; 66.6% of CQR-M studies) and online-questionnaires (one study; 33.3%). CQR-C studies have used video-recorded (three studies; 50% of CQR-C studies) or audio-recorded (three studies; 50%) psychotherapy sessions for data analysis. Diverse methods of data collection indicate that CQR is a flexible approach for conducting qualitative research.

## *Summary*

In closing, we are delighted to see so many CQR studies on such a wide range of topics, with diverse participants, and involving many researchers. The many important and interesting findings generated using the CQR method demonstrate its promise as a useful research tool. We encourage people to let us know about their experiences in using the method.

## TABLE 16.1

Summaries of Published Studies Using the Consensual Qualitative Research (CQR) Method

| Study | Topic | Sample | Team | Data collection | Brief results |
|---|---|---|---|---|---|
| | | **Psychotherapy** | | | |
| Rhodes, Hill, Thompson, and Elliot (1994) | Client perspectives on resolved and unresolved misunderstanding events in therapy | 19 (16 female, 3 male; all White) clients (age $M = 33.10$, $SD = 6.91$ years), most in long-term (> 25 sessions) therapy and who were themselves either therapists or therapists-in-training | 3 PhD researchers; 1 PhD auditor | 1 paper-and-pencil questionnaire | Resolution was typically associated with a good therapeutic relationship, clients' willingness to assert negative feelings, and therapist pursuit of repair with flexibility and acceptance. Unresolved events were typically associated with a poor therapeutic relationship, therapist unwillingness to discuss the event, lack of therapist acceptance, and a lack of awareness of client negative feelings. |
| Hill, Nutt-Williams, Heaton, Thompson, and Rhodes (1996) | Therapist perspectives on impasses that resulted in termination with long-term therapy clients | 12 (8 female, 4 male; all White; 11 PhD or EdD level, 1 social worker) therapists (39–67 years of age), 4 of whom did not complete the interview portion of the study | 2 doctoral student, 1 PhD researcher; 2 PhD auditors | Paper-and-pencil questionnaire and follow-up phone interview (length not specified) | Variables associated with impasses included client history of interpersonal problems, lack of agreement between therapist and client on goals and tasks of therapy, interference in the therapy by others, transference, therapist mistakes, and therapist personal issues. All but one therapist attempted to explore the impasse openly with their clients, intending to aid the client in gaining insight and reengaging in the therapy. |

*(continued)*

TABLE 16.1 (*Continued*)

**Summaries of Published Studies Using the Consensual Qualitative Research (CQR) Method**

| Study | Topic | Sample | Team | Data collection | Brief results |
|---|---|---|---|---|---|
| Ladany et al. (1997) | Predoctoral psychology interns' sexual attraction toward clients, use of supervision, and prior training | 13 (8 female, 5 male; 10 White, 2 Latina, 1 Middle Eastern) psychology predoctoral interns (27–39 years of age) | 3 doctoral student, 3 PhD researchers | 2 phone interviews (1st: 30–45 min; 2nd: 10–15 min) | Sexual attraction to clients included both physical and interpersonal aspects. Therapists were very invested and attentive when sexually attracted to clients, but also felt distant, distracted, and less objective. Only half of therapists disclosed their sexual attraction to supervisors, and supervisors rarely initiated discussion on sexual attraction. Therapists found it helpful when supervisors normalized sexual attraction and facilitated exploration of it in supervision. Training programs did not adequately address sexual attraction. |
| Knox, Hess, Petersen, and Hill (1997) | Client perceptions of helpful therapist self-disclosures in long-term therapy | 13 (9 female, 4 male; all White) clients (26–50 years of age) in long-term therapy | 3 doctoral student, 1 PhD researchers; 1 PhD auditor | 2 phone interviews (1st: 25–60 min; 2nd: 10–40 min) | Therapist self-disclosures were helpful when clients were discussing important personal issues, were perceived as intended to reassure clients, and revealed personal information unrelated to therapists' feelings toward clients or the therapeutic relationship. Helpful therapist self-disclosures typically resulted in client reassurance, promoted client insight, and improved the therapeutic relationship. |

| Study | Purpose | Sample | Researchers | Method | Findings |
|---|---|---|---|---|---|
| Hayes et al. (1998) | Therapist perspectives on countertransference | 8 (4 female, 4 male; 6 White; 2 African American) therapists (34–78 years of age; 5–42 years of postdoctoral experience) | 2 doctoral student, 3 PhD researchers; 1 PhD auditor | In-person interviews after each session of brief (12–20 sessions) psychotherapy | Three domains of therapist countertransference were identified: Origins, triggers, and manifestations. Patterns were observed among categories across domains (e.g., negative perceptions of clients [trigger] were associated with anxiety, nurturance, distancing from client, and thoughts about treatment). |
| Gelso, Hill, Rochlen, Mohr, and Zack (1999) | Therapist recollections about transference in successful long-term psychotherapy cases | 11 (6 male, 5 female; all White) psychodynamic therapists (33–64 years of age; 3–23 years of postdoctoral experience) | 3 doctoral student, 2 PhD researchers | 2 phone interviews (1st: 60 min; 2nd: 15 min) | Transference operated in a complex way with regards to its source, valence, content, and development over course of therapy. Dynamic therapists used both analytic and nonanalytic techniques to deal with transference. Strong working alliance, strong real relationship, client emotional insight, and countertransference management were associated with resolution. |
| Knox, Goldberg, Woodhouse, and Hill (1999) | Client internal representations of their therapists | 13 (7 female, 6 male; 10 White, 2 Asian American, 1 African American) clients (25–54 years of age) in long-term therapy | 3 doctoral researchers; 1 PhD auditor | 2 phone interviews (1st: 50 min; 2nd: 15 min) | Internal representations typically occurred in good therapeutic relationships and combined auditory, visual, and kinesthetic (i.e., the "felt presence" of the therapist) information. Representations were triggered when clients thought about sessions or were distressed. They occurred in a variety of locations; varied in length, duration, and intensity; *(continued)* |

TABLE 16.1 (Continued)

Summaries of Published Studies Using the Consensual Qualitative Research (CQR) Method

| Study | Topic | Sample | Team | Data collection | Brief results |
|---|---|---|---|---|---|
| Hill et al. (2000) | Client perspectives on focusing on dreams or loss in therapy for clients with troubling dreams and recent losses | 14 (8 female, 6 male; 12 White, 1 African American, 1 Iranian American) clients (19–50 years of age). All had troubling dreams and recent losses and were psychologically distressed | 10 doctoral student, 2 PhD researchers (rotating teams of coders and auditors) | 1 in-person interview (60 min; 1 week posttherapy) and 1 phone interview (15 min, 1 month posttherapy) | increased over the course of therapy, and benefitted the therapy and the therapeutic relationship, but were rarely discussed in therapy. Clients in both conditions were satisfied with therapy, gained insights about themselves, and made changes. Clients in the dream condition kept fewer secrets from therapists, liked the structure of therapy more, and understood their dreams better. Clients in loss condition gained more insight about the effects of the past and their loss and preferred therapist guidance. |
| Fuertes, Mueller, Chauhan, Walker, and Ladany (2002) | European American therapists' approach to counseling African American clients | 9 (6 female, 3 male; all White) therapists (age $M = 40$, $SD = 9$ years; postdoctoral experience $M = 9$, $SD = 8$ years) | 2 doctoral student, 1 PhD researchers; 1 doctoral student and 1 PhD auditor | 1 phone interview (length not specified) and an open-ended follow-up questionnaire (returned by mail) | Therapists attended directly and openly to racial differences with clients in the first two sessions of therapy. Therapists viewed race as a central focus and used a Rogerian approach to attain and maintain a strong working alliance. Race-related issues were typically viewed as related to clients' other concerns (e.g. mild depression, interpersonal issues). Therapists focused both on their own and their clients' |

| Study | Purpose | Sample | Data collection | Findings |
| --- | --- | --- | --- | --- |
| | | | | racial identity development throughout therapy. |
| Hill et al. (2003) | Therapist experience of hostile versus suspected-unasserted client anger and factors associated with resolution of anger events | 13 (9 female, 4 male; 12 White, 1 Latina) therapists in private practice (age $M = 51.62$, $SD = 4.21$ years; postdoctoral experience $M = 15.54$, $SD = 7.31$ years) | 5 doctoral student, 1 PhD researchers | 2 phone interviews (1st: 60 min; 2nd: 20 min) | All anger events were triggered by a disliked therapist action or inaction. Therapists reported more difficulty addressing hostile anger events than suspected-unasserted events. For hostile events, resolution was associated with therapist expression of negative feelings, a goal of connecting with clients, exploring client anger, and attributing client anger to problems in the therapeutic relationship rather than to personality deficits. For suspected-unasserted events, resolution was associated with a good therapeutic relationship and therapists' work to aid clients in exploring anger and gaining insight. |
| Knox, Burkard, Johnson, Suzuki, and Ponterotto (2003) | African American and European American therapists' experiences of addressing race in cross-racial psychotherapy dyads | 12 (6 female, 6 male; 5 African American, 7 European American) licensed psychologists (2–26 years of therapy experience) | 1 doctoral student, 2 PhD researchers; 2 PhD auditors | 2 phone interviews (1st: 30–60 min; 2nd: 5–15 min) | African American therapists routinely addressed race with clients, but European American therapists addressed race only when clients raised the issue. African American therapists addressed race more often than did European American therapists because of perceived client discomfort. European American therapists reported feeling uncomfortable addressing |

*(continued)*

TABLE 16.1 (Continued)

**Summaries of Published Studies Using the Consensual Qualitative Research (CQR) Method**

| Study | Topic | Sample | Team | Data collection | Brief results |
|---|---|---|---|---|---|
| | | | | | race with clients. All therapists positively evaluated the discussion of race. |
| Knox, Hess, Williams, and Hill (2003) | Therapist responses to client gifts | 12 (7 male, 5 female; all White) therapists (41–60 years of age; 7–29 years of therapy experience) | 3 PhD researchers; 1 PhD auditor | 2 phone interviews (1st: 40–60 min; 2nd: 5–20 min) | All participants had received gifts, usually of low monetary value. Gifts that raised concerns were typically given in the middle of therapy, and variantly at termination, early in therapy, or at specific events in therapists' lives (e.g., wedding, return from maternity leave). Participants discussed unproblematic gifts with clients but discussed problematic gifts only with persons other than the clients. |
| DiGiorgio, Arnkoff, Glass, Lyhus, and Walter (2004) | Therapist integration of eye-movement desensitization and reprocessing (EMDR) into other approaches | 3 experienced White male therapists (1 psychodynamic, 1 humanistic, 1 cognitive–behavioral; 57–71 years of age) | 3 doctoral student, 1 PhD researchers; 1 PhD auditor | 1 in-person or phone interview (50–72 min) | All participants deviated from the standard EMDR protocol, modifying it based on theoretical orientation. Client need was the primary reason therapists considered incorporating EMDR into treatment. |
| Ladany, Hill, Thompson, and O'Brien (2004) | Therapist perspectives on using silence in psychotherapy | 12 (7 male, 5 female; all White) psychotherapists (37–56 years of age; 10–25 years of experience providing psychotherapy) | 3 PhD researchers; 1 PhD auditor | 1 phone interview (60 min) | Therapists reported using silence to convey empathy, respect, or support for clients; to gather thoughts while preparing to intervene; and to allow clients time to reflect |

| Study | Purpose | Sample | Research team | Data collection | Findings |
|---|---|---|---|---|---|
| | | | | | and space to express their emotions. Therapists noted no established rules for when and how long to use silence, but only used silence when there was a good therapeutic alliance. Therapists learned how to use silence from experiences as clients and from supervision. |
| Knox, Catlin, Casper, and Schlosser (2005) | Client perspectives on how religion and spirituality were addressed in psychotherapy | 12 (11 female, 1 male; all White) clients (21–56 years of age) | 2 doctoral student, 1 PhD researchers; 1 doctoral student auditor | 2 phone interviews (1st: 40–60 min; 2nd: 5–20 min) | All participants noted that religious-spiritual (RS) activities were an important part of their lives. Discussion of RS in therapy usually focused on existential issues. Participants perceived their therapists as open, accepting, and facilitative of discussing RS. It was unhelpful when therapists initiated the discussion, passed judgment, or imposed personal beliefs. |
| Whiston, Lindeman, Rahardja, and Reed (2005) | Common themes and factors in career counseling cases from expert vocational psychologists | 10 (5 female, 5 male; 4 White, 2 African Americans, 1 Latino, 1 Chinese, 1 Jewish, 1 Russian) career counseling clients (22–42 years of age), each discussed by an expert or group of expert vocational psychologists | 3 master's student, 1 doctoral student, 1 PhD researchers; 1 PhD auditor | Written case studies from Niles, Goodman, and Pope (2002) | All therapists used the same basic helping skills used in individual personal-social therapy, based their interventions on a theoretical foundation, made use of formal and informal assessments, addressed sociocontextual factors in the counseling, and explored family of origin influences on career decision making. |
| Burkard, Knox, Groen, Perez, and Hess (2006) | European American therapist self-disclosure in cross-cultural counseling | 11 (6 female, 5 male; all White) therapists (33–53 years of age; 1.5–29 years of therapy experience) | 2 doctoral student, 2 PhD researchers; 1 PhD auditor | 2 phone interviews (1st: 45–60 min; 2nd: 5–15 min) | Therapists often disclosed their reactions to clients' experiences of racism or oppression to their clients. Therapist self-disclosure improved the *(continued)* |

TABLE 16.1 (Continued)

**Summaries of Published Studies Using the Consensual Qualitative Research (CQR) Method**

| Study | Topic | Sample | Team | Data collection | Brief results |
|---|---|---|---|---|---|
| | | | | | counseling relationship and encouraged clients to explore important issues. |
| Fitzpatrick, Janzen, Chamodraka, and Park (2006) | Critical incidents during early therapeutic alliance development | 20 (16 female, 4 male; 15 White, 3 biracial, 1 Asian, 1 Caribbean) clients (20–54 years of age) | 1 master's student, 1 doctoral student, 1 PhD researchers; 1 PhD auditor | 1 in-person interview (30 min) | Therapist interventions varied considerably in early relationship incidents. Clients noted that therapists' interventions were key to incident outcome and alliance development. The authors posited a positive emotion-exploration spiral in which client openness to exploration and positive responses to therapist interventions aid in alliance development. |
| King et al. (2006) | Motives and experiences of people who chose online over face-to-face or telephone counseling | 39 participants who used online counseling in Australia (age, gender, and race not specified) | 2 graduate student researchers; 2 PhD auditors | Online focus groups (120 min) | Participants chose online counseling because it was perceived as less confronting than regular or telephone counseling because of the lack of personal contact. Participants generally reported long waiting times during online counseling and being concerned about being misunderstood. |
| Baird, Szymanski, and Ruebelt (2007) | Feminist identity development of male therapists | 12 (8 PhD or EdD level, 4 master's level) self-identified feminist, White male therapists (27–61 years of age) | 1 doctoral student, 2 PhD researchers; 1 auditor (education not specified) | 1 in-person or phone interview (60 min) | Personal and professional relationships and professional training, particularly with feminist women, revealed to these therapists the importance of feminism and challenged their acceptance of |

| Study | Topic | Participants | Researchers | Interview | Findings |
|---|---|---|---|---|---|
| | | | | | traditional gender roles. Participants described feelings of isolation, attributing their isolation to difficulty connecting with other men as well as to a lack of support from women who question whether men can truly understand and champion women's issues. |
| Johnson, Hayes, and Wade (2007) | Therapist experiences working with clients with spiritual problems | 13 (8 female, 5 male; 10 White, 1 Latino, 1 Cajun, 1 unknown race; 8 PhD level, 5 master's level) therapists | 2 doctoral student, 1 PhD researchers; 1 PhD auditor | 1 in-person interview (45–60 min); 1 phone interview (15–30 min) | Therapists used a pluralistic approach for addressing client spirituality and conceptualized spiritual issues as intertwined with other psychological and relational issues. Therapists intervened with explicitly religious practices and indicated that clients experienced positive spiritual change over the course of therapy. |
| Chang and Berk (2009) | Clients' experiences of cross-racial therapy | 16 (8 female, 8 male; 6 African American, 5 Latino/a, 3 Asian, 2 multiracial; age range from 19-50 years, $M = 33.5$, $SD = 8.8$) clients in cross-racial therapy dyads with White therapists. 8 were satisfied and 8 were unsatisfied with therapy | 5 doctoral student researchers; 1 PhD auditor | 1 in-person interview (60–180 min) | Client evaluations depended primarily on the amount of affective involvement in the relationships and client beliefs that his or her counselor was addressing core needs and working toward achievement of treatment goals. A relationship was found between therapist self-disclosure and treatment satisfaction, suggesting that self-disclosure bridges the power distance in cross racial therapy dyads. Several clients expected some direct guidance from their therapists |

(continued)

TABLE 16.1 (Continued)

Summaries of Published Studies Using the Consensual Qualitative Research (CQR) Method

| Study | Topic | Sample | Team | Data collection | Brief results |
|---|---|---|---|---|---|
| | | | | | and praised therapists who showed culture-specific knowledge. |
| Fitzpatrick, Janzen, Chamodraka, Gamberg, and Blake (2009) | Client relationship incidents with therapists in early therapy | 15 (12 female, 3 male; 11 White, 2 Asian, 1 Middle Eastern, 1 not specified) depressed clients (20–61 years of age) | 3 doctoral student researchers; 1 doctoral student, 1 PhD auditors | 1 in-person interview (40–55 min) | When clients described events involving the working relationship with therapists, they recalled that therapists helped them think or act in new ways and identified their openness with therapists as contributors to good working relationships. Positive relational incidents were associated with positive emotional tone in clients. |
| Knox, Dubois, Smith, Hess, and Hill (2009) | Client experiences giving gifts to therapists | 9 (8 female, 1 male; all White) clients (26–61 years of age) | 2 doctoral student, 1 PhD researchers; 2 PhD auditors | 2 phone interviews (1st: 45 min; 2nd: 10 min) | In events when clients gave a gift that was accepted by their therapists, clients reported good therapeutic relationships and perceived that gift-giving had a positive outcome. Gifts were relatively inexpensive and were given during a nontermination session. Discussion of gifts was brief and did not entail an exploration of deeper meaning. |
| Santiago-Rivera, Altarriba, Poll, Gonzalez-Miller, Cragun 2009) | Therapist views on working with bilingual Spanish-English speaking clients | 9 (6 female, 3 male; 6 Hispanic, 3 European American) bilingual therapists (4–28 years of experience) | 2 doctoral student, 2 PhD researchers; 1 doctoral student auditor | 1 phone interview (length not specified) | Therapists switched from English to Spanish to establish a bond with clients and encourage disclosure. Clients switched from English to Spanish when |

| Study | Topic | Participants | Researchers | Interviews | Findings |
|---|---|---|---|---|---|
| | | | | | recounting experiences involving emotions to improve communication. and connect with therapists. Clients represented themselves differently depending on which language they used. |
| Spangler, Hill, Mettus, Guo, and Heymsfield (2009) | Therapist dreams about their clients | 8 (4 female, 4 male; all White; 4 PhD level, 4 master's level) therapists (40–71 years of age) | 1 doctoral student, 11 undergraduate researchers; 1 PhD auditor | 2 phone interviews (1st: ~65 min; 2nd: ~45 min) | Dreams were about difficulties with clients, personal concerns, and negative interpersonal interactions. Therapists gained insight based on analyzing the dreams; they used insight to examine countertransference, make changes to enhance treatment, and make changes in their personal lives. |
| Vivino, Thompson, Hill, and Ladany (2009) | Perspectives on compassion in psychotherapy by therapists who were nominated as compassionate | 14 (11 female, 3 male; 12 White, 2 Asian American) psychotherapists (35–65 years of age; years providing therapy $M = 18.14$, $SD = 6.20$) | 3 PhD researchers; 1 PhD auditor | 2 phone interviews (1st: 60 min; 2nd: length not specified) | Therapists were nominated by professional peers as being exceptionally compassionate (i.e. connecting with their clients' suffering and promoting client change). Therapists indicated that compassion is deeper and stronger than empathy; and is an engrossing state of being connected with a struggling, suffering client. Compassion was facilitated by therapist identification with and liking of clients, a good therapeutic relationship, and client involvement in the therapy. Compassion was hindered when clients violated boundaries or were resistant or aggressive and when therapists experienced |

(continued)

TABLE 16.1 (Continued)

**Summaries of Published Studies Using the Consensual Qualitative Research (CQR) Method**

| Study | Topic | Sample | Team | Data collection | Brief results |
|---|---|---|---|---|---|
| Wonnell and Hill (2000)[a] | Effects of action in dream interpretation | 22 (15 female, 7 male; 17 White, 4 Asian American, 1 Asian) therapists (24–40 years of age; 1–6 years of experience providing therapy) | 3 doctoral student researchers | 1 paper-and-pencil questionnaire | interfering personal issues, feelings of incompetence, or a dislike for clients. Therapists attributed ease of implementing the action stage in dream work to client factors (e.g., motivation, involvedness, and psychological mindedness), dream factors (e.g., recent dreams), therapist factors (e.g., experience, confidence, comfort), and the attainment of goals in exploration and insight stages. |
| Gazzola and Stalikas (2004)[b] | Therapist interpretation and client processes in different therapeutic modalities | 12 therapist–client dyads (therapists included Carl Rogers, Fritz Perls, Albert Ellis) | 6 graduate student researchers; 2 PhD auditors | 12 videotaped sessions of individual (4 client-centered, 4 gestalt, 4 rational–emotive behavioral) therapy | The content, goals, and styles of delivery of interpretations differed among therapists but were consistent with their theoretical orientations. Clients rarely rejected interpretations but they explored thoughts and feelings after interpretations. |
| Hill et al. (2007)[b] | Attainment of insight in the Hill Dream Model (Hill, 1996, 2004) | 29-year-old White female therapist trainee and 23-year-old female client of Arabic descent | 2 graduate student, 2 PhD researchers; 2 PhD auditors | 1 audiotaped dream session (75 min) | Gains in insight were associated with the salience and emotion-arousing aspect of the client dream, the therapeutic relationship, and client readiness, motivation and involvement. Therapist adherence to and competence in the Hill dream model likely |

| Study | Variable | Participants | Researchers | Data | Findings |
|---|---|---|---|---|---|
| Kasper, Hill, and Kivlighan (2008)[b] | Therapist immediacy in brief psychotherapy | 51-year-old White male therapist and 24-year-old "first generation" female client | 1 doctoral student, 1 PhD researchers | 12 videotaped psychotherapy sessions (50 min each) | enhanced client involvement. Therapists' probes for insight and reflection of feelings were associated with immediate client insight. Therapist immediacy focused on parallels between therapy relationship and external relationships, encouraging expression of immediate feelings, processing termination, expressing sadness, and inquiring about client reactions. Immediacy seemed to help client express immediate feelings about the therapist, feel closer to therapist, and become less defended, but client felt somewhat awkward and pressured. |
| Hill et al. (2008)[b] | Therapist immediacy in brief psychotherapy | 55 year-old White male therapist and 25-year-old African American female client | 4 doctoral student, 1 PhD researchers | 17 videotaped psychotherapy sessions (50 min each) | Therapist immediacy focused on reinforcing client for in-session behavior, inviting client to collaborate, inquiring about client reactions to therapy, and reminding client that it was okay to disagree with therapist. Immediacy enabled therapist and client to negotiate the relationship, helped client express immediate feelings to therapist, deepened exploration, and provided client with a corrective relational experience. |
| Knox, Hill, Hess, and Crook-Lyon (2008)[b] | Attainment of insight in dream sessions | 2 cases: One insight achieved (25-year-old White female therapist trainee and 19-year-old | 4 PhDs served as researchers and auditors, rotating roles across cases | 2 audiotaped dream sessions (80 min for each case) | Client who achieved insight compared to client who did not achieve insight from a single dream session was *(continued)* |

TABLE 16.1 (Continued)

Summaries of Published Studies Using the Consensual Qualitative Research (CQR) Method

| Study | Topic | Sample | Team | Data collection | Brief results |
|---|---|---|---|---|---|
| | | White female client) and one insight not achieved (24-year-old White female therapist trainee and 22-year-old African American female client) | | | more trusting, less resistant, and less emotionally overwhelmed. Therapist of the dream session that generated greater client insight was more competent in adhering to the Hill dream model and managing unproductive countertransference. |
| Sim et al. (2010)[b] | Problems and action ideas in dream sessions for first- and second-generation East Asian females | 7 1st-generation female Asian clients (came to the U.S. in past 6 years) and 7 2nd-generation female Asian clients (all 18–23 years of age) | 4 undergraduate student, 1 doctoral student researchers; 1 PhD auditor | Single audiotaped dream sessions (90 min) | Both first- and second-generation Asian women discussed interpersonal and academic/career issues. First-generation women disclosed more concerns about immigration/adjustment/ culture and physical distress and proposed more changes in thoughts and feelings than did second-generation women. |
| **Psychotherapist/counselor training and supervision** | | | | | |
| E. N. Williams, Judge, Hill, and Hoffman (1997) | Trainee, client, and supervisor perceptions of prepracticum students' reactions and management strategies | 7 (6 female, 1 male; 6 White, 1 African American) prepracticum trainees (22–44 years of age) | 2 doctoral student, 1 PhD researchers; 1 PhD auditor | Written responses to open-ended questions | Trainees experienced anxiety, distraction, self-focus, frustration, anger, inadequacy, and empathy in sessions. These reactions sometimes interfered with their ability to provide effective counseling. Trainees managed their reactions by focusing on the |

| Study | Topic | Participants | Researchers | Method | Findings |
|---|---|---|---|---|---|
| Ladany, Constantine, Miller, Erickson, and Muse-Burke (2000) | Supervisor countertransference with predoctoral interns | 11 (8 female, 3 male; 10 White, 1 African American) psychotherapy supervisors (31–59 years of age; 4–20 years of supervision experience) | 1 doctoral student, 4 PhD researchers | 1 phone interview (60 min) | client, using self-awareness, and suppressing their feelings. Supervisor countertransference could be manifested in affective (e.g., emotional distress), cognitive (e.g., questioning own competence), and behavioral (e.g., disengagement) components. Sources of countertransference included interpersonal styles of the interns and unresolved issues of supervisors. Participants lacked training in countertransference. |
| Gray, Ladany, Walker, and Ancis (2001) | Trainee experience of counterproductive events in supervision | 13 (10 female, 3 male; 12 White, 1 person of color) doctoral students in counseling psychology (23–29 years of age) | 2 doctoral student, 2 PhD researchers (rotating teams of researchers and auditors) | 1 phone interview (30–45 min) | Counterproductive events in supervision involved supervisors dismissing trainees' thoughts or feelings. Trainees experienced negative interactions with their supervisors, a weakened supervisory relationship, and negative effects on their work with clients as a result of the counterproductive events, but most did not think supervisors were aware that the events were counterproductive. Trainees did not disclose about these counterproductive experiences with their supervisors. |
| Hendrickson, Veach, and LeRoy (2002) | Student and supervisor perceptions of live supervision in genetic counseling | 15 (14 female, 1 male) genetic counseling master's students and 11 female genetic counseling clinical | 1 doctoral student, 1 PhD researchers; 1 mental health counselor as auditor | Focus group (40–90 min; 3 student groups and 3 supervisor groups) | Live supervision was a vital, viable method for training genetic counseling students. Students and supervisors both described appropriate *(continued)* |

TABLE 16.1 (Continued)

Summaries of Published Studies Using the Consensual Qualitative Research (CQR) Method

| Study | Topic | Sample | Team | Data collection | Brief results |
|-------|-------|--------|------|-----------------|---------------|
| | | supervisors (1–12 years of supervision experience) | | | supervisor behavior as taking notes, correcting and supplementing information, and allowing students to be the primary counselor in sessions. Perceptions of the limitations of live supervision differed: Students focused on the problematic effects of live supervision and negative experience of feedback challenges, whereas supervisors focused on problematic student behaviors, such as defensiveness. |
| Schlosser, Knox, Moskovitz, and Hill (2003) | Advisee perspective of graduate advising relationships | 16 (14 female, 2 male; 14 White, 2 biracial) third year counseling psychology doctoral students (24–50 years of age) | 1 master's student, 1 doctoral student, 1 PhD researchers; 1 PhD auditor | 2 phone interviews (1st: 60 min; 2nd: 10 min) | Satisfied advisees were more able than unsatisfied advisees to choose their advisors, had more frequent meetings with their advisors, had more benefits and fewer costs associated with their advising relationships, and dealt appropriately with conflict. Satisfied advisees reported that their advising relationships became more positive over time, whereas unsatisfied advisees reported that their advising relationships got worse over time. |

| Study | Purpose | Participants | Data collection | Findings |
|---|---|---|---|---|
| E. N. Williams, Polster, Grizzard, Rockenbaugh, and Judge (2003) | Novice therapist distracting self-awareness and management strategies | 6 (3 male, 3 female; 4 White, 2 biracial) first-year doctoral practicum students (22–42 years of age); 6 (3 male, 3 female; all White) experienced therapists (35–60 years of age; at least 3 years of postdoctoral experience) | 3 undergraduate student, 1 PhD researchers; 1 PhD auditor | 1 phone interview (60 min) | Novice therapists experienced more anxiety and critical self-talk, fewer external distracters, and less boredom than did experienced therapists. In terms of management, both groups refocused on clients and self-coached. Novices more often engaged in self-disclosure, whereas experienced therapists used thought-stopping techniques. |
| Dillon et al. (2004) | Counselor preparation for lesbian/gay/bisexual (LGB) affirmative counseling | 10 (8 male, 2 female; 8 White, 1 Latino, 1 Pacific Islander) graduate students (age not specified) in mental health counseling | 4 doctoral student researchers; 2 PhD auditors | Written responses to 4 open-ended questions | Participants emphasized self-reflection about their sexual identity development, and attitudes about LGB individuals in counselor training. Some had future plans to engage more LGB-affirmative behaviors in personal and professional lives. |
| Hoffman, Hill, Holmes, and Freitas (2005) | Supervisor perspectives on giving easy, difficult, or no feedback to supervisees | 15 (10 female, 5 male; 12 White, 3 African Americans) counseling center supervisors (age $M = 43.73$, $SD = 5.02$; 10.8 years of postdoctoral supervision experience | 2 doctoral student, 2 PhD researchers; no auditor | 2 phone interviews (1st: 60 min; 2nd: 20 min) | Easy feedback was most often about clinical problems (e.g. use of clinical skills, client welfare), difficult feedback was most often about nonclinical issues (e.g., trainee personality issues or professional issues). Supervisors refrained from giving difficult feedback when it implicated trainee personal issues and crossed the boundary between supervision and psychotherapy, and when trainees were not open to feedback. |
| Jennings, Sovereign, Bottorff, Mussell, and Vye (2005) | Ethical values of master therapists | 10 (7 female, 3 male; all White; 6 PhD level, 3 master's level social | 2 doctoral student, 1 PhD researchers; 1 PhD auditor | Reanalysis of interview data from a previous study: | Master therapists identified that building and maintaining personal connections, |

(continued)

TABLE 16.1 (Continued)

Summaries of Published Studies Using the Consensual Qualitative Research (CQR) Method

| Study | Topic | Sample | Team | Data collection | Brief results |
|---|---|---|---|---|---|
| | | worker, 1 MD) master therapists (50–72 years of age) | | Jennings and Skovholt (1999) | and building and maintaining expertise were central ethical values in their clinical practices. Therapists identified relational connections with clients, colleagues, family, friends, and community members as their most prized ethical values. |
| Burkard, Johnson, et al. (2006) | Supervisor cultural responsiveness and unresponsiveness in cross-cultural supervision | 26 (all females; 13 European American, 6 African American, 6 Asian American, 1 Latina) supervisees (24–48 years of age) | 5 doctoral student, 2 PhD researchers; 2 PhD auditors | 2 phone interviews (1st: 45–60 min; 2nd: 15–30 min) | Supervisees felt supported for exploring cultural issues when supervisors were culturally responsive. Culturally unresponsive supervisors ignored, discounted, or dismissed cultural issues. Supervisees of color reported more culturally unresponsive supervision than did European American supervisees. |
| Knox, Schlosser, Pruitt, and Hill (2006) | Advisors' perspective of graduate advising relationships | 19 (11 male, 8 female; 12 White, 2 African American, 3 Latino/a, 2 other) advisors (33–69 years of age) in APA-accredited counseling psychology doctoral programs | 2 doctoral student, 1 PhD researchers; 1 PhD auditor | 2 phone interviews (1st: 30–60 min; 2nd: 5–20 min) | Advisors, who learned how to advise from their advisors and advisees, viewed the advising role as supporting and advocating for advisees. The benefit of advising is personal satisfaction, whereas the cost is the time demand. In good advising relationships, advisees had positive personal/ professional characteristics |

| Study | Purpose | Sample | Data collection | Findings |
|---|---|---|---|---|
| | | | | and there was mutual respect, open communication, similarity in career path between advisor and advisee, and lack of conflict. In difficult advising relationships, advisees had negative personal/ professional characteristics, and there was a lack of respect, struggles about research, communication problems, feelings of ineffectiveness in working with advisees, disruption or rupture of the relationship, and conflict avoidance. |
| De Stefano et al. (2007) | Trainee experience of impasses in counseling and the impact of group supervision on their resolution | 8 (5 female, 3 male; all White) master's students in first practicum course (23–28 years of age) | 2 in-person interviews (length not specified) | Trainees experienced impasses as failures and reacted with negative emotions. After experiencing an impasse, trainees sought and got support/validation and a new perspective on the impasse from supervisors. In addition, trainees reported increased self-awareness after group supervision. |
| Gazzola and Thériault (2007) | Trainee experience in supervision | 10 (9 female, 1 male; race not specified) master's-level graduate students in counseling (24–47 years of age) | 1 in-person interview (60 min) | Supervisees reported disengagement from supervisory relationships in which they felt one-down and unequal; they reported more positive affect, creativity, and collaboration in relationships they perceived as egalitarian. Supervisees also reported more positive affect and creativity when supervisors provided challenges along with support. |

*(continued)*

TABLE 16.1 (*Continued*)

Summaries of Published Studies Using the Consensual Qualitative Research (CQR) Method

| Study | Topic | Sample | Team | Data collection | Brief results |
|---|---|---|---|---|---|
| Hill, Sullivan, Knox, and Schlosser (2007) | The experiences of novice psychotherapy trainees | 5 (3 female, 2 male; 4 White; 1 multiracial) students in helping skills course in 1st semester of a counseling psychology doctoral program (22–46 years of age) | 1 doctoral student, 1 PhD researchers; 2 PhD auditors | Weekly journals. Researchers sent feedback each week, and students responded to feedback in their next journal entry | Trainees identified several challenges to becoming psychotherapists (e.g., self-criticism, difficulty utilizing helping skills, and negative reactions that kept them from connecting with clients). Trainees managed anxiety through of positive self-talk in sessions and journaling outside of sessions. Trainees benefited from supervision but also had some negative experiences. |
| Lloyd, King, and Ryan (2007) | Perceptions of newly graduated occupational therapists about challenges of working in mental health settings | 15 (14 female, 1 male) occupational therapists (22–42 years of age) with less than 2 years postgraduate clinical experience in mental health settings | 3 researchers; 1 auditor (education not specified) | 1 in-person interview (60 min) | The challenges identified by the new graduates included the use of discipline-specific assessments, counseling, boundary setting, and experiencing a high level of stress and responsibility when working with clients. |
| Hess et al. (2008) | Predoctoral interns' non-disclosure in supervision | 14 (11 female, 3 male; 10 White, 2 African American, 2 Asian American) predoctoral interns (27–38 years of age) at university counseling centers | 4 doctoral student, 2 PhD researchers; 2 PhD auditors | 1 phone interview (45–60 min) | In good supervisory relationships, nondisclosures involved personal reactions to clients; in problematic relationships, nondisclosures involved global dissatisfaction with the supervisory relationship. Interns attributed nondisclosure to concerns about evaluation and negative feelings. In addition, interns who |

| Study | Focus | Sample | Researchers | Interviews | Findings |
|---|---|---|---|---|---|
| | | | | | experience problematic supervision did not disclose because of power dynamics, inhibiting demographic variables, and the supervisors' theoretical orientation. Interns reported negative effects of nondisclosure on themselves and on their relationships with clients. In addition, interns in problematic supervision indicated negative effects of nondisclosure on supervisory relationships. |
| Knox, Burkard, Edward, Smith, and Schlosser (2008) | Supervisor report of effects of supervisor self-disclosure on supervisees | 16 (9 male, 7 female; 15 White, 1 Asian) supervisors (30–67 years of age) | 1 doctoral student, 3 PhD researchers; 1 PhD auditor | 2 phone interviews (1st: 50–60 min; 2nd: 5–20 min) | Supervisors used self-disclosure to enhance supervisees' development and to normalize supervisees' experiences. Self-disclosure had positive effects on supervisor, supervisee, the supervisory relationship, and supervision of others. |
| Burkard, Knox, Schultz, and Hess (2009) | LGB supervisees' experiences of LGB-affirmative and non-affirmative supervision | 17 (6 lesbians, 8 gay men, 2 bisexual men, 1 bisexual woman; 16 White, 1 Native American) doctoral students (24–49 years of age; 10 counseling psychology, 6 clinical psychology, 1 counselor education) | 3 PhD researchers; 1 PhD auditor | 2 telephone interviews (1st: 45–60 min, 2nd: 10–20 min) | Supervisees described both an affirmative and a nonaffirmative event from their past supervision. All affirmative events positively affected the supervision relationship, client outcome, and supervisees themselves. In nonaffirming events, supervisors were perceived to be biased or oppressive and these events negatively affected the supervisory relationship, client outcomes, and the experiences of the supervisees themselves. |

*(continued)*

TABLE 16.1 (Continued)

Summaries of Published Studies Using the Consensual Qualitative Research (CQR) Method

| Study | Topic | Sample | Team | Data collection | Brief results |
|---|---|---|---|---|---|
| Hernández, Taylor, and McDowell (2009) | Ethnic minority marriage and family therapy supervisors' reflections on their experiences as supervisees | 10 (9 female, 1 male) ethnic minority supervisors (36–62 years of age; 4–20 years of supervisory experience) | 3 master's student, 2 PhD researchers | 1 in-person or phone interview (40–75 min) | Ethnic minority supervisors' experience as supervisees was characterized as having (a) lack of processing social location and diversity dimensions, (b) misuse of power by supervisors, and (c) lack of mentorship in the profession. |
| Stahl et al. (2009) | Intern-level trainees' perceived learning from clients | 12 (9 female, 3 male; 7 White, 2 African American, 1 biracial, 1 Asian American, 1 Middle Eastern) intern-level trainees (age $M = 34.0$, $SD = 7.11$ years) | 1 doctoral student, 3 postbaccalaureate, 1 undergraduate student researchers; 1 PhD auditor | 2 phone interviews (1st: 60–90 min; 2nd: 15–30 min) | Participants learned about doing therapy, themselves, client dynamics, human nature, the therapy relationship, and the usefulness of supervision from working with clients. Participants also indicated the importance of consultation and self-reflection to help them recognize what they had learned. |
| | | | **Multiculturalism** | | |
| Friedlander et al. (2000) | Bicultural identification and the experiences of internationally adopted children and their parents | 12 (7 female, 5 male) children of Korean or Latin American heritage (6–16 years of age) and 12 White parents of these children (age of parents not specified) | 8 researchers (education not specified); 1 PhD auditor | 1 in-person parent interview; 1 in-person child interview (5–90 min) | Parents identified their families as multicultural and promoted ethnic pride among their children. Parents' ways of educating their children about race varied greatly. Children showed good psychosocial adjustment but indicated that they struggled with a perception of being different, some experiencing feelings of sadness and loss. |

| Authors | Topic | Participants | Researchers | Data collection | Findings |
|---|---|---|---|---|---|
| Kim, Brenner, Liang, and Asay (2003) | Adaptation experiences of 1.5-generation Asian Americans | 10 (7 male, 3 female) Asian American college students (18–23 years of age; 9–18 years in the United States) | 2 doctoral student, 1 PhD researchers; 1 doctoral student auditor | Participants e-mailed 1-page responses to 10 sets of questions. Follow-up questions sent as needed. | Most participants identified with U.S. and Asian cultures. Some had experienced racism. Most had no difficulty making friends with culturally different persons but felt closest to friends of similar background. They sought support from friends, family, and religious organizations instead of psychologists or counselors. |
| Constantine, Anderson, Berkel, Caldwell, and Utsey (2005) | Cultural adjustment experience of African international college students | 12 (8 male, 4 female) African international undergraduate students (20–31 years) | 5 PhD researchers; 1 doctoral student auditor | 1 in-person interview (50–90 min) | Themes related to African international college students' cultural adjustment included presojourn perceptions of the United States, postsojourn perceptions of the United States, cultural adjustment problems, responses to prejudicial or discriminatory treatment, family and friendship network, strategies to cope with cultural adjustment problems, and openness to seeking counseling. |
| Yeh et al. (2005) | Cultural negotiations of Korean immigrant youth | 13 (10 female, 3 male) Korean immigrant youths (11–17 years of age) | 6 graduate student researchers; 2 graduate student auditors | 1 in-person interview (60 min) | Korean youths were expected to negotiate and shift identities to meet different expectations across interpersonal contexts. They also struggled to balance Korean and U.S. values and norms. Friends and families helped lower acculturative stress. |
| Inman, Howard, Beaumont, and Walker (2007) | Influence of contextual factors on Asian Indian immigrant parents | 16 (8 male, 8 female) first-generation Asian Indian immigrant parents | 2 doctoral student, 1 PhD researchers; 1 PhD auditor | 1 phone interview (90–180 min) | Ethnic identity retention was influenced by engagement in cultural celebrations, the *(continued)* |

TABLE 16.1 (Continued)

**Summaries of Published Studies Using the Consensual Qualitative Research (CQR) Method**

| Study | Topic | Sample | Team | Data collection | Brief results |
|---|---|---|---|---|---|
| | | (44–71 years of age; age of immigration range from 21–35 years) | | | need to hold onto tradition, family ties, social support, and rejection of Western values. Specific strategies and challenges to transmit ethnic identity to their children were identified. |
| Rich and Cinamon (2007) | Spirituality among Israeli Arab and Jewish adolescents | 36 (21 female, 15 male; 18 Jewish, 18 Arab) adolescents | 2 PhD, 2 graduate student researchers; 1 PhD, 1 doctoral student auditors | 1 in-person interview (length not specified) | A majority of participants viewed themselves as religious and indicated an emotional connection with a transcendent, supreme being (religious spirituality), whereas others described feelings of transcendence that were not related to a supreme being (humanistic spirituality). Participants attributed legitimacy to both types of spirituality. Most believed that the essence of spirituality, regardless of religious practice, is transcendence. |
| Tuason, Taylor, Rollings, Harris, and Martin (2007) | Exploring Filipino American identity | 30 (20 female, 10 male; 16 born in Philippines, 14 born in United States) participants (18–63 years of age) | 3 undergraduate student, 1 PhD researchers; 1 graduate student auditor | 1 in-person or phone interview (45–60 min) | U.S.-born Filipino Americans considered American lifestyle as a distinguishing feature of their identities, whereas Philippine-born individuals described the importance of valuing family relationships; being hospitable, polite, and respectful; having faith in God; and speaking Tagalog. |

| Study | Purpose | Participants | Researchers | Data collection | Findings |
|---|---|---|---|---|---|
| Ali, Mahmood, Moel, Hudson, and Leathers (2008) | Muslim and Christian women's views of religion and feminism | 7 (5 African American, 2 White) Christian women and 7 (3 White, 2 Arab, 1 Afghan American, 1 Turkish) Muslim women (25–38 years of age) | 4 doctoral student, 1 PhD researcher; 1 doctoral student auditor | 1 phone interview (45–90 min) | Both Muslim and Christian women indicated that religion played a significant positive role in their lives, indicated that women should play a primary role in rearing their children, and endorsed feminist beliefs about equality for and empowerment of women. However, Muslim women were more likely than Christian women to identify as feminist. |
| Park-Taylor et al. (2008) | Perceptions and experiences of second-generation Americans about being a "true" American | 10 (5 female, 5 male; 5 Asian American, 3 Hispanic, 1 Caribbean, 1 biracial) second generation graduate students (age not specified) | 5 doctoral student, 1 PhD researchers; 1 doctoral student auditor | 1 in-person interview (30–45 min) and 1 phone or online instant messaging interview (length not specified) | Participants perceived a "true" American as having white skin, blonde hair, and blue eyes and acting in a patriotic way. Participants indicated that 9/11 and the war against Iraq changed attitudes about "true" Americans. Participants' American identities grew gradually, and their feelings of being a "true" American depended on who they were with and where they were. |
| Spanierman et al. (2008) | White university students' responses to societal racism | 11 (7 female, 4 male; 9 undergraduate, 2 graduate) White participants (18–23 years of age) | 2 undergraduate student, 4 graduate student, 1 PhD researchers; 1 graduate student auditor | 1 in-person interview (60–90 min) | White students' reactions to racism were categorized into affective responses (such as empathic reaction, guilt, etc.), social responses (such as limited exposure to people of color, tension, avoidance, or fear in relation to people of color, disapproval of racism), and cognitive responses (such as distortion and denial of race and racism, acknowledgement of racism and |

(continued)

TABLE 16.1 (Continued)

**Summaries of Published Studies Using the Consensual Qualitative Research (CQR) Method**

| Study | Topic | Sample | Team | Data collection | Brief results |
|---|---|---|---|---|---|
| | | | | | White privilege, and perceived disadvantages of being White in U.S. society). |
| Constantine, Kindaichi, Okazaki, Gainor, and Baden (2009) | Cultural adjustment experiences of Asian internationals | 15 Asian international college women (18–21 years of age) | 1 doctoral student, 4 PhD researchers; 1 doctoral student auditor | 1 in-person interview (45–60 min) | Participants were excited about the opportunities offered in the United States but also sad about moving here. They perceived English proficiency as a major academic challenge. Participants experienced various forms of discrimination such as being mistaken as member of another Asian ethnic group or being teased for poor English ability. Coping strategies included seeking advice from friends and family, learning to be more independent or self-sufficient, and minimizing or denying their problems. |
| Liu, Stinson, Hernandez, Shepard, and Haag (2009) | Homelessness, masculinity, and social class among homeless men | 15 (11 White, 2 African American, 2 biracial) homeless men (29–61 years of age) | 3 doctoral student researchers; 3 doctoral student auditors | 1 in-person interview (length not specified) | Participants became more empathic with the homeless after becoming homeless themselves, and indicated that they retained their sense of masculinity regardless of homelessness. Participants identified substance use, inadequate health care, and social stigma as major barriers to overcoming homelessness. Participants identified |

| Study | Purpose | Participants | Research team | Interview(s) | Findings |
|---|---|---|---|---|---|
| | | | | | substance cessation, attainment of a steady job, moving to a higher and more respected social class, and providing for other family members as key ambitions. |
| Wing Sue, Torino, Capodilupo, Rivera, and Lin (2009) | White faculty members' perception and reaction to difficult dialogues on race | 8 (6 female, 2 male; all White) university faculty (43–68 years of age; 10–25 years of teaching experience) | 4 doctoral student researchers; 1 PhD auditor | 1 in-person interview (45–60 min) | Difficult racial dialogue involved intense emotions and anxiety in both professors and students. Major obstacles that interfered with teaching about competence included fears of revealing personal biases and prejudices, losing classroom control, inability to understand and recognize the causes of difficult dialogues, and lack of knowledge and skills to intervene. |
| Blustein et al. (2010) | Urban students' ideas about school, work, race, and ethnicity | 32 (19 female, 13, male; 13 Caribbean American, 6 African American, 5 multiracial, 4 Latino/a, 4 White) urban high school students (13–19 years of age) | 4 doctoral student researchers; 1 PhD auditor | 1 in-person interview (30–60 min) | Most students believed that society held low expectations for them on the basis of their racial and ethnic background, but they did not believe that success could be predicted on the basis of background. |

### Career development

| Study | Purpose | Participants | Research team | Interview(s) | Findings |
|---|---|---|---|---|---|
| E. N. Williams et al. (1998) | Career paths of prominent academic women in counseling psychology | 13 prominent White female counseling psychologists who had chosen careers primarily in academia (43–66 years of age; 16–31 years of postdoctoral working experience) | 1 doctoral student, 3 undergraduate/postbaccalaureate student researchers; 1 doctoral student, 1 PhD auditors | 1 phone interview (40–60 min) | Both chance and planning were important in participants' career paths. Chance events affected career choices by changing career paths altogether or by altering self-concepts. Both internal characteristics (abilities to take risks, self-confidence, *(continued)* |

TABLE 16.1 (*Continued*)

**Summaries of Published Studies Using the Consensual Qualitative Research (CQR) Method**

| Study | Topic | Sample | Team | Data collection | Brief results |
|---|---|---|---|---|---|
| | | | | | etc.) and external factors (a strong support system, few external barriers, etc.) helped participants take advantage of chance opportunities. |
| Juntunen et al. (2001) | American Indians' perspectives on the career journey | 18 (11 female, 7 male) American Indians (21–59 years of age) | 4 doctoral student, 1 PhD researchers; 1 doctoral student auditor | 1 in-person interview (length not specified) | Career was an important concept for American Indians, representing a long-term commitment, planning for the future, having a relationship with personal and family goals, and being viewed as part of one's identity. Community and family had an impact on the career decision regardless of the level of education. Education was a stronger supportive factor for participants who completed high school than for these who did not complete high school. The typical obstacle for participants who completed high school was the lack of support from significant others, whereas the typical obstacle for these who did not complete high school was discrimination. |
| Pearson and Bieschke (2001) | Familial influences on the career development of professional African American women | 14 African American women in the midpoint of their careers (age $M = 40$, $SD = 6.7$ years) | 4 master's level social workers, 3 doctoral student, 2 PhD | 1 interview (60–120 min; mode of interview not specified) | The most important family factors related to African American women's career development included |

| | | | | emphasis on education, relationships with family members, and family's social and economic resources. Other factors included family gender role socialization and value toward work. |
|---|---|---|---|---|
| | | | researchers; 1 auditor (education not specified) | |
| Schultheiss, Kress, Manzi, and Glasscock (2001) | Relational influences in career exploration and decision making | 14 (8 female, 6 male; 7 White, 5 African American, 1 Asian American, 1 Middle Eastern) undergraduate students (18–40 years of age) | 2 doctoral student, 1 PhD researchers; 1 PhD auditor | 1 in-person interview (60 min) | Participants described relationships with family members and significant others as positive sources of influence on their career development. Participants indicated that family members and significant others provided emotional support by boosting their self-confidence when they struggled to make career-related decisions. Family members and significant others also actively assisted participants by providing information regarding specific career paths and by aiding participants in completing important career-related tasks (e.g. writing a resume). |
| Schultheiss, Palma, Predragovich, and Glasscock (2002) | Sibling relational influence of career exploration and decision making | 13 (7 female, 6 male; 8 White, 5 African American; 12 undergraduate, 1 postbaccalaureate) students (age $M = 21.5$, $SD = 4.93$ years) | 2 doctoral student, 1 PhD researchers; 1 PhD auditor | 1 in-person interview (60 min) | Sibling relationships were predominant sources of support. Participants reported that they often approached siblings for advice and information and viewed siblings as role models when exploring educational/career decisions (e.g. choosing a job or choosing a college to attend) or transitions (e.g. from high school to college). |

(continued)

TABLE 16.1 (Continued)

Summaries of Published Studies Using the Consensual Qualitative Research (CQR) Method

| Study | Topic | Sample | Team | Data collection | Brief results |
|---|---|---|---|---|---|
| Cinamon and Hellman (2004) | Career development stages of Israeli school counselors | 15 Israeli female school counselors (24–57 years of age; 1–19 years of experience) | 1 graduate student, 1 senior clinical supervisor in school setting, and 2 PhD researchers; 1 doctoral student auditor | 1 in-person interview (90–120 min) | The development of school counselors follows 4 stages: exploration, establishment, maintenance, and specialization. In addition, Israeli school counselors typically viewed coordination of service in school and initiating and leading (change) process in school as their roles, and considered their profession as meaningful. In terms of work style, participants reported that their work involved responding to emergency, collaboration with other professionals, such as teachers and psychologists, and assessing clients' needs and planning specific programs to meet those needs. |
| Schaefer, Friedlander, Blustein, and Maruna (2004) | The work lives of child molesters | 8 (7 White, 1 Hispanic) male convicted child molesters (36–52 years of age) recruited from an outpatient treatment facility after incarceration | 1 master's student, 3 doctoral student researchers; 1 doctoral student auditor | 1 in-person interview (120 min) | A reciprocal influence was found between participants' work experiences and their sexual offenses, such that excessive focus on work or boredom and frustration at work often triggered offenses and/or provided access to victims. Participants discussed dramatic loss in self-esteem, sense of personal control, and social support in |

| Study | Topic | Participants | Research team | Data collection | Findings |
|---|---|---|---|---|---|
| Constantine, Miville, Warren, Gainor, and Lewis-Coles (2006) | Religion, spirituality, and career development in African American college students | 12 (8 female, 4 male) African American college students (18–22 years of age) | 2 PhD researchers; 1 PhD auditor | 1 in-person interview (55–80 min) | their work lives after their disclosures and convictions. Participants who were viewed by their therapists as making progress were able to rebuild a secure social network, including work supervisors. Religion and spirituality are important contributors to career development. Religion affected career choice by guiding students to choose careers in which they could serve others through their work. Religion and spirituality also served as protective buffers to challenges faced by students pursuing their career goals. |
| Kenny et al. (2007) | Urban adolescents' perceptions of supports and barriers to educational and career attainment | 16 (10 female, 6 male; 8 African American, 7 Latino/a, 1 biracial) ninth-grade students (14–16 years of age) | 3 doctoral student, 2 PhD researchers; 2 doctoral student auditors | 1 in-person interview (length not specified) | A majority of students endorsed a goal of attending college. They identified schools and family as primary sources of support in working toward this goal. Conversely, students noted family misfortune and school inadequacies as significant barriers to reaching their goals. |
| Okubo, Yeh, Lin, Fujita, and Shea (2007) | The career decision-making process of Chinese American youth | 8 (5 female, 3 male) Chinese American youth (16–19 years of age) | 3 researchers; 1 auditor (education not specified) | 1 in-person interview (25–45 min) | Parents' academic and career expectations influenced Chinese American youths' career decisions. Participants experienced conflicts between their interests and internalized career expectations. |
| Shivy et al. (2007) | Ex-offenders' transition from prison to the workforce | 15 (9 female, 6 male; 8 African American, 6 White, 1 other) participants (21–46 years of age) | 2 staff from Department of Corrections, 4 doctoral student, 2 PhD | 2 in-person focus groups (90 min) | Social networks played a critical role in the reentry of ex-offenders, sometimes being supportive and other times hindering. Social *(continued)* |

TABLE 16.1 (Continued)

Summaries of Published Studies Using the Consensual Qualitative Research (CQR) Method

| Study | Topic | Sample | Team | Data collection | Brief results |
|---|---|---|---|---|---|
| | | | researchers; 1 doctoral student auditor | | skills and ability to socially navigate the transition also influenced the transition from prison to work. |
| Fouad et al. (2008) | Asian American career development | 12 (9 female, 3 male) Asian Americans (age ranged from 20s–80s) | 6 doctoral student, 1 PhD researchers; 1 auditor (education not specified) | 1 in-person or phone interview (60–90 min) | Both culture and family of origin influenced the construction of meaning of Asian Americans' career choices. Family influence included family expectations, family support, family obligations, friction between family of origin and American culture, etc. Cultural influences included differences between the culture of origin and the mainstream U.S. culture, cultural values and expectations, acting as a cultural representative, opportunities, discrimination, gender, and trust/mistrust. |
| Cinamon and Hason (2009) | Resources and barriers in family and career plans among at-risk Israeli youths | 15 (8 female, 7 male) at-risk Israeli adolescents (16–19 years of age) | 4 researchers (education not specified); 1 PhD auditor | 1 in-person interview (90–120 min) | Participants viewed work mainly as a way to get money; they considered few occupations as being available. Self was seen as both a barrier and resource to future plans. Participants wanted to provide a safe and stable place for their children unlike what they received. They felt obligated to family but realized |

| Authors | Purpose | Participants | Research team | Data collection | Findings |
|---|---|---|---|---|---|
| Schultheiss, Palma, and Manzi (2005) | Career development in middle childhood | 49 (30 female, 19 male; 29 White, 12 African American, 6 Latino/a, 2 other) urban elementary school students (9–12 years of age) | 1 doctoral student, 1 PhD researchers; 1 PhD aucitor | Written responses to 5 open-ended questions | that family could also prevent them from breaking the cycle of crime and unemployment. In middle childhood, participants began to form ideas about the importance of earning money, providing a home for one's family, and helping others through work. Important figures in their lives had significant influence on career development. |

**Trauma**

| Authors | Purpose | Participants | Research team | Data collection | Findings |
|---|---|---|---|---|---|
| Kasturirangan and Williams (2003) | The experience of Latina survivors of domestic violence and implications for counselors | 9 Latina women (24–51 years of age) | 1 undergracuate student, 1 PhD researcers; 1 PhD auditor | 1 in-person interview (45 min) | Women aligned themselves with traditional female gender roles, including being a good housekeeper, mother, and wife. Their descriptions were in line with the *marianismo* concept (i.e., women are submissive to men and are strong in that they endure abuse and bear suffering for the sake of their families). Women stayed in abusive relationships out of a sense of fear, helplessness, and a cultural pressure to maintain relationships. Participants wanted bilingual or bicultural counselors who could understand and support them. |
| Wettersten et al. (2004) | Impact of domestic violence on the working lives of women in shelter | 10 (5 Native American, 4 White, 1 Latina) women (20–47 years of age) | 2 master's students, 4 doctoral students, 1 PhD researchers; 1 PhD auditor | 1 in-person interview (55–100 min) | Domestic violence impeded efforts to maintain a job and concentrate at work. Participants' vocational self-concept and ability to work were inversely related to the *(continued)* |

TABLE 16.1 (*Continued*)

Summaries of Published Studies Using the Consensual Qualitative Research (CQR) Method

| Study | Topic | Sample | Team | Data collection | Brief results |
|---|---|---|---|---|---|
| | | | | | amount of physical and psychological violence experienced. Women noted community resources that facilitated and impeded meaningful employment. |
| Brown et al. (2005) | Battered women's processes of leaving abusive relationships | 13 (9 African American, 3 White, 1 other) women (22–46 years of age) | 5 doctoral student, 1 PhD researchers; 1 PhD auditor | 1 in-person interview (length not specified) | Typical goals involved obtaining employment and stable housing. Perceived ability to leave an abusive relationship depended upon housing transition options provided by shelters. Participants expressed interest in working or attaining a professional career, and this goal served as a source of hope throughout the process of exiting abusive relationships. |
| Constantine, Alleyne, Caldwell, McRae, and Suzuki (2005) | Coping responses of Asians, Blacks, and Latino/a New York City residents after 9/11 terrorist attacks | 24 (16 female, 8 male; 8 Asian, 8 Black, 8 Latino/Latina) residents of New York City (19–53 years of age) | 2 PhD researchers; 1 PhD auditor | 1 in-person interview (40–68 min) | Participants sought support from family members, friends, and peers. They coped by providing support and assistance to others, praying, attending church services, and keeping busy to avoid thinking about the tragedy. |
| Jacob and Veach (2005) | Intrapersonal and familial effects of child sexual abuse on female partners of male survivors | 10 White female partners (27–51 years of age) of male survivors of childhood sexual abuse | 1 master's student, 1 doctoral student researchers; 1 PhD auditor | 1 in-person interview (120–195 min) | Findings conformed to components (threatened beliefs, chronic stress, and reenactment of aspects of childhood |

| Authors | Topic | Participants | Analysis team | Method | Findings |
|---|---|---|---|---|---|
| | | | | | sexual abuse) of Maltas and Shay's (1995) trauma contagion model. Unlike other trauma survivors, male survivors of sexual trauma may contribute unique problems in sexual intimacy with their female partners. |
| Cinamon and Hellman (2006) | Coping and professional development of Israeli counselors in schools affected by terrorism | 12 Israeli Jewish female school counselors (22–56 years of age) | 2 PhD researchers; 2 auditors (education not specified) | 1 phone interview (90–120 min) | Participants experienced role confusion when facing terror-induced crisis. Vicarious traumatization led to symptoms similar to posttraumatic stress disorder. Novice counselors compared with experienced counselors depended more on written directives and had more difficulty separating work and private lives. |
| Inman, Yeh, Madan-Bahel, and Nath (2007) | Bereavement and coping of South Asian families between 9 and 10 months post 9/11 terrorist attack | 11 (7 female, 4 male) first-generation South Asians (age not specified) who lost a family member to 9/11 attack | 2 doctoral students, 1 PhD researchers; 1 PhD auditor | 1 in-person or phone interview (90 min) | Participants experienced difficulty achieving closure after the death of a family member due in part to the lack of opportunity to engage in traditional mourning practices in the United States. Culturally specific bereavement was especially important for unexpected losses. |
| **Medical and health-related studies** | | | | | |
| Veach, Bartels, and LeRoy (2001) | Ethical and professional challenges posed by patients with genetic concerns | 97 (74 female, 19 male, 4 unknown gender) physicians, nurses, and genetic counselors (three fourths of participants between 25–45 years of age) | 1 master's level genetic counselor, 2 PhD researchers; 1 genetic counseling master's student auditor | 12 focus groups (120 min each) | Concerns in genetic counseling included informed consent, uncertainty, resource allocation, and value conflicts. Issues raised often touched upon multiple, and at times conflicting, ethical principles and professional obligations. |

*(continued)*

## TABLE 16.1 (Continued)

### Summaries of Published Studies Using the Consensual Qualitative Research (CQR) Method

| Study | Topic | Sample | Team | Data collection | Brief results |
|---|---|---|---|---|---|
| J. Williams, Wyatt, Resell, Peterson, and Asuan-O'Brien (2004) | Psychosocial issues in HIV-positive African American and Latino men who have sex with men (MSM) | 23 (12 African American, 11 Latino; 10 gay-identifying, 13 non-gay-identifying) male participants (age $M = 33.87$ years) | 5 researchers (2 PhD, education not specified for other 3) | 4 focus groups (60 min; groups divided by ethnicity and gay versus non-gay identification) | MSM of color struggled with fulfilling gender roles and social expectations while attempting to maintain their attachments to their respective ethnic communities. Sociocultural and gender roles shaped definitions of sexuality and were related to sexual and drug risk-taking experiences among HIV-positive African American and Latino MSM with sexual abuse histories. |
| Parr, Kavanagh, Young, and McCafferty (2006) | Views of benzodiazepine (BZ) use among general practitioners (GP) and users | 28 (20 male, 8 female) GP and 23 (14 female, 9 male) BZ users (25–79 years of age) | 3 researchers; 1 auditor (education not specified) | 1 in-person interview (GP: 15–30 min; BZ users: 30–60 min) | Users felt that BZ was too easily prescribed. They wanted more advice from doctors on long-term adverse effects of BZ, beneficial lifestyle change, nonpharmacological management of problems, cessation, and strategies to manage withdrawal and anxiety. |
| Brown, Pikler, Lavish, Keune, and Hutto (2008) | Surviving childhood leukemia: Career, family, and future expectations | 11 (7 male, 4 female; 10 White, 1 Latino) people diagnosed with childhood leukemia (age of diagnosis: 2–15 years; current age 19–24 years) | 3 doctoral student, 1 PhD researchers; 1 PhD auditor | 1 in-person or phone interview (length not specified) | Participants initially wanted to be doctors or nurses, but current career choices were outside of the medical field. Participants thought about positive growth from their cancer experiences, and perceived support from family for their career plans. |

| Reference | Topic | Sample | Researchers | Method | Findings |
|---|---|---|---|---|---|
| Corneille, Tademy, Reid, Belgrave, and Nasim (2008) | Sexual safety and risk taking among African American men who have sex with women | 28 African American men (18–35 years of age) who have sex with women | 2 doctoral student researchers; 1 PhD auditor | 1 in-person interview (15–50 min) or focus group (58–70 min) | Pregnancy prevention was the most frequently endorsed motivation for condom use, followed by concern for STI. Condom nonuse was driven by perception of a stable monogamous relationship and "heat of the moment." |
| Heppner et al. (2009) | Coping with lymphedema in breast cancer survivors | 10 women (race not specified) with breast cancer and lymphedema (47–88 years of age) | 3 graduate student researchers; 2 PhD auditors | 1 in-person interview (length not specified) | Stressors associated with lymphedema include interference with daily activities and job performance, and lack of concern and caring of health care providers. Women coped by actively seeking information and treatment options, accepting the limitations associated with lymphedema, focusing on positive aspects of life, and giving and receiving social support. |
| **Same-sex relationships** | | | | | |
| Rostosky et al. (2004) | Same-sex couples' perceptions of family support | 14 (7 male, 7 female) same-sex couples (25 White, 1 African American, 1 Native American, 1 other; 18–50 years of age; 7 months to 22 years in length of relationship) | 3 doctoral student researchers; 1 doctoral student auditor | Videotaped conversation (30 min) between partners based on written prompts | Couples perceived family as supportive, non-supportive, or ambivalent, resulting in positive or negative emotional reactions. Family support influenced couples' relationship quality, such that positive relationships with extended families resulted in stronger relationships. |
| Castro-Convers, Gray, Ladany, and Metzler (2005) | Interpersonal contact with gay men by heterosexuals | 8 (6 female, 2 male; 1 White, 2 Jewish, 1 Jamaican, 4 Latinas) self-identified heterosexuals (18–34 years of | 2 doctoral student researchers; 1 PhD auditor | Analysis conducted on archival interviews (20–35 min) conducted as part of a human | Participants had positive or neutral initial attitudes towards gay men. Experiences at a gay bar generated initial discomfort but were overall |

*(continued)*

TABLE 16.1 (Continued)

**Summaries of Published Studies Using the Consensual Qualitative Research (CQR) Method**

| Study | Topic | Sample | Team | Data collection | Brief results |
|---|---|---|---|---|---|
| | | age) who had at least one interpersonal contact with a gay man | | sexuality course assignment | positive. Open formative experiences and meaningful interpersonal contact contributed to openness towards gays. Contact with gays did not change personal sense of morality. |
| Rostosky, Riggle, Dudley, and Wright (2006) | Commitment in same-sex relationship | 14 (7 male, 7 female) same-sex couples (24 White, 4 non-White; 19–54 years of age; 7 months to 22 years in length of relationship) | 3 researchers; 1 auditor (2 PhD, 2 master's level) | Videotaped conversations (30 min) between partners based on written prompts | Participants defined commitment through comparisons, costs, intracouple differences, investments, personal and relationship values and ideals, rewards, and sexual boundaries. Decisions about monogamy were key to perceived commitment. |
| Sánchez, Greenberg, Liu, and Vilain (2009) | Gay men's perception of the effects of masculine ideals | 547 self-identified gay men (18–80 years of age; 83% White, 6.8% Latino, 4.4% Asian American, 2.0% African American, 1.1% Native American) | 1 doctoral student, 2 undergraduate student researchers; 2 PhD auditors | Responded online to 6 open-ended questions | Participants reported more adverse than positive effects of masculine ideals on self-image and romantic relationships, including difficulty being emotional and affectionate, pressure to be physically attractive and to appear masculine for societal acceptance and desirability with other gay men. |

[a]Study used the CQR—modified (CQR-M) method.
[b]Study used the CQR—case study (CQR-C) method.

# References

Ali, S., Mahmood, A., Moel, J., Hudson, C., & Leathers, L. (2008). A qualitative investigation of Muslim and Christian women's views of religion and feminism in their lives. *Cultural Diversity and Ethnic Minority Psychology, 14*(1), 38–46. doi:10.1037/1099-9809.14.1.38

Baird, M., Szymanski, D., & Ruebelt, S. (2007). Feminist identity development and practice among male therapists. *Psychology of Men & Masculinity, 8*(2), 67–78. doi:10.1037/1524-9220.8.2.67.

Blustein, D., Murphy, K., Kenny, M., Jernigan, M., Pérez-Gualdrón, L., Castañeda, T., . . . Davis, O. (2010). Exploring urban students' constructions about school, work, race, and ethnicity. *Journal of Counseling Psychology, 57*(2), 248–254. doi:10.1037/a0018939

Brown, C., Linnemeyer, R., Dougherty, W., Coulson, J., Trangsrud, H., & Farnsworth, I. (2005). Battered women's process of leaving: Implications for career counseling. *Journal of Career Assessment, 13*(4), 452–475. doi:10.1177/1069072705277928

Brown, C., Pikler, V., Lavish, L., Keune, K., & Hutto, C. (2008). Surviving childhood leukemia: Career, family, and future expectations. *Qualitative Health Research, 18*(1), 19–30. doi:10.1177/1049732307 309221

Buboltz, W., Miller, M., & Williams, D. (1999). Content analysis of research in the *Journal of Counseling Psychology* (1973–1998). *Journal of Counseling Psychology, 46*(4), 496–503. doi:10.1037/0022-0167.46.4.496

Burkard, A. W., Johnson, A. J., Madson, M. B., Pruitt, N. T., Contreras-Tadych, D. A., Kozlowski, J. M., Hess, S. A., & Knox, S. (2006). Supervisor cultural responsiveness and unresponsiveness in cross-cultural supervision. *Journal of Counseling Psychology, 53*, 288–301. doi:10.1037/0022-0167.53.3.288

Burkard, A., Knox, S., Groen, M., Perez, M., & Hess, S. (2006). European American therapist self-disclosure in cross-cultural counseling. *Journal of Counseling Psychology, 53*(1), 15–25. doi:10.1037/ 0022-0167.53.1.15

Burkard, A. W., Knox, S., Hess, S., & Schultz, J. (2009). Lesbian, gay, and bisexual affirmative and non-affirmative supervision. *Journal of Counseling Psychology, 56*, 176–188. doi:10.1037/0022-0167.56.1.176

Castro-Convers, K., Gray, L., Ladany, N., & Metzler, A. (2005). Interpersonal contact experiences with gay men: A qualitative investigation of "fag hags" and gay-supportive heterosexual men. *Journal of Homosexuality, 49*(1), 47–76. doi:10.1300/J082v49n01_03

Chang, D. F., & Berk, A. (2009). Making cross-racial therapy work: A phenomenological study of clients' experiences of cross-racial therapy. *Journal of Counseling Psychology, 56*(4), 521–536. doi:10.1037/a0016905.

Cinamon, R., & Hason, I. (2009). Facing the future: Barriers and resources in work and family plans of at-risk Israeli youth. *Youth & Society, 40*(4), 502–525. doi:10.1177/0044118X08328008

Cinamon, R., & Hellman, S. (2004). Career development stages of Israeli school counselors. *British Journal of Guidance & Counselling, 32*(1), 39–55. doi:10.1080/03069880310001648085

Cinamon, R., & Hellman, S. (2006). Israeli counsellors facing terrorism: Coping and professional development. *British Journal of Guidance & Counselling, 34*(2), 191–207. doi:10.1080/03069880600583246

Constantine, M., Alleyne, V., Caldwell, L., McRae, M., & Suzuki, L. (2005). Coping responses of Asian, Black, and Latino/Latina New York City residents following the September 11, 2001 terrorist attacks against the United States. *Cultural Diversity and Ethnic Minority Psychology, 11*(4), 293–308. doi:10.1037/1099-9809.11.4.293

Constantine, M., Anderson, G., Berkel, L., Caldwell, L., & Utsey, S. (2005). Examining the cultural adjustment experiences of African international college students: A qualitative analysis. *Journal of Counseling Psychology, 52*(1), 57–66. doi:10.1037/0022-0167.52.1.57

Constantine, M., Kindaichi, M., Okazaki, S., Gainor, K., & Baden, A. (2005). A qualitative investigation of the cultural adjustment experiences of Asian international college women. *Cultural Diversity and Ethnic Minority Psychology, 11*(2), 162–175. doi:10.1037/1099-9809.11.2.162

Constantine, M., Miville, M., Warren, A., Gainor, K., & Lewis-Coles, M. (2006). Religion, spirituality, and career development in African American college students: A qualitative inquiry. *The Career Development Quarterly, 54*(3), 227–241.

Corneille, M., Tademy, R., Reid, M., Belgrave, F., & Nasim, A. (2008). Sexual safety and risk taking among African American men who have sex with women: A qualitative study. *Psychology of Men & Masculinity, 9*(4), 207–220. doi:10.1037/a0012768

De Stefano, J., D'Iuso, N., Blake, E., Fitzpatrick, M., Drapeau, M., & Chamodraka, M. (2007). Trainees' experiences of impasses in counselling and the impact of group supervision on their resolution: A pilot study. *Counselling & Psychotherapy Research, 7*(1), 42–47. doi:10.1080/14733140601140378

DiGiorgio, K., Arnkoff, D., Glass, C., Lyhus, K., & Walter, R. (2004). EMDR and theoretical orientation: A qualitative study of how therapists integrate eye movement desensitization and reprocessing into their approach to psychotherapy. *Journal of Psychotherapy Integration, 14*(3), 227–252. doi:10.1037/1053-0479.14.3.227

Dillon, F., Worthington, R., Savoy, H., Rooney, S., Becker-Schutte, A., & Guerra, R. (2004). Counselor preparation: On becoming allies: A qualitative study of lesbian-, gay-, and bisexual- affirmative counselor training. *Counselor Education and Supervision, 43*(3), 162–178.

Fitzpatrick, M. R., Janzen, J., Chamodraka, M., Gamberg, S., & Blake, E. (2009). Client relationship incidents in early therapy: Doorways to collaborative engagement. *Psychotherapy Research, 19*(6), 654–665. doi:10.1080/10503300902878235

Fitzpatrick, M., Janzen, J., Chamodraka, M., & Park, J. (2006). Client critical incidents in the process of early alliance development: A positive emotion-exploration spiral. *Psychotherapy Research, 16*(4), 486–498. doi:10.1080/10503300500485391

Fouad, N., Kantamneni, N., Smothers, M., Chen, Y., Fitzpatrick, M., & Terry, S. (2008). Asian American career development: A qualitative analysis. *Journal of Vocational Behavior, 72*(1), 43–59. doi:10.1016/j.jvb.2007.10.002

Friedlander, M. L., Larney, L. C., Skau, M., Hotaling, M., Cutting, M. L., & Schwam, M. (2000). Bicultural identification: Experiences of internationally adopted children and their parents. *Journal of Counseling Psychology, 47*, 187–198. doi:10.1037/0022-0167.47.2.187

Fuertes, J. N., Mueller, L. N., Chauhan, R. V., Walker, J. A., & Ladany, N. (2002). An investigation of European American therapists' approach to counseling African American clients. *The Counseling Psychologist, 30*, 763–788. doi:10.1177/0011000002305007

Gazzola, N., & Stalikas, A. (2004). Therapist interpretations and client processes in three therapeutic modalities: Implications for psychotherapy integration. *Journal of Psychotherapy Integration, 14*(4), 397–418. doi:10.1037/1053-0479.14.4.397

Gazzola, N., & Thériault, A. (2007). Relational themes in counselling supervision: Broadening and narrowing processes. *Canadian Journal of Counselling, 41*(4), 228–243.

Gelso, C. J., Hill, C. E., Rochlen, A., Mohr, J., & Zack, J. (1999). Describing the face of transference: Psychodynamic therapists' recollections of transference in successful long-term therapy. *Journal of Counseling Psychology, 46*, 257–267. doi:10.1037/0022-0167.46.2.257

Gray, L. A., Ladany, N., Walker, J. A., & Ancis, J. R. (2001). Psychotherapy trainees' experience of counterproductive events in supervision. *Journal of Counseling Psychology, 48*, 371–383. doi:10.1037/0022-0167.48.4.371

Hayes, J. A., McCracken, J. E., McClanahan, M. K., Hill, C. E., Harp, J. S., & Carozzoni, P. (1998). Therapist perspectives on countertransference: Qualitative data in search of a theory. *Journal of Counseling Psychology, 45*, 468–482. doi:10.1037/0022-0167.45.4.468

Hendrickson, S. M., Veach, P. M., & LeRoy, B. S. (2002). A qualitative investigation of student and supervisor perceptions of live supervision in genetic counseling. *Journal of Genetic Counseling, 11*, 25–49. doi:10.1023/A:1013868431533

Heppner, P., Tierney, C., Wang, Y., Armer, J., Whitlow, N., & Reynolds, A. (2009). Breast cancer survivors coping with lymphedema: What all counselors need to know. *Journal of Counseling & Development, 87*(3), 327–338.

Hernández, P., Taylor, B., & McDowell, T. (2009). Listening to ethnic minority AAMFT approved supervisors: Reflections on their experiences as supervisees. *Journal of Systemic Therapies, 28*(1), 88–100. doi:10.1521/jsyt.2009.28.1.88.

Hess, S., Knox, S., Schultz, J. M., Hill, C. E., Sloan, L., Brandt, S., . . . Hoffman, M. A. (2008). Pre-doctoral interns' non-disclosure in supervision. *Psychotherapy Research, 18,* 400–411. doi:10.1080/105033 00701697505

Hill, C. (1996). *Working with dreams in psychotherapy.* New York, NY: Guilford Press.

Hill, C. (2004). *Dream work in therapy: Facilitating exploration, insight, and action.* Washington, DC: American Psychological Association.

Hill, C. E., Kellems, I. S., Kolchakian, M. R., Wonnell, T. L., Davis, T. L., & Nakayama, E. Y. (2003). The therapist experience of being the target of hostile versus suspected-unasserted client anger: Factors associated with resolution. *Psychotherapy Research, 13,* 475–491. doi:10.1093/ptr/kpg040

Hill, C., Knox, S., Hess, S., Crook-Lyon, R., Goates-Jones, M., & Sim, W. (2007). The attainment of insight in the Hill dream model: A case study. In L. G. Castonguay & C. E. Hill (Eds.), *Insight in psychotherapy* (pp. 207–230). Washington, DC: American Psychological Association.

Hill, C. E., Knox, S., Thompson, B. J., Williams, E. N., Hess, S.A., & Ladany, N. (2005). Consensual Qualitative Research: An update. *Journal of Counseling Psychology, 52,* 196–205. doi:10.1037/0022-0167.52.2.196

Hill, C. E., Nutt-Williams, E., Heaton, K. J., Thompson, B. J., & Rhodes, R. H. (1996). Therapist retrospective recall of impasses in long-term psychotherapy: A qualitative analysis. *Journal of Counseling Psychology, 43,* 207–217. doi:10.1037/0022-0167.43.2.207

Hill, C. E., Sim, W., Spangler, P., Stahl, J., Sullivan, C., & Teyber, E. (2008). Therapist immediacy in brief psychotherapy: Case study II. *Psychotherapy: Theory, Research, Practice, Training, 45,* 298–315. doi:10.1037/a0013306

Hill, C. E., Sullivan, C., Knox, S., & Schlosser, L. Z. (2007). Becoming psychotherapists: Experiences of novice trainees in a beginning graduate class. *Psychotherapy: Theory, Research, Practice, Training, 44,* 434–449. doi:10.1037/0033-3204.44.4.434

Hill, C. E., Thompson, B. J., & Williams, E. N. (1997). A guide to conducting consensual qualitative research. *The Counseling Psychologist, 25,* 517–572. doi:10.1177/0011000097254001

Hill, C. E., Zack, J. S., Wonnell, T. L., Hoffman, M. A., Rochlen, A. B., Goldberg, J. L., . . . Hess, S. (2000). Structured brief therapy with a focus on dreams or loss for clients with troubling dreams and recent loss. *Journal of Counseling Psychology, 47,* 90–101. doi:10.1037/0022-0167.47.1.90

Hoffman, M. A., Hill, C. E., Holmes, S. E., & Freitas, G. F. (2005). Supervisor perspective on the process and outcome of giving easy, difficult, or no feedback to supervisees. *Journal of Counseling Psychology, 52,* 3–13. doi:10.1037/0022-0167.52.1.3

Inman, A., Howard, E., Beaumont, R., & Walker, J. (2007). Cultural transmission: Influence of contextual factors in Asian Indian immigrant parents' experiences. *Journal of Counseling Psychology, 54*(1), 93–100. doi:10.1037/0022-0167.54.1.93

Inman, A., Yeh, C., Madan-Bahel, A., & Nath, S. (2007). Bereavement and coping of South Asian families post 9/11. *Journal of Multicultural Counseling and Development, 35*(2), 101–115.

Jacob, C., & Veach, P. (2005). Intrapersonal and familial effects of child sexual abuse on female partners of male survivors. *Journal of Counseling Psychology, 52*(3), 284–297. doi:10.1037/0022-0167.52.3.284

Jennings, L., & Skovholt, T. M. (1999). The cognitive, emotional, and relational characteristics of master therapists. *Journal of Counseling Psychology, 46,* 3–11. doi:10.1037/0022-0167.46.1.3

Jennings, L., Sovereign, A., Bottorff, N., Mussell, M., & Vye, C. (2005). Nine ethical values of master therapists. *Journal of Mental Health Counseling, 27*(1), 32–47.

Johnson, C., Hayes, J., & Wade, N. (2007). Psychotherapy with troubled spirits: A qualitative investigation. *Psychotherapy Research, 17*(4), 450–460. doi:10.1080/10503300600953520

Juntunen, C. L., Barraclough, D. J., Broneck, C. L., Seibel, G. A., Winrow, S. A., & Morin, P. M. (2001). American Indian perspectives on the career journey. *Journal of Counseling Psychology, 48,* 274–285. doi: 10.1037/0022-0167.48.3.274

Kasper, L., Hill, C. E., & Kivlighan, D. (2008). Therapist immediacy in brief psychotherapy: Case study I. *Psychotherapy: Theory, Research, Practice, Training, 45,* 281–297. doi:10.1037/a0013305

Kasturirangan, A., & Williams, E. N. (2003). Counseling Latina battered women: A qualitative study of the Latina perspective. *Journal of Multicultural Counseling and Development, 31,* 162–178.

Kenny, M., Gualdron, L., Scanlon, D., Sparks, E., Blustein, D., & Jernigan, M. (2007). Urban adolescents' constructions of supports and barriers to educational and career attainment. *Journal of Counseling Psychology, 54*(3), 336–343. doi:10.1037/0022-0167.54.3.336

Kim, B. S. K., Brenner, B. R., Liang, C. T. H., & Asay, P. A. (2003). A qualitative study of adaptation experiences of 1.5-generation Asian Americans. *Cultural Diversity & Ethnic Minority Psychology, 9,* 156–170. doi:10.1037/1099-9809.9.2.156

King, R., Bambling, M., Lloyd, C., Gomurra, R., Smith, S., Reid, W., & Wegner, K. (2006). Online counselling: The motives and experiences of young people who choose the Internet instead of face to face or tele-phone counseling. *Counselling & Psychotherapy Research, 6*(3), 169–174. doi:10.1080/14733140600848179

Knox, S., Burkard, A. W., Edwards, L., Smith, J., & Schlosser, L. Z. (2008). Supervisors' reports of the effects of supervisor self-disclosure on super-visees. *Psychotherapy Research, 18,* 543–559. doi:10.1080/105033008 01982781

Knox, S., Burkard, A. W., Johnson, A. J., Suzuki, L. A., & Ponterotto, J. G. (2003). African American and European American therapists' expe-riences of addressing race in cross-racial psychotherapy dyads. *Journal of Counseling Psychology, 50,* 466–481. doi:10.1037/0022-0167.50.4.466

Knox, S., Catlin, L., Casper, M., & Schlosser, L. Z. (2005). Addressing religion and spirituality in psychotherapy: Clients' perspectives. *Psychotherapy Research, 15,* 287–303. doi:10.1080/10503300500090894

Knox, S., Dubois, R., Smith, J., Hess, S. A., & Hill, C. E. (2009). Clients' experiences giving gifts to therapists. *Psychotherapy: Theory, Research, Practice, Training, 46,* 350–361. doi:10.1037/a0017001

Knox, S., Goldberg, J. L., Woodhouse, S. S., & Hill, C. E. (1999). Clients' internal representations of their therapists. *Journal of Counseling Psychology, 46,* 244–256. doi:10.1037/0022-0167.46.2.244

Knox, S., Hess, S., Petersen, D., & Hill, C. E. (1997). A qualitative analy-sis of client perceptions of the effects of helpful therapist self-disclosure in long-term therapy. *Journal of Counseling Psychology, 44,* 274–283. doi:10.1037/0022-0167.44.3.274

Knox, S., Hess, S. A., Williams, E. N., & Hill, C. E. (2003). "Here's a little something for you": How therapists respond to client gifts. *Journal of Counseling Psychology, 50,* 199–210. doi:10.1037/0022-0167.50.2.199

Knox, S., Hill, C., Hess, S., & Crook-Lyon, R. E. (2008). Case studies of the attainment of insight in dream sessions: Replication and exten-sion. *Psychotherapy Research, 18*(2), 200–215. doi:10.1080/105033007 01432242

Knox, S., Schlosser, L. Z., Pruitt, N. T., & Hill, C. E. (2006). A qualitative examination of graduate advising relationships: The advisor perspec-tive. *The Counseling Psychologist, 34,* 489–518. doi:10.1177/001100000 6290249

Ladany, N., Constantine, M. G., Miller, K., Erickson, C., & Muse-Burke, J. (2000). Supervisor countertransference: A qualitative investigation into its identification and description. *Journal of Counseling Psychology, 47,* 102–115. doi:10.1037/0022-0167.47.1.102

Ladany, N., Hill, C. E., Thompson, B. J., & O'Brien, K. M. (2004). Therapist perspectives on using silence in therapy: A qualitative study. *Counselling & Psychotherapy Research, 4,* 80–89. doi:10.1080/147331404 12331384088

Ladany, N., O'Brien, K. M., Hill, C. E., Melincoff, D. S., Knox, S., & Petersen, D. A. (1997). Sexual attraction toward clients, use of supervision, and prior training: A qualitative study of predoctoral psychology interns. *Journal of Counseling Psychology, 44*, 413–424. doi:10.1037/0022-0167.44.4.413

Liu, W., Stinson, R., Hernandez, J., Shepard, S., & Haag, S. (2009). A qualitative examination of masculinity, homelessness, and social class among men in a transitional shelter. *Psychology of Men & Masculinity, 10*(2), 131–148. doi:10.1037/a0014999

Lloyd, C., King, R., & Ryan, L. (2007). The challenge of working in mental health settings: Perceptions of newly graduated occupational therapists. *British Journal of Occupational Therapy, 70*(11), 460–470.

Maltas, C., & Shay, J. (1995). Trauma contagion in partners of survivors of childhood sexual abuse. *American Journal of Orthopsychiatry, 65*(4), 529–539. doi:10.1037/h0079673

Niles, S. G., Goodman, J., & Pope, M. (2002). *The career counseling casebook: A resource for practitioners, students, and counselor educators.* Tulsa, OK: National Career Development Association.

Okubo, Y., Yeh, C., Lin, P., Fujita, K., & Shea, J. (2007). The career decision-making process of Chinese American youth. *Journal of Counseling & Development, 85*(4), 440–449.

Park-Taylor, J., Ng, V., Ventura, A., Kang, A., Morris, C., Gilbert, T., . . . Androsiglio, R. A. (2008). What it means to be and feel like a "true" American: Perceptions and experiences of second-generation Americans. *Cultural Diversity and Ethnic Minority Psychology, 14*(2), 128–137. doi:10.1037/1099-9809.14.2.128

Parr, J., Kavanagh, D., Young, R., & McCafferty, K. (2006). Views of general practitioners and benzodiazepine users on benzodiazepines: A qualitative analysis. *Social Science & Medicine, 62*(5), 1237–1249. doi:10.1016/j.socsimed.2005.07.016

Pearson, S. M., & Bieschke, K. J. (2001). Succeeding against the odds: An examination of familial influences on the career development of professional African American women. *Journal of Counseling Psychology, 48*, 301–309. doi: 10.1037/0022-0167.48.3.301

Rhodes, R., Hill, C. E., Thompson, B. J., & Elliott, R. (1994). Client retrospective recall of resolved and unresolved misunderstanding events. *Journal of Counseling Psychology, 41*, 473–483. doi:10.1037/0022-0167.41.4.473

Rich, Y., & Cinamon, R. (2007). Conceptions of spirituality among Israeli Arab and Jewish late adolescents. *Journal of Humanistic Psychology, 47*(1), 7–29. doi:10.1177/0022167806291324

Rostosky, S., Korfhage, B., Duhigg, J., Stern, A., Bennett, L., & Riggle, E. (2004). Same-sex couple perceptions of family support: A consensual qualitative study. *Family Process, 43*(1), 43–57. doi:10.1111/j.1545-5300.2004.04301005.x

Rostosky, S., Riggle, E., Dudley, M., & Wright, M. (2006). Commitment in same-sex relationships: A qualitative analysis of couples' conversations. *Journal of Homosexuality, 51*(3), 199–222. doi:10.1111/j.1545-5300.2004.04301005.x

Sánchez, F., Greenberg, S., Liu, W., & Vilain, E. (2009). Reported effects of masculine ideals on gay men. *Psychology of Men & Masculinity, 10*(1), 73–87. doi: 10.1037/a0013513

Santiago-Rivera, A. L., Altarriba, J., Poll, N., Gonzalez-Miller, N., & Cragun, C. (2009). Therapists' views on working with bilingual Spanish–English speaking clients: A qualitative investigation. *Professional Psychology: Research and Practice, 40*, 436–443. doi:10.1037/a0015933

Schaefer, B. M., Friedlander, M. L., Blustein, D. L., & Maruna, S. (2004). The work lives of child molesters: A phenomenological perspective. *Journal of Counseling Psychology, 51*(2), 226–239. doi:10.1037/0022-0167.51.2.226

Schlosser, L. S., Knox, S., Moskovitz, A. R., & Hill, C. E. (2003). A qualitative examination of graduate advising relationships: The advisee perspective. *Journal of Counseling Psychology, 50,* 178–188. doi:10.1037/0022-0167.50.2.178

Schultheiss, D. E. P., Kress, H. M., Manzi, A. J., & Glasscock, J. M. J. (2001). Relational influences in career development: A qualitative inquiry. *The Counseling Psychologist, 29,* 216–239. doi: 10.1177/0011000001292003

Schultheiss, D., Palma, T., & Manzi, A. (2005). Career development in middle childhood: A qualitative inquiry. *The Career Development Quarterly, 53*(3), 246–262.

Schultheiss, D. E. P., Palma, T. V., Predragovich, K. S., & Glasscock, J. M. J. (2002). Relational influences on career paths: Siblings in context. *Journal of Counseling Psychology, 49,* 302–310. doi: 10.1037/0022-0167.49.3.302

Shivy, V., Wu, J., Moon, A., Mann, S., Holland, J., & Eacho, C. (2007). Ex-offenders reentering the workforce. *Journal of Counseling Psychology, 54*(4), 466–473. doi:10.1037/0022-0167.54.4.466

Sim, W., Hill, C. E., Chowdhury, S., Huang, T. C., Zaman, N., & Talavera, P. (2010). Problems and action ideas discussed by first- and second-generation female East Asian students during dream sessions. *Dreaming, 20,* 42–59. doi:10.1037/a0018993

Spangler, P., Hill, C. E., Mettus, C., Guo, A. H., & Heymsfield, L. (2009). Therapist perspectives on the dreams about clients: A qualitative investigation. *Psychotherapy Research, 19,* 81–95. doi:10.1080/10503300802430665

Spanierman, L., Oh, E., Poteat, V., Hund, A., McClair, V., Beer, A., & Clarke, A. M (2008). White university students' responses to societal racism: A qualitative investigation. *The Counseling Psychologist, 36*(6), 839–870. doi:10.1177/0011000006295589

Stahl, J. V., Hill, C. E., Jacobs, T., Kleinman, S., Isenberg, D., & Stern, A. (2009). When the shoe is on the other foot: A qualitative study of intern-level trainees' perceived learning from clients. *Psychotherapy: Theory, Research, Practice, Training, 46,* 376–389. doi:10.1037/a0017000

Tuason, M. T. G., Taylor, A. R., Rollings, L., Harris, T., & Martin, C. (2007). On both sides of the hyphen: Exploring the Filipino-American identity. *Journal of Counseling Psychology, 54,* 362–372. doi:10.1037/0022-0167.54.4.362

Veach, P. M., Bartels, D. M., & LeRoy, B. S. (2001). Ethical and professional challenges posed by patients with genetic concerns: A report of focus group discussions with genetic counselors, physicians, and nurses. *Journal of Genetic Counseling, 10,* 97–119. doi:10.1023/A:1009487513618

Vivino, B. L., Thompson, B., Hill, C. E., & Ladany, N. (2009). Compassion in psychotherapy: The perspective of psychotherapists nominated as compassionate. *Psychotherapy Research, 19,* 157–171. doi:10.1080/10503300802430681.

Wettersten, K., Rudolph, S., Faul, K., Gallagher, K., Trangsrud, H., Adams, K., . . . Terrance, C. (2004). Freedom through self-sufficiency: A qualitative examination of the impact of domestic violence on the working lives of women in shelter. *Journal of Counseling Psychology, 51*(4), 447–462. doi:10.1037/0022-0167.51.4.447

Whiston, S., Lindeman, D., Rahardja, D., & Reed, J. (2005). Career counseling process: A qualitative analysis of experts' cases. *Journal of Career Assessment, 13*(2), 169–187. doi:10.1177/1069072704273126

Williams, E. N., Judge, A. B., Hill, C. E., & Hoffman, M. A. (1997). Experiences of novice therapists in prepracticum: Trainees', clients', and supervisors' perceptions of therapists' personal reactions and management strategies. *Journal of Counseling Psychology, 44,* 390–399. doi:10.1037/0022-0167.44.4.390

Williams, E. N., Polster, D., Grizzard, M. B., Rockenbaugh, J., & Judge, A. B. (2003). What happens when therapists feel bored or anxious? A qualitative study of distracting self-awareness and therapists' management strategies. *Journal of Contemporary Psychotherapy, 33,* 5–18. doi:10.1023/A:1021499526052

Williams, E. N., Soeprapto, E., Like, K., Touradji, P., Hess, S. & Hill, C. E. (1998). Perceptions of serendipity: Career paths of prominent academic women in counseling psychology. *Journal of Counseling Psychology, 45,* 379–389. doi:10.1037/0022-0167.45.4.379

Williams, J., Wyatt, G., Resell, J., Peterson, J., & Asuan-O'Brien, A. (2004). Psychosocial issues among gay- and non-gay-identifying HIV-seropositive African American and Latino MSM. *Cultural Diversity and Ethnic Minority Psychology, 10*(3), 268–286. doi:10.1037/1099-9809.10.3.268

Wing Sue, D., Torino, G., Capodilupo, C., Rivera, D., & Lin, A. (2009). How White faculty perceive and react to difficult dialogues on race: Implications for education and training. *The Counseling Psychologist, 37*(8), 1090–1115. doi:10.1177/0011000009340443

Wonnell, T., & Hill, C. E. (2000). The effects of including the action stage in dream interpretation. *Journal of Counseling Psychology, 47*, 372–379. doi:10.1037/0022-0167.47.3.372.

Yeh, C., Ma, P., Madan-Bahel, A., Hunter, C., Jung, S., Kim, A., . . . Sasaki, K. (2005). The cultural negotiations of Korean immigrant youth. *Journal of Counseling & Development, 83*(2), 172–182.

# MODIFICATIONS AND EXTENSIONS OF CONSENSUAL QUALITATIVE RESEARCH

# IV

*Patricia T. Spangler, Jingqing Liu, and Clara E. Hill*

# Consensual Qualitative Research for Simple Qualitative Data
## *An Introduction to CQR-M*

17

magine that you are conducting a large online quantitative survey of countertransference management strategies used by therapists in training. In addition to the quantitative measures included in the survey, you decide to add a single open-ended question asking participants to describe components of their unique clinical experiences that were not captured by the measures in the survey (e.g., "How do specific client characteristics or presenting issues relate to your unresolved issues?"). The written responses obtained from your 300 participants contain three or four sentences each and are relatively straightforward and easy to understand. Constructing core ideas as you would for a traditional consensual qualitative research (CQR) analysis seems excessive because the comments are already succinct and there is no context to consider. A briefer alternative to CQR that would produce domains and categories consensually derived from the data would be useful, but you are unsure of how to structure the coding teams, code the data, report the results, or discuss the qualitative findings within the context of the overall study. Fortunately, consensual qualitative research—modified (CQR-M) allows you to do just this task. This chapter provides a brief definition and background of CQR-M followed by a rationale for using CQR-M. We then provide a step-by-step guide to conducting CQR-M analyses.

## Definition and Background

CQR-M is a qualitative research method that was adapted from CQR for use with large samples and relatively brief, simple, qualitative data. In addition to its basis in original CQR, CQR-M borrows from both discovery-oriented research (Mahrer, 1988) and exploratory research (Hill, 1990). These methods are bottom-up approaches through which researchers derive categories from the data rather than imposing a predetermined structure on the data. Once categories are developed, discovery-oriented and exploratory researchers train a new team of judges to code data into the derived categories, calculate interrater reliability, and retrain judges to code more reliably if necessary. We eschew the approach of training judges to high reliability, however, because our experience has been that focusing on reliability stifles judges' clinical judgment and inhibits discussion and thereby prevents the team from coming to the best, most comprehensively informed judgment. CQR-M merges the discovery-oriented and exploratory approaches with the consensual component of CQR to create a method that allows us to code relatively simple data directly into categories using consensus among judges.

## Rationale for CQR-M

### CQR-M VERSUS INTERRATER AGREEMENT

We favor CQR-M over quantitative methods that emphasize interrater agreement for several reasons. First, human communication is often nuanced and ambiguous. Being able to think and talk about shades of meaning helps researchers arrive at a more faithful representation of participants' responses than can typically be achieved by coders working independently. Relatedly, in quantitative research, judges often code data independently, and thus their unchecked biases may cause them to overlook important things. By contrast, CQR-M judges discuss their expectations, biases, and disagreements with each other at length and can thus help each other keep true to the data. Having multiple perspectives typically helps to reduce individual biases and thereby yields a better understanding of the data. Lastly, in quantitative research judges often consciously or unconsciously strive for high levels of agreement, which may cause them to constrain their clinical intuition and try to guess what other judges will say so that they can attain a specific level of agreement. In contrast, with CQR-M, judges are not required to force data into particular domains just to attain high agreement levels. Instead, they are encouraged to use their experience and wisdom to provide thoughtful reasons for their coding.

## PURPOSES OF CQR-M

CQR-M is an effective tool for exploring phenomena for new and unexpected ideas. For example, in a recently completed study (Spangler et al., 2009), we investigated specific teaching methods for training undergraduates to use the helping skill of immediacy. Through qualitative analysis of participants' written responses to questions about their experience of learning immediacy, we were able to explore participants' reactions to what they liked and disliked about training. Using CQR-M enabled discovery of two unanticipated domains in immediacy training: (a) what the students would have liked in their training and (b) how the training affected the closeness of lab group members.

In addition to exploration and discovery, CQR-M can be used for describing little-studied phenomena; results can help to expand the knowledge base and can serve as the basis for further research. Such newly described phenomena can also be combined with quantitative data to gain a fuller understanding of the topic under investigation. For example, in a study of interpersonal patterns in dreams (Hill, Spangler, Sim, & Baumann, 2007), written descriptions of dreams were taken from 67 participants. One purpose of the study was to identify and describe interpersonal themes in dreams and another was to examine the associations between these relational themes and the quantitative data on session process and outcome. CQR-M was used to derive five basic relational themes: positive, negative, interpersonal nightmare, interpersonal agency, and noninterpersonal. In addition to describing the patterns, quantitative analyses were used to determine whether different patterns of process and outcome occurred in dream sessions for the five different types of dreams.

*Triangulation*—another rationale for using CQR-M—refers to the notion that multiple views of a phenomenon provide a better understanding of the phenomenon of interest (Heppner, Kivlighan, & Wampold, 1999). Denzin (1978) described methodological triangulation as using multiple methods to examine a phenomenon. CQR-M can be used in combination with quantitative methods for the purpose of methodological triangulation. For example, in the aforementioned study on immediacy training (Spangler et al., 2009), the overall purpose of the study was to investigate how specific instructional components contributed to students' self-efficacy for using immediacy. After each component of training (e.g., reading, lecture, practice), participants were asked to rate their self-efficacy for using immediacy using a four-item scale. We triangulated quantitative results from these items with CQR-M-analyzed results of participants' responses to four open-ended questions: What was difficult about learning to do immediacy? What was most helpful about the training? What was least helpful? How do you think your culture affected your ability (either positively or negatively) to learn immediacy? Comparison of qualitative and quantitative results revealed that students' perception of their immediacy training experience was very different in retrospect (the open questions were asked at the end of training) than it was during the process of training, when the quantitative measures were completed. CQR-M analyses indicated that 72% of the sample believed that practicing immediacy was the most effective part of the training, whereas quantitative results showed that the greatest increase in immediacy self-efficacy occurred after the lecture component. The varying results illustrate the benefit of triangulating perspectives from multiple time points.

Clearly, then, the qualitative component in this study raised interesting questions about the comparative effectiveness of teaching components and supported our thinking that the quantitative measure was subject to a ceiling effect (i.e., additional benefits of practice cannot be captured on the quantitative measure when ratings after lecture were already extremely high). In addition, the exploratory questions shed new light on culture as a factor in helping skills training, in particular, specific cultural variables unknown to the investigators that thus could not be preconceived and incorporated into the quantitative measure.

## CQR-M: A Step-by-Step Guide

In this section we provide a detailed description of how to conduct CQR-M analyses. We begin with design considerations, including determining the purpose of the qualitative data and the issue of sample size. Next are steps for data collection, followed by steps for recruiting and training judges. We then describe the procedures for analyzing brief qualitative data, including development of domains and categories, and the consensual coding process. Finally, we provide some guidance for writing up CQR-M results and discussion sections. The steps of the CQR-M process are shown graphically in Figure 17.1. To compare the CQR-M process with that of CQR as originally conceived, compare Figure 17.1 with Figure 1.1 in Chapter 1 (see p. 13).

### DESIGN CONSIDERATIONS

#### Purposes of the Qualitative Data

A key consideration in deciding whether CQR-M is appropriate is how the qualitative data will be used. Whether the data will be used for

## FIGURE 17.1

**GETTING STARTED**

1. Determine purpose of qualitative data.

2. Determine sample size.

3. Determine appropriate length of questionnaire.

4. Determine medium for data collection.

5. Collect data.

6. Determine which data to include in data set.

**DATA ANALYSIS**

1. Develop domains and list of categories.

2. Select a coding team.

3. Train judges.

4. Revise domains and categories.

5. Code data into categories.

**WRITING THE MANUSCRIPT**

1. Write, rewrite, rewrite.

2. Give quotes to illustrate categories.

3. Get feedback and revise.

4. Keep rewriting until you convey a good, clear, story that reflects the data.

Steps involved in consensual qualitative research—modified.

exploration and description of phenomena or for triangulation with quantitative data will help determine how much data to collect and which topics should be the focus of inquiry. For example, for the immediacy training study (Spangler et al., 2009), we began by speculating about variables that might relate to students gaining immediacy self-efficacy. Among those variables were specific training components, student aptitude and prior experience with helping, and lab group climate. Specific training components were quantitatively tested, as were helping aptitude and group climate. However, we were concerned that our quantitative measures might not capture the complexity of the students' experience of learning such an advanced and socially uncomfortable helping skill. We were interested in triangulating the quantitative data with qualitative analyses that provided a more participant-constructed view of the experience. However, given the large sample size, we wanted to limit their written responses to a length that could capture their individual experience and that could be analyzed in a reasonable length of time, which could not be done with full CQR interview-based data.

## Sample Size

Although CQR traditionally has been used to analyze small samples (eight to 15 participants), larger samples can be accommodated with CQR-M. To date, two studies (Hill et al., 2007; Spangler et al., 2009) have used the CQR-M approach with samples sizes of 67 and 132, respectively. There are benefits and costs of studying a large sample using CQR-M. Obviously, studying a large number of cases with the amount of rich data that are collected with traditional CQR would be unrealistic because of the time and effort it would require. CQR-M sacrifices depth and richness in analyzing a small amount of qualitative data collected from a large number of cases, but it allows for a more complete description of the population (assuming the sample has been selected randomly). Thus, when the focus of research is not a thorough, contextual understanding of individual cases but rather a more comprehensive understanding of the population, CQR-M can be used. For instance, for the immediacy training study (Spangler et al., 2009), the qualitative component was an essential piece of the study, but our sample size ($N = 132$) made the use of traditional CQR unfeasible. Thus, we determined that we would ask a small set of structured questions that focused on attaining a fuller description of the participants' experience of learning this skill than could be captured by our quantitative measures alone.

In addition, a large sample allows researchers to divide the sample into subgroups when there is unexpected variability in cases that makes it difficult to analyze the sample as a whole. For example, having 67 participants in the Hill et al. (2007) study enabled us to examine quantitative process and outcome variables for the six subgroups of qualitatively derived patterns of interpersonal dreams.

## DATA COLLECTION

In approaching data collection with CQR-M, it is helpful to think about balancing the desired richness of content with the practical concerns presented by sample size. Traditional CQR analysis is a rather labor-intensive process: The interview transcript for each participant is read by the group of judges word by word, domains and core ideas are derived from the data, feedback between auditor and coding groups may go through several iterations, and cross-analysis of core ideas across all cases is also done consensually. The process for the recommended eight to 15 participants typically takes from 6 to 18 months. Clearly, then, for a large sample, analyzing such lengthy and detailed data would not be feasible. Thus, when larger samples are involved, it is recommended that researchers collect relatively brief and simple qualitative data.

One major departure of CQR-M is that researcher relationship to participant is much less of a factor than it is with CQR. Because a large sample size typically precludes the use of interviews, there is no direct interpersonal contact. The researcher's impact on the participant thus is typically solely through indirect means, and their coconstruction of the participant's reality is not influenced by follow-up probes that can be asked when there is direct contact between researcher and participant. Data typically is collected in written form, and questionnaires are the typical mode of communication between researcher and participant.

## Developing the Questionnaire

In developing the questionnaire for CQR-M, it is crucial to have a clear idea of the purpose of the qualitative investigation. Depending on the purpose, steering a course between specificity and openness will inform construction of the items. For example, in Hill et al. (2007), the purpose of analyzing the qualitative data was to explore interpersonal themes of dreams and relate them to quantitative process and outcome results. Thus, the question was very open and simply asked participants to describe a recent dream. Participants were given no indication as to how much or how little to write, which encouraged openness in their responses.

If control over the scope and length of responses is desired, a set amount of space can be indicated, as was done for Spangler et al.'s (2009) investigation of immediacy training. For that study, participants were given half a page in which to type their responses to each question, thus indicating to them the length of their expected responses and providing a degree of consistency in the scope of responses. In addition to controlling length of response, one goal of collecting the qualitative responses was to triangulate with the immediacy self-efficacy measures as to effectiveness of specific teaching components. Thus, two of the questions corresponded to the quantitative immediacy self-efficacy measure. Specifically, we asked "What was most helpful about the training?" and "What was least helpful about the training?" The other two questions were more exploratory: "What was difficult about learning to do immediacy?" and "How did your culture affect your ability (either positively or negatively) to learn immediacy?"

The medium of data collection is also an important practical point for large samples, and we strongly encourage researchers to use electronic data collection methods. Electronic collection is less costly and more environmentally friendly than paper-and-pencil collection, facilitates anonymity, and generally streamlines data management with the added advantage of not having to transcribe the data. For the immediacy training study, the questionnaire was either posted on the class website or emailed to participants. To gather impressions of the experience while it was still fresh, participants were required to submit their response papers to their instructors via e-mail prior to the start of the next lecture class. Because the questions asked were not likely to elicit responses that required keeping a high level of confidentiality, e-mail was deemed an acceptable medium for collecting the responses. We did, however, ask students to use only their student ID numbers on their responses. We wanted to maintain the participants' anonymity because judges for the study were recruited from among the helping skills instructors and teaching assistants, and we wanted to minimize instructor bias or expectations of their students' responses.

## Handling Missing and Unsuitable Data

If the goal of a study is to use CQR-M to describe and explore events, then missing data is not so much of a problem. If, however, the intent of a study is to triangulate qualitative and quantitative results on a particular phenomenon, then researchers must decide whether a participant's missing qualitative or quantitative data necessitates omitting all of that participant's data. For the immediacy training study (Spangler et al., 2009), because we wanted to compare qualitative responses with quantitative results, we omitted all data from any participant who did not complete both qualitative and quantitative measures.

CQR-M researchers also may be faced with the dilemma of having collected data that are unsuitable for addressing the research questions at hand. The data may not work for either theoretical or methodological reasons. For example, in the interpersonal dream study (Hill et al., 2007), deriving very simple relational patterns for the categories was essential to investigating how interpersonal patterns related to process and outcome data; theoretically, it was important to have pure categories to conduct the analysis. However, many of the dreams were relationally complex, with multiple scenes and images that made it impossible for the judges to come to consensus on which pattern the dream fit. Thus, these complex dreams, as well as the quantitative data for these participants, were eliminated from the final analysis of the particular questions in the study (although they may have provided important data for a different study).

## RECRUITING AND TRAINING JUDGES

When assembling coding teams for CQR-M analyses, researchers should consider the amount of data to be coded and any constraints on time or availability of judges. For very large samples, it is helpful to have two or more teams working simultaneously (but trained together to ensure a shared understanding of the domains and categories). Another consideration is judges' prior coding experience and familiarity with the phenomena of interest. Although training novice coders can serve to minimize biases and expectations, some qualitative data require that judges have a more sophisticated understanding of the topics being investigated. Finally, because biases and expectations are as likely to influence judges' interpretation of phenomena in CQR-M as they are in CQR, it is important that prior to coding, members of the coding teams discuss their biases and expectations as they pertain to the material being reviewed.

When recruiting judges for the coding team for the immediacy training study (Spangler et al., 2009), we determined that it would be helpful to have coders who were familiar with the processes of both teaching and learning immediacy and who had some understanding of the theoretical bases and clinical uses of this helping skill. We thus decided to ask the course instructors and teaching assistants to serve as judges (and authors), and we were able to recruit six individuals to work on coding. The combination of judges making up the team varied from session to session, but because the categories and subcategories were clearly defined and the data were simple (and all judges were trained), shifting the composition of the teams did not seem to be problematic. The judges met as a large group during the early stages of domain development to discuss their expectations and biases about immediacy training in general, their own experiences of both teaching and learning the skill, and how they thought culture might affect immediacy self-efficacy. For training, we talked as a group about each of the domains and categories and tried to reach a common understanding of the meaning of each. We then practiced on several transcripts to ensure a common understanding of each category. Only after reaching high agreement did we separate into smaller subgroups.

## THE CODING PROCESS

### Developing Domains and Categories

Domains and categories in CQR-M are directly derived from the data, making this a bottom-up process. Typically, we have two people read through perhaps 30 or so transcripts and develop domains. We then write out the list of domains and edit it and put similar items close together on the list. In the next step, we meet with the larger team and work together to apply the domains and categories to a different set of 30 or so transcripts, modifying the system until everyone feels comfortable that we have captured all the relevant ideas in the most elegant structure. Again, we draw up the list and edit it for clarity. Once the list is fairly well developed, we start the coding.

As an example, when determining the categories for the interpersonal dream content study (Hill et al., 2007), two of the authors derived the categories of interpersonal content of dreams by reading through a sample of approximately 50 dreams and identifying four types of interpersonal dreams and one type of dream that was devoid of interpersonal content. The first author had many years of dream research and CQR experience, and the second author had detailed knowledge of the dream descriptions because she had worked with the data at many steps in the process. In the immediacy training study (Spangler et al, 2009), deriving domains and categories was more complicated and required developing a fairly complex list (see Exhibit 17.1 for part of the list). The two initial coders began by using the questions asked to derive domains and

---

### EXHIBIT 17.1

**Example List of Coding Categories and Subcategories for CQR-M**

---

Domain: Most Helpful Component of Training (He)
1. Video vignettes
2. Lecture/didactic
3. Readings
   a. Textbook
   b. Extra article
   c. Reading quiz
4. Practice
   a. Chain exercise (e.g., feedback chain, feedback loop, first lab exercise)
      i. normalizing
      ii. fact that it was compulsory
      iii. liked positive feedback
      iv. playing both client and helper roles
   b. Disclosure to classmates
   c. Practice was real and immediate (not artificial)
   d. Lab leader
      i. role-play/model (demonstration)
      ii. supportiveness
   e. Lab group members
      i. watching them (modeling)
      ii. supportive presence (group climate, respect)
   f. Feedback
      i. from lab leaders
      ii. from peers/classmates
   g. Mindfulness/relaxation exercise
5. Sequence of training components (getting didactic before practice)
6. Other

---

then reviewed a sample of cases to derive categories and subcategories. They also created a coding table (see Exhibit 17.2) to track the responses of each participant, which facilitated determining frequencies. In addition, if coders came upon a particularly descriptive response, they marked that response number with an asterisk so that the text could be considered later as an illustrative quotation.

## EXHIBIT 17.2

**Example Coding Sheet for CQR-M**

Judge: _____

Instructions: Write last 4 # of ID at top of column; asterisk if well-articulated good example.

| Domain/Category | ID# 1234 | ID# 5678 | ID# | ID# | ID# |
|---|---|---|---|---|---|
| Most Helpful | | | | | |
| He1 | √ * | √ | | | |
| He2 | | √ | | | |
| He3 | | | | | |
| He3a | | | | | |
| He3b | | | | | |
| He3c | | | | | |
| He4 | | | | | |
| He4a | | | | | |
| I | | | | | |
| Ii | √ | | | | |
| Iii | | | | | |
| He4b | | | | | |
| He4c | | | | | |
| He4d | | | | | |
| I | √ | √ * | | | |
| Ii | | √ | | | |
| He4e | | | | | |
| I | | | | | |
| Ii | √ | | | | |
| He4f | | | | | |
| He4g | | | | | |
| He5 | | | | | |
| He6 | | | | | |

A major departure from CQR is that in CQR-M, we do not construct core ideas. Because CQR-M data typically are not as detailed, complex, or lengthy and do not have much context, it is not necessary to make sure we have interpreted the data within the context; rather, we simply place the data directly into the categories (the step that is similar to the cross-analysis in CQR). For example, for the interpersonal dream study (Hill et al., 2007), dream descriptions were simply placed into one of the six types (positive, negative, interpersonal agency, interpersonal nightmares, noninterpersonal dreams, other).

Written CQR-M responses are especially prone to ambiguity because there is no opportunity for researchers to ask clarifying questions. Although the data are comparatively simple, the fact that no follow-up questions are asked of participants makes the judges' ability to clarify ambiguous data a key factor in the analysis. For this reason, the consensual analytical process is particularly beneficial; rather than one person coding unclear data, the judges offer their interpretations of any ambiguities and come to a consensus about the participant's intent.

The judges rotate reading the responses and offering their opinion of the appropriate categories. Differences of opinion are discussed until consensus is reached. In Spangler et al. (2009), the judges read the responses to all four questions and considered them for all categories because participants' responses did not necessarily correspond to the question asked. Using this very thorough process, an entirely new domain (Outcomes of Training) emerged during the final coding, and judges went back over all papers to code this domain.

The next step in CQR-M analyses is to determine the response frequency, which we typically do by presenting the proportion of each category (the frequency of each category divided by the total number of responses). This step represents another departure from CQR as originally conceived in which frequencies are reported as *general, typical,* or *variant* rather than as proportions. For example, in the immediacy training study (Spangler et al., 2009), 72% of the sample indicated that practice was a helpful component of the immediacy training, whereas only 14% indicted that lecture was helpful. Using an a priori determined criterion of a 30% difference being the threshold for an "important" difference (see justification for this criterion in Chapter 12 in this volume), we could thus say that practice was considered to be more helpful than lecture.

As a final step we look at all categories to determine if there are categories that occur infrequently, that seem minor, or that overlap, and we edit them as needed. We try to combine small categories into larger, more abstract categories (e.g., Reading First and Modeling Before Practice were subsumed into the category Sequence of Training), or we might drop miscellaneous, small, less relevant categories that occur infrequently (< 1%).

## No Auditing

Auditing is not done with CQR-M because discrepancies among judges in interpreting relatively brief responses are easily resolved through discussion and consensus among members of the coding team. Given the lack of context and the simplicity of the data, the multiple perspectives of the team members typically seem sufficient. If, however, judges have concerns about the quality of the codings, they might submit a subset of the data to an auditor to provide a check on their coding.

# WRITING UP CQR-M

## Writing Up Results

Because of the richness and complexity of qualitative data, it can be particularly challenging to present qualitative results in a clear, succinct manner. One suggestion to facilitate clarity is to organize results on the basis of the research questions. Specifically, researchers may restate the research question and then follow it with the results for that question. For example, in the immediacy training study (Spangler et al., 2009), one purpose of the study was to explore specific components and events that influenced undergraduate participants' experiences of learning immediacy. Four domains related to this research question were presented in Results section: difficulties involved in learning immediacy, effects of culture on learning immediacy, most helpful components of training, and least helpful components of training.

As described earlier, we report the proportion of each category in the Results section. For example, in Spangler et al. (2009), under the domain Difficulties of Learning Immediacy, the authors started with the most frequently described difficulty (i.e., it can feel awkward, uncomfortable, and socially inappropriate to use immediacy) and noted that 55% of the sample reported experiencing this difficulty in their responses. We then reported the results for the remainder of the categories. Following Hill et al.'s (2005) suggestion that CQR researchers report all data in tables and present only general and typical results in the text, we recommend that CQR-M researchers report all of the data in tables and present only the most frequent categories in the text of the Results section. Finally, just as it is helpful in traditional CQR studies, we strongly advocate the use of quotations to illustrate domains and categories when presenting CQR-M results. Participants' actual words can give the reader a vivid feel of the data and help the reader understand what the categories mean (Hill et al., 2005).

### Writing the Discussion

In their article updating the use of CQR, Hill et al. (2005) stated that authors should not simply repeat the results in the Discussion section. We share this view and recommend that authors using CQR-M use the Discussion section to elaborate on the full richness of their findings in describing new or unexpected phenomena and to provide a sense of how the data fit with the literature. In addition, we recommend that authors discuss how their qualitative findings triangulate with quantitative results. Points of particular interest are consistencies and inconsistencies between qualitative and quantitative results and consideration of how these results inform our understanding of the phenomena of interest. For example, in Spangler et al. (2009), both quantitative and qualitative results indicated that immediacy training was effective, which provided stronger evidence for the effectiveness of immediacy training than if our support had been from only quantitative or only qualitative data. However, qualitative and quantitative results diverged in terms of the relative importance of each component of the training. Specifically, quantitative results suggested that lecture was the most effective component of training, whereas qualitative results indicated that practice was the most helpful component. The difference between quantitative and qualitative results posed an interesting question that we addressed in the Discussion.

## Conclusions

CQR-M can be a particularly useful approach for dealing with simple data taken from large samples. It is an adaptation that retains the practice of consensus among multiple judges while integrating components of discovery-oriented and exploratory methods. By eliminating components of traditional CQR that would make its use with large samples impracticable, CQR-M provides researchers a means to explore and describe phenomena and to triangulate their qualitative findings with quantitative results. It is our hope that the preceding CQR-M primer has elucidated the method sufficiently to enable interested readers to make use of this practical and efficient means for coding qualitative data.

## References

Denzin, N. K. (1978). *The research act: A theoretical introduction to sociological methods.* New York, NY: McGraw-Hill.

Heppner, P. P., Kivlighan, D. M., & Wampold, B. E. (1999). *Research design in counseling* (2nd ed.). Belmont, CA: Wadsworth.

Hill, C. E. (1990). A review of exploratory in-session process research. *Journal of Consulting and Clinical Psychology, 58,* 288–294. doi:10.1037/0022-006X.58.3.288

Hill, C. E., Knox, S., Thompson, B. J., Williams, E. N., Hess, S.A., & Ladany, N. (2005). Consensual qualitative research: An update. *Journal of Counseling Psychology, 52,* 196–205. doi:10.1037/0022-0167.52.2.196

Hill, C. E., Spangler, P., Sim, W., & Baumann, E. (2007). The interpersonal content of dreams: Relation to the process and outcome of single sessions using the Hill dream model. *Dreaming, 17*(1), 1–19. doi:10.1037/1053-0797.17.1.1

Hill, C. E., Thompson, B. J., & Williams, E. N. (1997). A guide to conducting consensual qualitative research. *The Counseling Psychologist, 25,* 517–572. doi:10.1177/0011000097254001

Mahrer, A. R. (1988). Discovery-oriented psychotherapy research. *American Psychologist, 43,* 694–702. doi:10.1037/0003-066X.43.9.694

Spangler, P., Hill, C. E., Dunn, M. G., Hummel, A., Liu, J., Walden, T., . . . Salahuddin, N. (2009). *Helping in the here-and-now: Teaching undergraduates to use immediacy.* Manuscript in preparation.

*John L. Jackson, Harold T. Chui, and Clara E. Hill*

# The Modification of Consensual Qualitative Research for Case Study Research

## An Introduction to CQR-C

**18**

S ince its development (Hill et al., 2005; Hill, Thompson, & Williams, 1997), consensual qualitative research (CQR) has relied primarily on interviews for data collection so that researchers can gain an in-depth understanding of the inner experiences, attitudes, or beliefs of participants. Although this interview approach is excellent for directly asking participants about their experiences, attitudes, or beliefs, it is often inadequate for analyzing phenomena that are best observed as they occur (e.g., events in which a client and therapist process their relationship during a session). Because psychotherapy researchers are particularly interested in qualitatively analyzing data obtained through the observation of cases of psychotherapy, Hill and colleagues have been experimenting with modifications of CQR for case study research. Hill (in press) first articulated some of the principles of this modification, and we extend this description in the current chapter. Specifically, we provide a justification for using qualitative methods in case study research and then outline the steps that researchers can use to conduct CQR—case study (CQR-C). In this chapter, we focus only on the application of CQR-C to psychotherapy, although other applications are certainly possible and encouraged (e.g., studies of legal cases, conversations between friends).

## Justification for a Qualitative Case Study Approach

For well over a century, researchers have developed and refined a breadth of quantitative and qualitative approaches to examine and understand the corrective nature of psychotherapy. The *case study approach,* which may be defined roughly as a design that examines data from a single case of psychotherapy, has existed and evolved as a prevalent domain of research throughout this time.

We recognize two trends in psychotherapy case study research. First, researchers have increasingly emphasized the use of replicable, quantitatively oriented case study designs. Notably, psychotherapy researchers have promoted time series designs for obtaining objective, inferential data regarding client change and psychotherapy process (Borckardt et al., 2008; Kazdin, 1981). Despite the promise of quantitative methods to produce replicable results across cases, they are often inadequate for examining novel, complex phenomena in psychotherapy because they involve the use of predetermined, standardized assessment instruments or coding schemes. Such fixed research methods involve a reduction in the scope of data obtained and analyzed from a case. Data falling outside the realm of quantitative instruments are relegated as "noise" or error. Quantitative case study approaches thus often preclude the discovery of unique and novel features of the phenomena of interest. In our research group, we have conducted a number of case studies (Hill, 1989; Hill, Carter, & O'Farrell, 1983; O'Farrell, Hill, & Patton, 1986) that involved judges coding relevant client and therapist variables using measures that have received considerable psychometric attention. We note that judges in these case studies were trained to achieve high reliability, showing that it is possible to conduct case study research systematically and with considerable fidelity to the data.

Second, we recognize that qualitative case study approaches have maintained an influential and dynamic presence throughout the history of psychotherapy research. Case study research historically involved passive observation of anecdotal data from cases. Studies were often assembled from clinical notes and impressions of a single practitioner writing about his or her work with a client (Hilliard, 1993). Building and improving on this more anecdotal type of case study (as opposed to the experimental quantitative case studies mentioned earlier), a number of researchers have conducted qualitative case studies using more rigorous observational methods.

A qualitative case study approach offers researchers the opportunity to observe and analyze intricate, sometimes novel phenomena (e.g., relational processes, alliance formation and maintenance, affect expression) regarding human experience and behavior in the psychotherapy process.

Consensual qualitative research (Hill et al., 1997, 2005) modified for case studies (CQR-C; Hill, 2011) is one such method that offers researchers both rigor and depth in the examination and description of complex social science phenomena. In contrast to the observational case studies mentioned earlier in the chapter, CQR-C does not rely on calculating reliability statistics and averaging independent judges' scores on existing rating systems. Instead, the method invites in-depth discussion among research team members to reach consensus judgment on a domain of interest. Each team member's experience of the case is thus invoked and incorporated to render a rich, constructive understanding and presentation of a phenomenon.

For CQR-C, we define a *case study* as research focusing on the unfolding of phenomena of interest over a single case or a small number of cases of psychotherapy. CQR-C essentially involves the identification and description of events that evince the phenomena of interest over a course of psychotherapy. If several cases are examined, data collected from events can be summarized within and across cases. To date, precursors to CQR-C have been used in a number of case studies (Berman et al., in press; Hill et al., 2008, 2011; Kasper, Hill, & Kivlighan, 2008). Though the method itself is still evolving, we describe in this chapter our current thinking about the basic steps for conducting CQR-C.

## Influential Sources in the Development of CQR-C

In our development of CQR-C, we have been influenced by Bill Stiles, who described case study research as the process of integrating observations from a single case with the statements of an existing theory (Stiles, 2003). Stiles focused on the capability of case study research to provide numerous observations that could be brought to bear on related elemental statements of broad psychotherapy theories. He asserted that case study research serves not only to confirm or disconfirm existing theory but, more important, to extend, modify, or elaborate on a theory. Stiles (2007) explained that in order to draw on observations from a case, a rich case record is essential. Stiles indicated that such rich case records should include both qualitative and quantitative data, such as recordings of treatment sessions, data from session-by-session quantitative questionnaires, and quantitative and narrative data on treatment outcome. In addition, Stiles emphasized utilizing data from the case record to apply the case to the theory rather than theory to the case. Simply fitting an existing theory to the case likely requires that researchers ignore important details of the data and places restrictions on the potential depth and breadth of theory elaboration. Stiles also noted that although case study research should be systematic and intentional, it is unwise to adhere to an inflexible study protocol; doing so would limit the variety in the data gathered and essentially reduce a case study to a lab exercise rather than informative research.

Given that CQR-C is an observation-based, discovery-oriented approach that deems attention to the depth and uniqueness of data as paramount to confirmation or disconfirmation of existing theories, it reflects a number of Stiles's (2003, 2007) views on case study research. We agree that fitting theory to data through a process of theory elaboration and modification is preferred to fitting data to an existing theory. Furthermore, CQR-C relies on a rich case record, and we recommend using both qualitative and quantitative data when conducting case studies using this method. Lastly, CQR-C is a flexible approach, allowing the researchers to make a number of choices at each point during the orchestration of a study, from data collection to manuscript composition.

Elliott et al.'s (2009) case study approach, which involves explicit attention to confirmatory and disconfirmatory evidence of therapeutic efficacy, has also influenced us. Elliott's hermeneutic single-case efficacy design (HSCED) involves gathering affirmative and disconfirming evidence specifically regarding the sequence of events that leads to client change. Elliott et al. revised the HSCED method by incorporation of a more formal "adjudication" approach in which an affirmative team and a skeptic team evaluate a case on the basis of qualitative and quantitative data and debate the extent to which therapy led to positive change for the client. We find Elliott's HSCED method and adjudication approach to be a useful means of guarding against groupthink and the predominance of individual group members in CQR-C. Although CQR does not include a formal adjudication approach, we have made efforts, based on Elliott's work, to ensure that conflicting ideas can be freely expressed and discussed by each research team member during the consensus process.

A final influence is Schielke, Fishman, Osatuke, and Stiles's (2009) qualitative approach to case study research known as the Ward method (named for Ward's 1987 approach to team development of architectural designs). This method takes advantage of both individual creative work and group information exchange among a team of psychotherapy researchers. After the research team has developed a topic of interest (e.g., the use of immediacy in a case of psychotherapy) and a number of questions about the topic (e.g., "How is immediacy used in the case?"; "What determines the quality of an immediacy event?"), each member evaluates the case record individually and creates a conceptualization of the case addressing the questions. Team members then meet as a group and discuss each conceptualization. During the presentation of each conceptualization, other team members ask for elaboration rather than provide criticism so that each team member can fully expand on her or his conceptualization. After this meeting, members independently modify their work to incorporate ideas they have gained from the other members. Through an iterative process of independent work and group information exchange, the group eventually reaches a point of convergence such that a common conceptualization is endorsed by all members. We find Schielke et al.'s (2009) Ward method an inventive way to promote creativity and productive group interaction while minimizing the criticism or member dominance that often hampers the consensus process. We have adapted the Ward method in the data summary steps of CQR-C, using a similar iterative process of independent work and group information exchange.

# Initial Steps in CQR-C

Initial steps in CQR-C are similar to those in CQR (see Chapter 3 in this volume). We briefly review them here to highlight some important differences (See Figure 18.1 for a flow chart of all CQR-C steps).

## CHOOSING A TOPIC

Developing a focused topic area is critical to obtaining rich, meaningful results in CQR-C, just as it is in CQR. The topic guides the selection of an appropriate case and identification of the events of interest within the case. Once a topic area has been selected, researchers develop several research questions to guide the study (although these questions may change as researchers immerse themselves in the case and discover more refined interests).

## SELECTING A TEAM OF JUDGES

In the study of psychotherapy using CQR-C, the optimal research team is made up of members who have had at least some experience, either through training or professional work, in providing psychotherapy. Familiarity with basic theoretical orientations (e.g., psychodynamic, cognitive–behavioral) and aspects of psychotherapy process (e.g., the therapeutic relationship, transference, therapist intervention types) may also help members contribute meaningful perspectives when discussing cases because one or more of these concepts are typically related to the phenomena of interest in psychotherapy research. It is also advisable that team members differ in their level of expertise, given that novice members can often add a fresh perspective, whereas experienced members can offer wisdom from their experience. We recommend that

**FIGURE 18.1**

**GETTING STARTED**

1. Choose a topic and review the literature.

2. Select a team of judges, keeping in mind that larger teams (e.g., 4 to 6 members) are recommended for CQR-C.

3. Obtain a case and gain familiarity with the case.

4. Define event(s) of interest.

5. Develop domains.

**DATA COLLECTION**

1. Watch case material (e.g., psychotherapy sessions).

2. Identify event. Stop tape and rewatch.

3. Prepare narrative description of event.

4. Code event according to each predetermined domain.

5. Repeat Steps 1 through 4 until all events have been identified, recorded, and coded.

**CROSS-ANALYSIS**

1. Create a summary table.

2. Develop categories within domains.

3. Triangulate event data with other case data.

4. Develop a narrative document that answers research questions and provides a synopsis of the data.

    a. Individual team members develop separate *initial conceptualizations*.

    b. Research team develops a joint *final conceptualization*.

**WRITE THE MANUSCRIPT**

1. Write, making sure to appropriately familiarize the reader with the case.

2. Revise, revise, revise.

Steps involved in conducting consensual qualitative research—case study (CQR-C).

larger teams (e.g., four to six members) be used for CQR-C than for CQR because more perspectives are often valuable when observing complicated data and because auditors are not as often used. Once a team has been selected, the researchers discuss their biases and expectations related to the topic (see also Chapter 5, this volume).

## OBTAINING A CASE

Researchers have two main options for obtaining case material. First, they can recruit a client and therapist to complete a course of therapy for the purposes of the study (e.g., in the study of therapist immediacy, Kasper et al., 2008, recruited an interpersonally oriented psychotherapist and a client who responded positively to probes for immediacy during a recruitment interview). A second option is to obtain case materials from a case that has already been completed (e.g., Berman et al., in press, examined an existing set of three cases of individual psychotherapy with clients who had anorexia nervosa to see how relational work unfolds naturally). An important caveat here is that it is useful to have video rather than just audio recordings of psychotherapy sessions because video allows judges to consider both the verbal and nonverbal behavior of the therapist and client in segments of interest.

# *Preparing for Data Collection*

Researchers should first familiarize themselves with the case because they need a context within which to make judgments about the case. In some instances, watching the video of the case in its entirety may be helpful. In other instances, knowledge about the entire case could be problematic if it biases how team members perceive the phenomenon of interest given that they are aware of later events and the outcome of the case. In such instances, it may be preferable for team members to familiarize themselves with the case by reading intake notes and viewing several early sessions.

## DEFINING EVENTS

An *event* is a segment in a session of therapy during which the phenomenon of interest is transpiring. An event can be defined by its beginning (e.g., when the phenomenon initially appears) and its end (e.g., when the therapist and client start to talk about something else, or when the phenomenon disappears). For example, in Hill et al.'s (2008) study of immediacy in psychotherapy, the authors defined an immediacy event as beginning when either the therapist or client initiated a discussion of the therapeutic relationship and the other person accepted the bid to engage in the discussion; the event ended when the discussion shifted to another topic. If the discussion was resumed later in the session or in subsequent sessions, it was coded as either the same event or a separate event depending on the similarity of the content (i.e., occasionally participants returned to the topic after an interlude, e.g., ". . . as I was saying earlier . . . "). Events can range from a few seconds to an entire session, but both participants must be engaged in the topic for it to be considered an event (e.g., if the therapist brings up a topic but the client ignores the therapist, we do not consider that to be an event; rather it is a bid for an event that does not come to fruition).

## DEVELOPING DOMAINS

Once the events have been defined and their data captured throughout the therapy, the team develops a list of domains (see Chapter 8, this volume) that they will use to capture different dimensions of the event. Domains are developed to initially categorize information related to the phenomenon of interest. For example, for each relationship event (when the client talked about her relationship with the therapist or with a person outside of the therapy) in the Hill et al. (2011) study, the authors consensually described actions within the domains of Wish, Response of Self, Response of Other, Activating Affect, and Inhibitory Affect. These domains were developed on the basis of the topic of interest in the study (relational themes and their change over a course of therapy) and through a review of literature on methods for assessing relational themes. Because new research questions may emerge as the team becomes familiar with the case (e.g., unanticipated questions may arise as the team works with the data), the generation of domains is a flexible process, with new and better domains added and ineffective domains deleted to better fit the emerging understanding of the data.

## *Data Collection*

Researchers watch sessions of a case sequentially (so that they have the context) and stop the recording when the team members identify the occurrence of a predefined event. After identifying the event and recording the beginning and end of the event, the team rewatches and prepares a narrative description of the event—for example,

> The therapist asked the client how he felt about her arriving late for the session. The client expressed that he felt upset because he thought that the therapist didn't respect him or care about him. He noted that the therapist had been late two other times. The

therapist apologized for being late and stated that she did respect the client and was invested in their work.

Consensus is important in developing the narrative description because it ensures that the perspectives of all team members are reflected. To encourage each team member to share equally and achieve optimal collaboration, we recommend that team members rotate providing initial descriptions of events and then having the rest of the team amend the description consensually.

After describing the event, the team members code the event according to each of the predetermined domains. Here, too, it is important that each team member share his or her thinking before moving to consensual discussion. Consensus takes precedence over reliability during observation and coding of events. For example, in the Hill et al. (2011) article on relational events in psychotherapy, a relational event in which the client appeared anxious and/or expressed anxiety was coded as "anxiety" in the *inhibitory affect* domain. Codes or phrases in each domain for an event are recorded under the narrative description of the event. Through successive meetings, the team continues this process and thereby develops a running narrative of events, complete with domain coding (Exhibit 18.1 provides an example of a narrative event summary

## EXHIBIT 18.1

**An Example of the Narrative Summary and Domain Information for a CQR-C Event**

**RE2 (8:45):** Cl was in a rush to leave the house and housemate R called her name. Cl abruptly told him that she was busy. Later, housemate R told Cl that he just wanted to let her know that the morning coffee was ready. Cl believed that housemate R wanted to sit her down to chat, a typical example of his attention-seeking behavior.

**Wish:** On one level, Cl wanted housemate R to get out of her way and not be such an obstacle to leaving the house. On another level, Cl likes to be needed.

**RO:** R retreated and returned to explain why he approached the client.

**RS:** Cl thought that housemate R was demanding, self-centered, and that she was needed all the time; she felt annoyed.

**Action:** Cl sat down to have coffee with housemate R, neglecting her own needs to leave the house on time.

**AA:** self-assertion (needs to politely assert her need to go and follow through with leaving)
    Rating: 24

**IA:** shame (not lovable if others don't need her)
    Rating: 56

*Note.* The second relational event (RE2) in an observed therapy session began at 8 minutes and 45 seconds into the session. Below the brief event summary are the domains of interest. The numerical ratings below AA and IA indicate the extent to which the client expressed AA and IA on a scale of 0 to 100, as determined via team consensus. CQR-C = consensual qualitative research—case study; Cl = client; RO = response of other (i.e., the client's perception of his interactant's response in the event); RS = response of self, the client's response to the RO; AA = the client's activating affect in the event (i.e., the affect that the team believed would have been adaptive given the circumstances of the event); IA =the client's inhibitory affect (i.e. the maladaptive affect that inhibited the client from more fully expressing the AA).

composed during the data collection phase of the Hill et al., 2011, study of relational events). Judges sometimes use nominal categories (e.g., emotion-focused, cognitive-focused) and sometimes assign numbers reflecting the strength of the variable (e.g., amount of activating affect). As coding progresses, research teams may find that they need to redefine domains to fit the emerging case material better. If domains change, the team needs to reexamine any sessions previously coded to ensure consistent coding throughout the project. At each team meeting, the team member assigned the role of note taker (again we suggest rotating this responsibility) takes responsibility for recording all of the information about the event (e.g., session number, time markers of beginning and end of event, narrative description, all codings).

## Summarizing the Data (Cross-Analysis)

### CREATING A SUMMARY TABLE

After the data have been collected, the researchers can then enter the data for all events into a table (see Table 18.1 for an example from Hill et al., 2011), the purpose of which is to create a concise, organized document that allows the team to identify and discuss patterns in the data across events. Hill et al. (2011) coded segments from a course of therapy when the client spoke either about her relationship with the therapist or about her interactions with others outside of therapy. The researchers used Luborsky and Crits-Christoph's (1990) core conflictual relationship theme as a framework for capturing the client's attitudes and reactions in the interactions and McCullough et al.'s (2003) affect expression framework to capture the client's activating and inhibitory affect during the interactions and to consensually rate affect using a 0 to 100 scale. Table 18.1 illustrates how this information initially was organized in tabular form, also showing how the event numbers and the "target" (i.e. the initials of the individuals with whom the client was interacting) were represented. To save space, this particular table does not include a narrative description of each event. However, researchers may want to include an abbreviated version of the narrative description in its own column. As illustrated in Table 18.1, each domain is presented in its own column.

### DEVELOPING CATEGORIES WITHIN DOMAINS

In category development, team members consensually identify themes or patterns within domains. To accomplish this task, we suggest that the

**TABLE 18.1**

**Session 1 From Hill et al. (2011) Relational Psychotherapy Study**

| Event | Target | Wish | RO | RS | AA | IA |
|-------|--------|------|-----|-----|-----|-----|
| 1-1 | R | Closeness | Cooperatively discussed his perspective nonargumentatively | Relieved—easier than expected. | Closeness (35) | Fear/ anxiety (40) |
| 1-2 | R | To control others | He disagrees with her, telling her that honesty is important | Feels incredulous and angry. | Pain (20) | Anger (50) |
| 1-3 | R | Closeness | Rejected her, saying she was too old and he wanted a family | Hurt and shocked. Said conversation is over and left the room. | Hurt (35) | Shame (40) |
| 1-4 | R | To be respected | He shows sensitivity to cl regarding age issue | She feels respected. | Self-respect (41) | Shame (25) |
| 1-5 | A | To control | Roommate resists control | Cl feels outraged, appalled, frustrated, angry. | Hurt (31) | Anger (91) |
| 1-6 | A | To be recognized as having a valid opinion | Roommate validated her opinion | Feels vindicated. | Self-respect (41) | Guilt (36) |
| 1-7 | T | To be reassured, to not offend T | T reassures Cl | Hopeful but still doubtful. | Pain (25) | Fear of rejection (55) |

*Note.* The Event column includes the session number followed by the event number within that session. The Target column indicates the person with whom the client (Cl) interacted in the event (R = roommate R; A = roommate A; T = therapist). The RO column includes information for the Response of Other domain. The RS column includes information for the Response of Self domain. The AA column includes information and ratings for the client's activating affect during the event. The IA column includes information and ratings for the client's inhibitory affect during the event.

team hold an initial meeting in which each team member shares his or her ideas about patterns that emerge across events within each domain. Following this discussion, each member then spends time alone with the data and creates categories independently before meeting again as a team to discuss the individually developed categories. At this next meeting, or through a series of meetings if necessary, the team consensually determines the best-fitting categories for each domain by integrating the categories that each member created. Data that appear infrequently or that do not fall cleanly under these categories can be reexamined to determine whether a new category should be created or whether the data should be put into a general Other category. Table 18.2 is a complete summary table reproduced by permission from the Hill et al. (2011) study referenced earlier in the chapter. The table organizes coded events by "Target" individual in the first and final three sessions of therapy and includes standardized categories within each of the five domains of interest. Additionally, categories are labeled General, Typical, or Variant to denote how often they occurred across all events.

## TRIANGULATION

Once CQR-C has been conducted with observational data, as outlined previously, we recommend that the themes identified in the cross-analysis be triangulated with other qualitative data (e.g., interviews with the therapist and client). Such data can confirm or disconfirm the team's themes. For example, in the Kasper et al. (2008) case study of immediacy, categories did not capture some of the negative reactions to immediacy that the client expressed in a posttherapy interview. The interview data thus added a valuable perspective to what was observed by the team members when coding psychotherapy sessions and was included in the Kasper et al. study.

Qualitative data based on observation and interviews can also be triangulated with quantitative data to enhance researchers' understanding of the case. For example, in Hill et al.'s (2011) study on relational events, analysis of pre- to posttherapy change showed a significant improvement in the client's overall interpersonal distress. Analysis of the qualitative data, however, indicated that although the client showed improvement in her interactions with some significant others, her desires and behavior in other relationships remained problematic. The nuances of these data, which were presented and discussed in the manuscript, thus provided different perspectives and insights into the complex process of interpersonal change.

## ANSWERING THE RESEARCH QUESTIONS

After triangulating the data from different sources, the primary team now develops a narrative document (referred to here as a *case conceptualization*) that answers the research questions and serves as a major synopsis of the themes and nuances found in the data. The conceptualization process entails (a) team members individually developing an *initial conceptualization*, (b) a number of team meetings during which these conceptualizations are explored and enhanced, leading to (c) the team's joint *final*

**TABLE 18.2**

Completed Summary Table From Hill et al. (2011): Client's Wishes (W), Response of Other (RO), Response of Self (RS), Activating Affect (AA), and Inhibiting Affect (IA) in the First Three and Final Three Sessions

| Target of interaction | No. of events | W | RO | RS | AA | IA |
|---|---|---|---|---|---|---|
| | | | | First three sessions | | |
| Ex-boss C | 4 | Close/needed (T), Respected (V) | Opposed/rejected her (V), Validated her (V) | Disappointed/hurt (V) | Anger/self-assertion (T), Pain/hurt (V) Overall intensity (M = 32.00, SD = 6.68) | Shame/guilt (T) Overall intensity (M = 47.00, SD = 7.26) |
| Housemate D | 7 | Control (T), Respected (V), Close (V) | Opposed/rejected her (T), Validated her (V), Complied with her (V) | Frustrated/angry (T), Positive/connected/ opened up (V), Disappointment/ hurt (V) | Pain/hurt (T), Anger/ self-assertion (V) Overall intensity (M = 29.29, SD = 7.93) | Shame/guilt (T) Overall intensity (M = 64.43, SD = 23.15) |
| Housemate E | 8 | Close/needed (V), Control (V) Respected (V) | Opposed/rejected her (T), Complied with her (V) | Disappointed/hurt (V), Positive/connected/ opened up (V) | Pain/hurt (T) Overall intensity (M = 29.62, SD = 9.81) | Shame/guilt (T) Overall intensity (M = 39.12, SD = 8.22) |
| Across all interactions | 30 | Close/needed (T), Control (V), Respected (V), Avoid conflict (V) | Opposed/rejected her (T), Validated her (V), Complied with her (V) | Frustrated/angry (V), Disappointed/ hurt (V), Positive/ connected/opened up (V) | Pain/hurt/sadness (T), Anger/ self-assertion (V), Self-respect/ pride (V), Closeness/ tenderness (V) Overall intensity (M = 30.27, SD = 7.40) | Shame/guilt (T), Fear/anxiety (V), Anger/contempt/ distrust (V), Confusion/ conflicted/ stuck (V) Overall intensity (M = 47.67, SD = 17.44) |

*(continued)*

**TABLE 18.2** (*Continued*)

| Target of interaction | No. of events | W | RO | RS | AA | IA |
|---|---|---|---|---|---|---|
| | | | | Final three sessions | | |
| Ex-boss C | 9 | Close/needed (T), Respected (T) | Opposed/rejected her (T), Validated her (V) | Disappointed/hurt (V), Self-respect/pride (V), Pain/hurt (V), Anger/self-assertion (V) | Pain/hurt (T), closeness/tenderness (V) Overall intensity ($M = 29.22$, $SD = 13.65$) | Confused/conflicted (V), Pain/sadness (V), Shame/guilt (V) Overall intensity ($M = 32.44$, $SD = 10.74$) |
| Housemate D | 2 | Control (G) | Opposed/rejected her (G) | Frustrated/angry (G) | Pain/hurt (G) Overall intensity ($M = 10.50$, $SD = .71$) | Fear/anxiety (G) Overall intensity ($M = 20.00$, $SD = 0$) |
| Housemate E | 1 | Respected | Accepted her | Positive/connected/opened up | Positive self-feelings Intensity = 58 | Sadness/Pain Intensity = 18 |
| Across all interactions | 19 | Close/needed (T), Respected (V), Control (V), Avoid conflict (V) | Opposed/rejected her (T), Validated her (V) | Positive/connected/opened up (V), Frustrated/angry (V), Disappointed/hurt (V), Confused/conflicted (V) | Pain/hurt/sadness (T), Anger/self-assertion (V), Self-respect/pride (V), Closeness/tenderness (V) Overall intensity ($M = 30.63$, $SD = 13.95$) | Pain/sadness (V), Fear/anxiety (V), Confusion/conflicted (V), Shame/guilt (V) Overall intensity ($M = 25.79$, $SD = 13.38$) |

*Note.* The information entered within each domain has been categorized and thus is represented by one of the developed categories from the study. G = general (occurred in all events); T = typical (occurred in more than half of the events); V = variant (occurred in at least 2 events). From "Hitting the Wall: A Case Study of Interpersonal Changes in Psychotherapy," by C. E. Hill, H. Chui, T. Huang, J. Jackson, J. Liu, and P. Spangler, 2011, *Counselling and Psychotherapy Research, 11,* p. 38. Copyright 2011 by the British Association for Counselling and Psychotherapy. Reprinted by permission of Taylor & Francis, Ltd. (http://www.tandf.co.uk/journals) on behalf of the British Association for Counselling and Psychotherapy.

*conceptualization*. We describe each of these steps more fully in the next paragraphs.

The conceptualization begins with a meeting in which team members meet to clarify what it is that they want to conceptualize. After developing a clear idea of the essential area of interest in the conceptualization, team members go their separate ways, consult the raw data and the codings, and individually create an initial conceptualization.

In the next team meeting, members present their conceptualizations one at a time and are queried by other members regarding their answers to the research questions so that each person has a chance to expand on his or her ideas and hear other members' ideas in full (a process similar to that used by Schielke et al., 2009). If some consensus seems to be emerging through this prolonged discussion, the team moves to jointly developing the final conceptualization. If no consensus is readily apparent, the team members separate again to continue working individually. Members each modify their original conceptualizations by reflecting on and integrating what they consider to be valuable ideas shared by others during the previous meeting. Members then return for subsequent meetings and go through the process again. The process of presentation of ideas, discussion, and rewriting continues until consolidation of ideas occurs. Consolidation is marked by team members' consensual identification of the most pertinent material from each individual's conceptualization. This consolidated, pertinent material is discussed and recorded during a meeting to provide a frame for the final consensual case conceptualization. In addition, team members continue to attend to the raw data so that the emerging conceptualization remains faithful to the case material. For the final conceptualization, each team member takes responsibility for writing a section of the document by collating all the important ideas.

The Berman et al. (in press) study of relational work in psychotherapy provides an illustration of the conceptualization process. After qualitatively coding data from three psychotherapy cases, the members of the research team met and agreed that they wanted to answer the following three questions in their conceptualizations: (a) What was the context in which the relational events occurred? (b) What were the effects of the relational events? (c) What client, therapist, and relationship factors contributed to the effects? Each member individually wrote a conceptualization for each of the three clients that answered these questions. They individually presented their conceptualizations in a team meeting and were questioned by other members so that their opinions could be fully expressed and understood. The team members continued working on their own and meeting with each other until they reached consensus. They discussed the consensual conceptualization of the cases and then divided responsibilities for writing the final conceptualization.

## Writing Up CQR-C Results

Writing up the CQR-C results parallels the writing process for traditional CQR data (see Chapter 11, this volume). In addition, however, it is important to appropriately familiarize the reader with the case (taking care, of course, to disguise the identity of the participants; see Chapter 15, this volume). Relevant therapist and client demographic information should be included. Additional information for therapists might include years of experience providing therapy, theoretical orientation, and therapist demeanor and style of interventions throughout the case. Additional client information might include marital status, sexual orientation, reasons for seeking therapy, diagnosis, appearance, and overall demeanor throughout the case. A brief description of the therapy process and relationship is useful to allow the readers to become immersed in what took place throughout the therapist's and client's work together. Such information might include the predominant topics or themes discussed throughout sessions as well as any ruptures or corrective moments that occurred in the therapy. Following the description of these pieces of information, the data and conceptualization are presented, providing specific answers (with corroborating evidence) to each of the research questions and exploring the findings' implications for future practice and research.

## Important Considerations

### CONSENSUS

Consensus is vital to obtaining rich, clinically relevant conceptualizations of a case (see also Chapter 1, this volume). Accordingly, researchers need to attend to group dynamics of the research team to ensure that all members share their thoughts throughout data analysis (see also Chapter 6, this volume). Requiring each team member to take a turn and initiate discussion can provide a structure to ensure that everyone speaks. Groupthink is likely to occur and bias the findings if unbalanced power dynamics prevail and some members feel undervalued or incompetent to share their opinions openly during meetings.

### AUDITING

To date, we have not used auditors in CQR-C, primarily because auditors in CQR studies would need to be as intimately involved in the data as the primary team. To be effective, the auditors need as much information about the case as does the primary team, and obtaining this amount of information would require watching the case in its entirety and engaging in extensive discussions about the case. Without having a team with whom to discuss the case, the auditor would have a difficult time engaging with the material in the comparable way.

To compensate for not having auditors, we have used larger teams of four to six researchers rather than the two to three researchers used in traditional CQR studies. A larger team allows for more variation across team member perspectives. A second strategy is to view sessions multiple times to ensure that data are coded consistently. Third, it may prove helpful to ask the therapist and perhaps the client to provide their perspectives on the case. For example, in Hill et al. (2011), the therapist (also an author) watched and discussed a number of the initial psychotherapy sessions with the research team and provided team members with her impressions on the general context of the therapy. The research team watched and discussed the remainder of the sessions without the therapist so that they could be more comfortable and open regarding their impressions of the therapy. In Kasper et al. (2008), the therapist took part in a posttherapy interview to discuss his reactions to the study. He also read drafts of the manuscript and wrote his afterthoughts about the case and the research question regarding the use of immediacy throughout the therapy. Although incorporating therapist and client perspectives in the data analysis is not a proxy for auditors, it does provide a valuable outside (perhaps better called an inside) perspective on the data and helps the researchers question their conclusions, return to the data, and possibly revise their work.

## Conclusions

Although the CQR-C approach is relatively new and still evolving, we hope that the steps provided in this chapter will provide enough information so that other researchers can begin to use it. Though somewhat standardized, the procedures outlined in this chapter offer the case study researcher substantial flexibility regarding the nature of phenomena that can be studied, the types of therapy (e.g., individual therapy, career counseling, couples' counseling, group psychotherapy) that can be studied, and the types of data (e.g., videorecorded psychotherapy sessions, posttherapy interviews with the therapist and client, quantitative process and outcome measures) that can be integrated to investigate phenomena of interest. We encourage further innovation to refine and improve this emerging method.

# References

Berman, M., Hill, C. E., Liu, J., Jackson, J., Sim, W., & Spangler, P. (in press). Corrective relational events in the treatment of three cases of anorexia nervosa. In L. G. Castonguay & C. E. Hill (Eds.), *Transformation in psychotherapy: Corrective experiences across cognitive behavioral, humanistic, and psychodynamic approaches.* Washington, DC: American Psychological Association.

Borckardt, J. J., Nash, M. R., Murphy, M. D., Moore, M., Shaw, D., & O'Neil, P. (2008). Clinical practice as natural laboratory for psychotherapy research: A guide to case-based time-series analysis. *American Psychologist, 63*(2), 77–95. doi:10.1037/0003-066X.63.2.77

Elliott, R., Partyka, R., Alperin, R., Dobrenski, R., Wagner, J., Messer, S. B., . . . Castonguay, L. G. (2009). An adjudicated hermeneutic single-case efficacy design study of experiential therapy for panic/phobia. *Psychotherapy Research, 19*(4–5), 543–557. doi:10.1080/10503300902905947

Hill, C. E. (1989). *Therapist techniques and client outcomes: Eight cases of brief psychotherapy.* Newbury Park, CA: Sage.

Hill, C. E. (in press). Consensual qualitative research (CQR) methods for conducting psychotherapy process research. In O. Gelo (Ed.), *Psychotherapy research: General issues, outcome and process.* Vienna, Austria: Springer.

Hill, C. E., Carter, J. A., & O'Farrell, M. K. (1983). A case study of the process and outcome of time-limited counseling. *Journal of Counseling Psychology, 30*, 3–18. doi:10.1037/0022-0167.30.1.3

Hill, C. E., Chui, H., Huang, T., Jackson, J., Liu, J., & Spangler, P. (2011). Hitting the wall: A case study of interpersonal changes in psychotherapy. *Counselling and Psychotherapy Research, 11*, 34–42.

Hill, C. E., Knox, S., Thompson, B. J., Williams, E. N., Hess, S.A., & Ladany, N. (2005). Consensual qualitative research: An update. *Journal of Counseling Psychology, 52*, 196-205. doi:10.1037/0022-0167.52.2.196

Hill, C. E., Sim, W., Spangler, P., Stahl, J., Sullivan, C., & Teyber, E. (2008). Therapist immediacy in brief psychotherapy: Case study II. *Psychotherapy: Theory, Research, Practice, Training, 45*, 298–315. doi:10.1037/a0013306

Hill, C. E., Thompson, B. J., & Williams, E. N. (1997). A guide to conducting consensual qualitative research. *The Counseling Psychologist, 25*, 517–572. doi:10.1177/0011000097254001

Hilliard, R. B. (1993). Single-case methodology in psychotherapy process and outcome research. *Journal of Consulting and Clinical Psychology, 61*(3), 373–380. doi:10.1037/0022-006X.61.3.373

Kasper, L., Hill, C. E., & Kivlighan, D. (2008). Therapist immediacy in brief psychotherapy: Case study I. *Psychotherapy: Theory, Research, Practice, Training, 45,* 281–297. doi:10.1037/a0013305

Kazdin, A. E. (1981). Drawing valid inferences from case studies. *Journal of Consulting and Clinical Psychology, 49*(2), 183–192. doi:10.1037/0022-006X.49.2.183

Luborsky, L., & Crits-Christoph, P. (1990). *Understanding transference: The core conflictual relationship theme method.* New York, NY: Basic Books.

McCullough, L., Kuhn, N., Andrews, S., Kaplan, A., Wolf, J., & Hurley, C. L. (2003). *Treating affect phobia: A manual for short-term dynamic psychotherapy.* New York, NY: Guilford Press.

O'Farrell, M. K., Hill, C. E., & Patton, S. (1986). Comparison of two cases of counseling with the same counselor. *Journal of Counseling and Development, 65,* 141–145.

Schielke, H. J., Fishman, J. L., Osatuke, K., & Stiles, W. B. (2009). Creative consensus on interpretations of qualitative data: The Ward method. *Psychotherapy Research, 19,* 558–565. doi:10.1080/10503300802621180

Stiles, W. B. (2003). When is a case study scientific research? *Psychotherapy Bulletin, 38*(1), 6–11.

Stiles, W. B. (2007). Theory-building case studies of counselling and psychotherapy. *Counselling & Psychotherapy Research, 7*(2), 122–127. doi:10.1080/14733140701356742

Ward, A. (1987). Design archetypes from group processes. *Design Studies, 8,* 157–169.

*Clara E. Hill*

# Appendix: Frequently Asked Questions About Consensual Qualitative Research

A s I hope is evident from reading this book, consensual qualitative research (CQR) is a vibrant, exciting method of getting close to data, analyzing their meanings, and presenting the stories they tell. We have developed and refined this method by infusing qualitative approaches into more traditional quantitative designs, and we believe that the melding of the two paradigms has led to an integrative approach that combines the best of both methods. We have continued to modify CQR to fit new topics and data formats and expect such evolution to continue as we encounter new challenges and opportunities.

We hope that many of your questions about CQR have been answered by reading this book as well as empirical articles that have used this method. We have found, however, that new concepts are hard to grasp and need to be presented in a variety of formats. Hence, the authors of the book suggested questions that they are frequently asked about CQR. In this Appendix, I provide brief answers and refer readers to the relevant chapters for more detail. I break the questions into those about the overall method, the data analysis, and writing and publishing CQR studies.

## Questions About the Overall Method

1. What is consensual qualitative research (CQR)?

   ▪ CQR is an inductive approach to research that relies on words rather than numbers, involves a team of judges and auditors to code the data, relies on consensus for all judgments, and continually returns to the raw data to ensure accurate representation of the data. Data may be generated via interviews, brief written responses to open-ended questions, or case data.
   ▪ See Chapter 1 for more detail.

2. What are the advantages and disadvantages of using CQR?

   ▪ The advantages include staying close to the data, the ability to explore phenomena that are complex and context laden, the ability to examine data in depth, having multiple perspectives on the data, and the social aspect of working closely with a team.
   ▪ Disadvantages include the time and amount of detail involved in conducting analyses, the influence of unknown biases related to interviewers and judges, and difficulties related to transferability of data (i.e., replication of data across studies).
   ▪ See Chapters 1, 2, and 3.

3. What fields or disciplines are most appropriate for CQR?

   ▪ CQR has been used primarily for psychotherapy research, but it has also been used to study many other topics (e.g., health, abortion, sexuality).
   ▪ See Chapters 2 and 16 for more detail.

4. Should I use quantitative or qualitative methods? What kind of research question is appropriate for CQR?

   ▪ The choice of quantitative or qualitative methods depends on the research question. If the research question involves wanting to know about the amount of something in the population (e.g., what is the prevalence of psychopathology in the United States?), a statistical comparison between conditions (e.g., is psychodynamic psychotherapy better than cognitive–behavioral therapy?), or the relationship between variables (e.g., the relationship between working alliance and psychotherapy outcome), quantitative methods are the best approach. If the question, however, involves wanting rich description about inner experiences (e.g., how do therapists react to clients who act out with hostility toward

them?), attitudes (e.g., expectations about seeking psychotherapy), or beliefs (e.g., religious/spiritual convictions), or if not much is known about a topic, qualitative methods are excellent.
- See Chapter 3 for more detail.

5. How does CQR differ from other qualitative methods?

- CQR is more structured than many other qualitative methods in that it involves semistructured interviews to collect consistent data across participants, relatively clear-cut procedures for analyzing the data, and the use of consensus among multiple judges and auditors.
- See also Chapters 1 and 2.

6. How do you communicate with quantitative researchers about CQR?

- Emphasize the importance of multiple perspectives, problems with traditional assessments of interjudge reliability, the procedures of returning to the data to repeatedly check for consistency, and the ability to study phenomena in great depth and richness.
- See Chapters 1 and 2 for more detail.

7. How do you communicate with qualitative researchers about CQR?

- Emphasize the constructivist nature of the data analysis (there are not truths to be determined but rather understandings of phenomena to emerge from the data) and that analyses are bottom-up (results emerge from the data rather than being imposed from theory).
- See Chapters 1 and 2 for more detail.

8. How do I choose among CQR and the new modifications (CQR-M and CQR-C)?

- Traditional CQR is appropriate for use with interview data (these data may be collected via face-to-face interview, telephone, or e-mail). Consensual qualitative research—modified (CQR-M) is appropriate for responses to open-ended questions when these responses are brief and relatively simple to directly place into categories derived from the data without the need for constructing core ideas. Consensual qualitative research—case study (CQR-C) is appropriate when investigating case data (e.g., psychotherapy sessions) where specific questions are not being asked of the participant; researchers instead use a structure derived from the data for categorizing data.
- See Chapters 1, 7, 17, and 18 for more detail.

9. How long does a CQR project take?

- Our projects typically take about 2 to 3 years from start to finish: about 3 to 6 months planning, 3 months doing interviews and obtaining transcripts, 9 to 12 months doing data analyses (domains, core ideas, and cross-analyses), 6 months writing and rewriting, and 6 to 12 months from the time of submitting the manuscript until you see the article in print. This timeline fits when all is going well and the team is working about 2 hours a week on the project. Theses and dissertations tend to be completed faster because teams meet 6 to 10 hours a week.

10. CQR generally uses smaller sample sizes than quantitative studies, so how can findings be generalizable?

- Because CQR samples are not typically randomly selected from the population, we cannot generalize to the population with confidence. We do, however, hope that the data can be used to understand something about more than just the individuals included in the sample (i.e., we hope the findings apply to other people). To this end, we try hard to select homogeneous samples of well-defined participants who can speak clearly and cogently about the topic, and then we provide detailed information about the sample in the write-up so that readers know the characteristics of the sample. We also write about any anomalies or limitations of the sample in the write-up.
- We describe how much each finding is characteristic of the sample to give some idea of how much the results generalize to the sample. We use the terms *general* (applies to all or all but one), *typical* (applies to more than half up to the cutoff for general), and *variant* (applies to two or three up to the cutoff for typical).
- See Chapters 6 and 13 for more detail.
- We also recommend the use of qualitative meta-analyses to examine the consistency of results across samples, a direct test of transferability of CQR data.
- See Chapter 12 for more detail.

11. Why don't you assess for reliability among the judges?

- When judges have to code into predetermined categories and work to reliability, their task is to figure out the meaning of the category and how other judges are thinking. They cannot use their clinical judgment to think about the data in innovative ways. By instead using consensus among judges after considerable discussion and airing of lots of ideas, our experience is that we have richer, more meaningful data.

12. How do I locate a CQR expert for consultation?

- You might contact authors who have conducted CQR research on topics in which you are interested. But do be sensitive about such requests because adequate consultation takes a long time— a consultant may ask to be paid or be included on the publication (perhaps as an auditor).

# Questions About Conducting the Data Analysis

13. How do you do CQR?

   ■ Read this book thoroughly through before starting, and then read the relevant chapters again as you approach each new step. In addition, read several CQR studies to get an idea of how others have approached the process. If possible, work first on a team with others who have experience using CQR.

14. Should you review the extant literature on your topic before beginning the study or does doing so bias you even before you begin?

   ■ We recommend that you review the extant literature so that you do not recreate the wheel and so that you can learn from others and extend what has been done before. But when you are conducting the interviews and analyzing the data, it is important to set aside (or bracket) this previous knowledge as much as possible and focus completely on the data in front of you.
   ■ See Chapters 3, 5, 8, and 9 for more detail.

15. Given how much time we ask participants to invest in a study, how can we encourage more people to take part?

   ■ If you want people to participate in your study, it is important to choose a topic that is meaningful and salient to them and appeals to their desire to be helpful to you. It is also important to treat participants well and to provide a safe, confidential setting for them to talk.
   ■ See Chapter 6.

16. Why do you use semistructured interviews?

   ■ We want to obtain consistent data across participants so that we can compare findings, but we also want to probe the depths of the individual experiences, so semistructured interviews allow for both goals to be met.
   ■ See Chapter 7 for more detail.

17. How "old" can experiences be and still be included in a study?

   ■ It depends on the research topic. If the topic of interest is something fleeting (e.g., sighing or crying in psychotherapy sessions), it is best to conduct the interviews as soon as possible after the event. On the other hand, if the topic is something more profound and salient and you want the perspective of time (e.g., the effects of divorce), the experiences could have occurred quite some time ago and still be useful for the research.
   ■ See Chapter 6 for more detail.

18. What if you realize halfway through data collection that you forgot to explore a really important area with all of your participants thus far? Should you go back and reinterview the early participants?

   - You need to think through the consequences carefully. Data gathered from the "old" and "new" participants might be quite different because of the different context. You might want to just collect the data for the new sample and then report a smaller sample size for some of the data. You could also just report the new findings as a postscript in the Results section and recommend that other researchers gather data on this topic.
   - See Chapter 7 for more detail.

19. What is a domain?

   - A *domain* is a discrete topic area (e.g., antecedents, behaviors, consequences, contributing factors).
   - See Chapter 8 for more detail.

20. What is a core idea?

   - A *core idea* is a summary or abstract of the critical essence of what the participant has said in clear, more concise terms. The core ideas take into account everything that the participant has said so that the participant's views are adequately represented when taken out of context.
   - See also Chapter 8.

21. How many people should be on the primary research team?

   - We recommend at least three people on the primary team (the team making the initial judgments about domains, core ideas, and cross-analyses). There have been larger teams but rarely have there been smaller teams.
   - See Chapter 4 for more detail.

22. How do you select research team members?

   - Research team members should be motivated (i.e., willing to commit 1 to 2 years) and interested in the topic of the study, open-minded, able to think objectively (i.e., not having an agenda that they want the results to turn out a particular way), and enjoy working with a team of people. It helps to have some diversity of opinion on the team but also constitute a team of people who like each other and can talk to each other.
   - See Chapter 4 for more detail.

23. What are the responsibilities of team members?

   - It is important to negotiate roles early in the process. Typically, the principal investigator (PI) is the first author and takes primary responsibility for obtaining institutional review board approval, keeping track of the data flow, and writing the manuscript. All team members (including the PI) typically share responsibility for conducting the interviews and managing the data for the cases they interview. An exception to this work flow distribution often occurs with theses and dissertations, where the PI (the thesis student or dissertator) does all of the interviews and manages the data.

- See Chapter 4 for more detail.

24. How would you know if a team member isn't working out?

- A team member might not show up for meetings, not be prepared with having done the assignments, not voice any opinions, or dominate and not let others talk.
- See Chapter 4 for more detail.

25. What do you do if a member of your CQR team isn't working out?

- Try to prevent problems by wisely selecting team members. If problems arise, the group should first try to discuss the concerns within the group by using immediacy and concern. Group dynamics inevitably arise and need to be addressed sensitively and compassionately. If problems cannot be resolved, the PI may need to ask the team member to resign.
- See Chapter 4 for more detail.

26. How many auditors do I need to have?

- We typically use one to two auditors, with a preference for two auditors because they often have such different perspectives.
- See Chapter 10 for more detail.

27. What software program do you use to analyze your qualitative data?

- We have not used any commercial software programs. The only tool we use is a word processing program (e.g., Microsoft Word).
- See Chapter 8 for more detail.

## *Writing and Publishing CQR Studies*

28. What's the most effective way to present the Results and Discussion sections?

- It depends on the study. Sometimes the Results and Discussion sections are distinct, sometimes combined.
- See Chapter 11 for more detail.

29. Should I include core ideas or quotes in the results?

- We have done both, but we are beginning to use quotes more often because it provides more of a feel of what the participants actually said. Sometimes we present the core ideas or quotes in the Results section, sometimes in a table.
- See Chapter 11 for more detail.

30. How do I ensure that the Discussion is not just a dry regurgitation of the Results section?

- Tie the results back into the literature. Also think of the larger meaning of the findings—do they fit into some theory, or can you create a theory that explains them? The bottom line is to discern the story the findings tell.
- See Chapter 11 for more detail.

31. How do we decide authorship order?

- Typically, the PI is the first author. Others on the research team are then the next authors, with an author's note that indicates that they contributed equally (if such is the case) and their names placed alphabetically or in a random order. The auditors are typically last in the publication lineup. It is important that authorship be discussed early in the life of a project and that everyone contribute according to her or his place in the authorship order. One issue that has arisen in our work is whether undergraduates serving as judges and earning course credit for a thesis or dissertation project (wherein the PI does all the interviews and manages all the data) deserve authorship. We have gone both ways with this—it depends on the students' level of commitment and contribution.
- See the *Publication Manual of the American Psychological Association* (2010) for more detail about the ethics of assigning authorship.

32. Which journals are receptive to CQR studies?

- A perusal of the studies published shows that they have been published mostly in the *Journal of Counseling Psychology; Psychotherapy Research; Cultural Diversity and Ethnic Minority Psychology; The Counseling Psychologist;* and *Psychotherapy: Theory, Research, Practice, Training.* The predominance of counseling journals is probably because CQR was developed by counseling psychologists. Other journals are increasingly publishing CQR articles.
- See Chapter 16 for more detail.

33. How can we educate journal editors of the value of CQR research?

- Do high quality CQR, get on editorial boards, and talk to journal editors about the appropriateness of CQR. If manuscripts are rejected because of seeming bias against qualitative methods, write to the editor and tactfully explain the method and ask for another review by people who are qualified to review qualitative research, perhaps suggesting names.

## Final Thoughts

I expect that in 20 years, we will have evolved new qualitative methods that stretch us even further than what is reflected in this book about the current applications of CQR. It is exciting to contemplate what these developments might look like. I thus encourage researchers to continue to think of new approaches that will help continue to improve our research.

## Reference

American Psychological Association. (2010). *Publication manual of the American Psychological Association* (6th ed.). Washington, DC: Author.

# Index

# About the Editor

**Clara E. Hill** earned her PhD at Southern Illinois University in 1974. She started her career in 1974 as an assistant professor in the Department of Psychology, University of Maryland, College Park, and is currently there as a professor. She has been the president of the Society for Psychotherapy Research, the editor of the *Journal of Counseling Psychology*, and the editor of *Psychotherapy Research*. She was awarded the Leona Tyler Award from Division 17 (Society of Counseling Psychology) and the Distinguished Psychologist Award from Division 29 (Psychotherapy) of the American Psychological Association, the Distinguished Research Career Award from the Society for Psychotherapy Research, and the Outstanding Lifetime Achievement Award from the Section on Counseling and Psychotherapy Process and Outcome Research of the Society for Counseling Psychology. Her major research interests are helping skills, psychotherapy process and outcome, training therapists, dream work, and qualitative research. She has published more than 170 journal articles, 40 chapters in books, and nine books (including *Therapist Techniques and Client Outcomes: Eight Cases of Brief Psychotherapy; Helping Skills: Facilitating Exploration, Insight, and Action;* and *Dream Work in Therapy: Facilitating Exploration, Insight, and Action*).